LABOUR AND CONSERVATIVE
PARTY MEMBERS 1990-92

Labour and Conservative Party Members 1990-92

Social Characteristics, Political Attitudes and Activities

PATRICK SEYD
PAUL WHITELEY
and
JON PARRY

Dartmouth

Aldershot • Brookfield USA • Singapore • Sydney

Published by
Dartmouth Publishing Company Limited
Gower House
Croft Road
Aldershot
Hants GU11 3HR
England

Dartmouth Publishing Company
Old Post Road
Brookfield
Vermont 05036
USA

British Library Cataloguing in Publication Data
Seyd, Patrick
    Labour and Conservative party members 1990-92 : social
    characteristics, political attitudes and activities
    1. Labour Party (Great Britain) 2. Conservative Party 3. Party
    affiliation - Great Britain 4. Political parties - Great Britain
    I. Title II. Whiteley, Paul, 1946- III. Parry, Jon
    324.2'41

Library of Congress Cataloging-in-Publication Data
Seyd, Patrick.
    Labour and Conservative Party members 1990-92 : social
    characteristics, political attitudes, and activities / Patrick Seyd,
    Paul Whiteley, and Jon Parry.
        p.   cm.
    Includes bibliographical references and index.
    ISBN 1-85521-536-5
    1. Party affiliation–Great Britain. 2. Political activists-
    -Great Britain. 3. Labour Party (Great Britain) 4. Conservative
    Party (Great Britain) I. Whiteley, Paul. II. Parry, Jon.
    III. Title.
    JN1121.S49   1996
    324.24104–dc20   95-46955
                                                                          CIP

ISBN 1 85521 536 5

Printed and bound in Great Britain by Ipswich Book Co. Ltd., Ipswich, Suffolk

63833

Contents

Introduction

How to Use this Book

This is a reference book designed to provide direct comparisons between Labour and Conservative party members in relation to a wide variety of measures, including their social and political backgrounds, political activities, and attitudes. The tables are derived from surveys conducted in 1990 and 1992. Direct comparisons between the parties are facilitated by the fact that all the attitude questions in both surveys were asked within a few months of each other in 1992. In the case of the Labour party, the survey was the second wave of a panel sample, the first wave of which was conducted in 1990, and has been comprehensively analyzed in Seyd and Whiteley (1992). The social background questions for the Labour party respondents are taken from the first wave survey. Researchers interested in changes in attitudes can examine differences between respondents set out in the appendix of that book, and the responses of the same party members surveyed some two years later in the present volume.

The Conservative party survey was also conducted in 1992, and the results of this have been comprehensively analyzed in Whiteley, Seyd and Richardson (1994). However, such is the richness of this survey that many interesting relationships were not explored in that book, and can be examined for the first time in the present volume.

This reference book is designed for a number of audiences. Firstly, it is aimed at journalists, political researchers and commentators on public affairs, who would like to be able to compare easily Labour and Conservative party members on an issue like their attitudes to European integration; this can be done relatively quickly by looking up the appropriate sections of the questionnaires which are reproduced in the text. Secondly, it is aimed at students, who in the course of writing an essay on the British party system may, for example, want to find out the differences between Labour and Conservative women members, on an issue like support for the National Health Service. In this case they would simply look at the relevant table in the chapter on gender and party membership. Thirdly, it is aimed at fellow political scientists, who may have obtained a copy of the original survey data from the ESRC archive at the University of Essex, and who are embarking on secondary analysis of the data; they can use this book as a guide to help them identify key relationships between variables of interest, which can be explored in more detail using the original data.

Selection of the Variables

The original surveys of Labour and Conservative party members contained a number of issue questions which are specific to one party. For example, in the Labour survey there was a question about the respondent's views on who should succeed Neil Kinnock, the then party leader, if he should decide to resign. We asked Conservatives the same question, but about John Major, rather than Neil Kinnock.

However, there were a wide variety of questions which were put to both party members, using exactly the same wording. Thus one criterion for selecting variables for this book, is that exactly the same question was asked of both party members. The few exceptions to this are designated in the text. A second factor governing the choice of variables is the idea of comparing the social and political characteristics of party members on the one hand, with their attitudes to various issues and political activities on the other. We could, of course, have done direct comparisons between, say, views about government spending with views about a single European currency, but a comprehensive analysis of all attitude questions with all others would have made the book impossibly long.

Table Layouts

The tables in each of the chapters all contain row percentages, i.e. they add up to 100 percent by rows. Thus, for example, in Table 2.1 some 50 percent of all Labour party members agree with the proposition that the party should try to capture the middle ground of politics; 12.2 percent neither agreed nor disagreed, and 37.8 percent disagreed with the idea, making 100 percent altogether. Each table also contains the N, or the number of cases which fall into that row category, some 2,658 cases in the first row of Table 2.1.

The remaining two rows of Table 2.1 relate to responses to the same question classified by social class. Thus in the case of the Labour party, only 45.8 percent of the salariat - the middle class professionals - agreed with the proposition, and 40 percent disagreed with it. Thus the middle class radicals are rather less supportive of electoral pragmatism than the working class, some 61 percent of whom agreed with the statement. Interestingly enough, the same pattern exists for the Conservatives; in their case some 68.2 percent of the salariat support the

2

idea of 'capturing the middle ground' compared with 75.9 percent of the working class Conservatives.

There are some tables in each chapter, referred to as the 'thermometers' which differ slightly from the other tables. In a preamble to this set of questions, party members were asked to 'please think for a moment of a thermometer scale that runs from zero to 100 degrees, where 50 is the neutral point. If your feelings are warm and sympathetic towards something or someone, give them a score higher than 50; the warmer the feelings, the higher the score. If your feelings are cold and unsympathetic, give them a score less than 50; the colder your feelings the lower the score. A score of 50 means that your feelings are neither warm nor cold'.

There are five columns in the tables which describe the thermometer ratings; the left hand column is labelled 'Cd' meaning 'Cold' and refers to the percentage of respondents who gave that person or organization a score between zero and 25. The next column is labelled 'Cl' which means 'Cool' and refers to a score between 26 and 50; the third column is labelled 'W' for 'Warm' refers to scores between 51 and 75; and the fourth column labelled 'H' for 'Hot' relates to scores between 76 and 100. Finally, the fifth column gives the mean score on the thermometer for that person or organization.

It can be seen, for example, that in Table 9.44, some 76.1 percent of Labour party members gave the Conservative party a score between 0 and 25 in the 'Cd' category, and the mean score for the Conservative party among Labour members was 14.7. Interestingly enough in Table 9.45, the thermometer scale for the Labour party, only 50 percent of Conservative party members gave a 'Cd' code to Labour, and the mean score for Labour among Conservatives was 26.8. Thus Labour party members dislike the Conservative party more than Conservative party members dislike Labour.

Missing Observations

The tables always exclude missing values, or respondents for whom information is unavailable. This is usually because the respondent missed answering the question, for example, by turning over two pages in the survey at once, or by replying 'don't know'. The proportion of missing data in any one table is usually small and does not distort the true answers because for the most part missing cases are randomly distributed across respondents. For this reason, missing cases do not systematically differ from observed cases. The missing data does account for the slight difference in percent of the general frequencies in the Appendix and the 'All' categories of the respective tables in chapters 1 to 13. This is because the cross tabulations in these chapters take account of two variables and their missing values as opposed to only one variable in the frequencies.

The Representativeness of the Samples

The data are based on representative random samples of party members. In the case of the Labour party the first wave of the survey was a one-in-thirty sample of all party members in 480 constituencies in Great Britain. This type of sample was made possible by the fact that constitutional changes in the party in the 1980's led to the setting up of the first national database of party members in the late 1980's. This database was the 'sampling frame' or population from which our sample was selected. The surveys were conducted using a mail questionnaire with a number of reminders, the exact details of which appear in Seyd and Whiteley, (1992: 221-22). About three months after the initial data collection was completed, a follow-up random sample of non-respondents established that the original respondents were rather more middle class and more likely to be members of a trade union than members in general. The information from this 'non-respondent' survey was used to weight the original sample to make it representative of party members in general. The weighted file consisted of 5,071 respondents. When the members were surveyed again in 1992, the data was again weighted to correct for response bias, giving 2,935 individual respondents overall at that stage. The response rate for the original survey was 62.5 percent which is very good for a mail survey of this type.

In the case of the Conservative party all information about party members is held at the Constituency level, and so our survey of party members involved a two-stage stratified random sample design. A 5 percent sample of constituency associations in Great Britain was selected, stratified by region, and a random sample of one-in-ten party members were surveyed in those constituencies. The survey response rate was 63 percent giving 2,467 individual respondents after weighting for gender and strength of partisanship. Again, a follow-up survey of non-respondents provided the weights for this exercise. Further methodological details of the survey can be found in Whiteley, Seyd and Richardson, (1994: 239-41).

In the remainder of these notes we examine a limited number of the findings, as a way of illustrating the richness of these data sets.

An Overview of the Tables

Down at the grassroots, among Labour and Conservative party members, there are limits to political consensus. Not surprisingly, agreement between them is not common. However, both sets of members believe that they possess political influence. Sixty-six percent of Labour and fifty-seven percent of Conservative members believe that they 'can have a real influence in politics if ... prepared to get involved' (Table 14.42). On policy matters, there is a consensus among both sets of members that governments have a responsibility to spend money, first, to get rid of poverty (Table 14.26) and, secondly, on the National Health Service (Table 14.28). Finally, they both dislike the notion of coalition government (Table 14.25). For them, governing is about one party implementing its distinct

4

principles and programme. Of course, clear differences between them arise in relation to what these principles are in practice.

Asked how they would rank themselves on a Left-Right scale for British politics in general (from 1-Left to 9-Right), the mean scores of Labour and Conservative members were 3.3 and 6.8 respectively. This clear Left-Right divide is then reflected in a wide range of attitudinal differences, only some of which are highlighted here.

There is a clear division of opinion regarding the redistribution of income and wealth towards ordinary people. Labour members support such a commitment while Conservative members oppose it (Table 14.16). This view of redistribution is then further reflected in attitudes towards government expenditure (Table 14.29), taxation (Table 14.20), and private medicine (Table 14.27).

Whilst there is a predictable and fairly stable division of opinion between party members over redistribution, attitudes towards the European Union appear to be more volatile and less predictable. It was a Conservative government which took Britain into the EEC in 1973, while the Labour party promised withdrawal in its 1983 election manifesto. However, today it is Labour members who prefer further British integration within the European Union (Table 14.22) and the creation of a single European currency (Table 14.19) and their Conservative counterparts oppose both. Although opinions on European issues are more volatile, and are more responsive to particular issues and developments, Labour's grassroots are pro-European, in the sense of wanting further political and economic union, and Conservative grassroots are anti-European, in the sense of opposing any further union.

It is often claimed that one of the reasons for the Conservative party's electoral successes in the twentieth century has been its close identity with the dominant institutions of the nation state (Gamble, 1974). The Conservative party's historic attachments to church, crown and constitution have been exploited to its electoral advantage. The Labour party, on the other hand, has been more the voice of radical dissent. We see this distinction when, in the surveys, party members were asked to rank a whole range of institutions, organisations and groups of people in Britain. Conservatives rank such groups and institutions as the Police (Table 14.66), the House of Commons (Table 14.67), the Queen (Table 14.69), and the Judges (Table 14.70), significantly higher than do Labour members.

Turning next to social class, for over 30 years consistent claims have been made regarding the decline of working class political activity within the Labour party. There is extensive literature suggesting that the Labour party now has few claims to be a working-class party. Its leadership is overwhelmingly middle class (Burch and Moran, 1987) and its electoral support is increasingly middle class. Ivor Crewe wrote after the 1983 general election that 'the Labour party vote remained largely working class, but the working class was no longer largely Labour' (Crewe, 1983: Public Opinion). Election specialists might differ about the absolute and relative levels of working class support for the Labour party, but there is little doubt that the number of working-class Labour voters has declined (Heath, Jowell, and Curtice, 1991 and 1994). Furthermore, it has been argued that local Labour parties have been taken over by middle class professionals (Hindess, 1971; Forrester, 1976).

It is certainly the case, as is revealed in the Labour party survey, that the majority of party members are middle class. Some 59 percent are from the salariat and only 18 percent are traditional manual workers. However, the 'decline of working class politics' thesis should be carefully scrutinised. For example, in relative terms, the smaller group of working class members play a more active part in local Labour politics than their middle-class counterparts. They are more frequent attendees at party meetings and they are more active in delivering party leaflets and canvassing voters; they also have a stronger sense of political efficacy, or a belief that individual political involvement results in political influence. Furthermore, they regard party activism as a good way to meet people and to receive a political education. This suggests that grassroots activism is not, and need not, become solely a middle class preserve, if the Labour party provides appropriate incentives for working class recruits. However, working class members also feel more strongly that the party leadership does not listen to ordinary party members.

At the time of the publication of the initial party member surveys (Seyd and Whiteley, 1992; Whiteley, Seyd and Richardson, 1994) many commentators drew attention to the disparity in age profiles between the two sets of party members. Much was made of the fact that the mean age of a Conservative was 62, fourteen years greater than for a Labour member.

In terms of grassroots activities, however, it is the young who are prominent in Conservative politics. Those aged 25 and under are more likely than their older colleagues to attend party meetings (Table 11.22), to be party office-holders (Table 11.24), to give more time to the party (Table 11.25), to deliver party leaflets (Table 11.39), and to canvass voters (11.41).

The young in both parties are more committed to political principles even if this should mean losing a general election; Labour young are twice as likely, and Conservative young four times more likely, than their retired party colleagues to regard political principles as a higher priority (Table 11.4). Furthermore, they are far less likely to support a political strategy of 'capturing the middle ground' (Table 11.1).

Both young Labour and Conservative members are likely to place themselves more towards the Left and Right respectively, on their party political spectrum (Table 11.42). The Conservative young are more distinctive in their political opinions and would appear to be more 'Thatcherite' a group within the party. Conservatives up to age 25 are less in favour of the redistribution of income and wealth (Table 11.3), less supportive of government expenditure to relieve poverty (Table 11.13), more favourably inclined to private medicine (Table 11.14), and more favourably-inclined towards defence expenditure (Table 11.19) than their older colleagues.

In both parties the membership is more male than female; there are fewer female party office-holders (Table 10.24) and local councillors (Table 10.27). Whether this imbalance is a result of supply-side or demand-side factors is a matter of debate (Norris and Lovenduski, 1995). What is revealed here, however, is that both Labour and Conservative women are less likely to believe that they can influence politics by being active than their male counterparts (Table 10.29), that they could do a good job as a local councillor (Table 10.31), or that they would make successful MPs (Table 10.36), suggesting that their sense of political efficacy is low. Thus the 'supply-side' explanation of gender imbalance in both the Labour and Conservative parties has validity.

Both Labour and Conservative women are more committed to political principles than their male counterparts (Table 10.4). Clear differences exist between Labour and Conservative members over Europe; majorities of Labour members are in favour of moves towards further European integration while Conservative members are hostile to this (Table 10.9). However, women in both parties are less supportive of a single European currency (Table 10.6) and of further integration of the European Community (Table 10.9) than their male colleagues.

Not surprisingly, one of the most potent variables for discriminating between the attitudes of party members is strength of partisan attachments. Thus strong Labour partisans are much more likely to favour the redistribution of income and wealth than weak Labour partisans (Table 1.3); similarly strong Conservative partisans are much more likely to disagree with this than weak Conservative partisans. Similar large differences between strong and weak partisans appear in both parties in relation to attitudes to nuclear energy (Table 1.5), attitudes to income tax (Table 1.7), attitudes to European Integration (Table 1.9), beliefs about stricter laws to regulate trade unions (Table 1.17), and attitudes to defence spending (Table 1.19).

There are relatively few issues in which partisan attachments do not significantly influence attitudes. This appears to be true in relation to government spending to get rid of poverty (Table 1.13), and spending on the Health Service (Table 1.15). Interestingly enough, Labour members are more likely to have similar views when their strengths of partisan attachments vary, than do Conservatives; this is true of attitudes to 'capturing the middle ground of politics' (Table 1.1), to standing by principles (Table 1.4), and finally on attitudes to a European currency.

Differences between strong and weak partisans are particularly evident in relation to those who attended party meetings within the last twelve months (Table 1.22) and those who devote a lot of time to party activities in the average month (Table 1.25). Interestingly enough strong partisans are also the least likely to perceive that attending party meetings can be tiring after a hard days work (Table 1.30), although they are likely to think that party activity takes time away from one's family (Table 1.35).

Most notably all the indicators of activism, including delivering leaflets (Table 1.39), donating money (Table 1.38), and canvassing voters (Table 1.41) are strongly related to the strength of partisanship. Obviously, if the partisan attachments of grassroots party members weaken, they are likely to become less active and this will influence the success or failure of local election campaigns.

We hope this illustrates the richness of this data, which provides the first representative picture of the grassroots Labour and Conservative parties in Britain. Many relationships between variables remain to be explored, and we hope that the reader will find the task of exploring them to be rewarding.

1   Partisanship

Table 1.1 *The Labour/Conservative party should try to capture the middle ground in politics (%)*

Partisanship	Labour				Conservative			
	Agree	Neith-er	Dis-agree	N	Agree	Neith-er	Dis-agree	N
All	51.1	12.1	36.8	2843	69.7	13.4	16.9	2298
Very Strong	50.3	11.3	38.4	1536	64.3	12.6	23.1	748
Fairly Strong	52.6	12.7	34.7	1111	71.6	12.8	15.6	1147
Not Very Strong	47.9	15.3	36.8	144	74.2	15.6	10.2	314
Not At All Strong	50.0	11.5	38.5	52	74.2	19.1	6.7	89

Table 1.2 *A Labour/Conservative government should introduce a prices and Incomes policy as a means of controlling inflation (%)*

Partisanship	Labour				Conservative			
	Agree	Neith-er	Dis-agree	N	Agree	Neith-er	Dis-agree	N
All	57.5	18.9	23.6	2844	42.2	11.7	46.1	2343
Very Strong	58.3	17.0	24.7	1541	37.6	10.5	51.9	764
Fairly Strong	57.1	20.8	22.1	1110	43.2	10.3	46.5	1166
Not Very Strong	53.2	24.1	22.7	141	47.5	18.0	34.5	322
Not At All Strong	51.9	21.2	26.9	52	48.4	16.5	35.1	91

Table 1.3 *Income and wealth should be re-distributed towards ordinary working people (%)*

Partisanship	Labour				Conservative			
	Agree	Neith-er	Dis-agree	N	Agree	Neith-er	Dis-agree	N
All	86.0	9.1	4.9	2878	25.3	20.4	54.3	2333
Very Strong	88.7	7.2	4.1	1563	18.1	17.5	64.4	756
Fairly Strong	83.7	11.1	5.2	1120	25.5	21.1	53.4	1168
Not Very Strong	77.9	12.4	9.7	145	31.9	25.6	42.5	317
Not At All Strong	76.0	12.0	12.0	50	58.7	17.4	23.9	92

Table 1.4   *The Labour/Conservative Party should always stand by its principles even if this should lose it an election (%)*

Partisanship	Labour				Conservative			
	Agree	Neith-er	Dis-agree	N	Agree	Neith-er	Dis-agree	N
All	67.9	11.8	20.3	2874	81.2	8.3	10.5	2393
Very Strong	69.2	11.3	19.5	1555	82.7	6.5	10.8	788
Fairly Strong	66.0	12.1	21.9	1122	81.7	7.9	10.4	1191
Not Very Strong	69.0	14.5	16.5	145	80.4	11.2	8.4	321
Not At All Strong	65.4	13.5	21.1	52	64.5	18.3	17.2	93

Table 1.5   *Further nuclear energy development is essential for the future prosperity of Britain (%)*

Partisanship	Labour				Conservative			
	Agree	Neith-er	Dis-agree	N	Agree	Neith-er	Dis-agree	N
All	14.1	11.8	74.1	2861	60.2	16.9	22.9	2349
Very Strong	13.1	11.9	75.0	1553	67.8	14.9	17.3	763
Fairly Strong	13.5	12.0	74.5	1112	59.7	17.8	22.5	1175
Not Very Strong	22.9	9.7	67.4	144	47.3	19.4	33.3	319
Not At All Strong	30.8	13.5	55.7	52	48.9	13.0	38.1	92

Table 1.6   *A future Labour/Conservative government should not agree to a single European currency (%)*

Partisanship	Labour				Conservative			
	Agree	Neith-er	Dis-agree	N	Agree	Neith-er	Dis-agree	N
All	25.4	19.0	55.6	2852	57.8	12.1	30.1	2370
Very Strong	24.1	17.9	58.0	1545	65.3	10.6	24.1	770
Fairly Strong	27.0	20.1	52.9	1113	56.1	12.2	31.7	1186
Not Very Strong	28.7	18.9	52.4	143	51.6	13.4	35.0	322
Not At All Strong	21.6	25.5	52.9	51	40.2	17.4	42.4	92

Table 1.7 **High Income tax makes people less willing to work hard (%)**

Partisanship	Labour				Conservative			
	Agree	Neith-er	Dis-agree	N	Agree	Neith-er	Dis-agree	N
All	26.4	10.9	62.7	2879	82.0	6.0	12.0	2395
Very Strong	25.5	10.1	64.4	1559	86.1	4.3	9.6	789
Fairly Strong	26.6	11.0	62.4	1122	81.8	5.6	12.6	1190
Not Very Strong	31.7	15.9	52.4	145	76.2	9.6	14.2	323
Not At All Strong	32.1	18.9	49.0	53	68.8	11.8	19.4	93

Table 1.8 **Britain's electoral system should be replaced by a system of proportional representation (%)**

Partisanship	Labour				Conservative			
	Agree	Neith-er	Dis-agree	N	Agree	Neith-er	Dis-agree	N
All	57.8	13.1	29.1	2875	21.6	11.9	66.5	2360
Very Strong	52.4	12.7	34.9	1560	10.3	8.9	80.8	778
Fairly Strong	63.6	13.6	22.8	1118	22.4	12.7	64.9	1168
Not Very Strong	69.7	13.8	16.5	145	37.3	16.8	45.9	322
Not At All Strong	65.4	13.5	21.1	52	51.1	12.0	36.9	92

Table 1.9 **Further moves towards integration within the European Community should be resisted (%)**

Partisanship	Labour				Conservative			
	Agree	Neith-er	Dis-agree	N	Agree	Neith-er	Dis-agree	N
All	21.7	13.2	65.1	2867	54.1	15.5	30.4	2369
Very Strong	20.5	12.5	67.0	1562	62.8	12.4	24.8	775
Fairly Strong	22.2	14.0	63.8	1112	50.5	17.3	32.2	1179
Not Very Strong	27.0	12.1	60.9	141	48.6	15.8	35.6	323
Not At All Strong	32.7	17.3	50.0	52	45.7	17.4	36.9	92

Table 1.10   There is no need for a Bill of Rights in this country (%)

Partisanship	Labour				Conservative			
	Agree	Neith-er	Dis-agree	N	Agree	Neith-er	Dis-agree	N
All	11.4	10.0	78.6	2850	39.9	26.5	33.6	2285
Very Strong	11.9	9.0	79.1	1542	49.7	22.3	28.0	746
Fairly Strong	10.9	10.3	78.8	1113	37.9	27.3	34.8	1140
Not Very Strong	8.4	17.5	74.1	143	27.0	31.5	41.5	311
Not At All Strong	15.4	9.6	75.0	52	28.4	35.2	36.4	88

Table 1.11   A future Labour/Conservative government should introduce a directly elected Scottish Assembly with taxing powers (%)

Partisanship	Labour				Conservative			
	Agree	Neith-er	Dis-agree	N	Agree	Neith-er	Dis-agree	N
All	61.3	22.0	16.7	2875	22.7	26.5	50.8	2331
Very Strong	65.4	19.0	15.6	1562	18.1	21.2	60.7	769
Fairly Strong	56.3	25.6	18.1	1119	24.6	27.0	48.4	1156
Not Very Strong	57.7	25.4	16.9	142	24.9	34.7	40.4	317
Not At All Strong	57.7	25.0	17.3	52	31.5	37.1	31.4	89

Table 1.12   Coalition governments are the best form of government for Britain (%)

Partisanship	Labour				Conservative			
	Agree	Neith-er	Dis-agree	N	Agree	Neith-er	Dis-agree	N
All	8.6	16.7	74.7	2871	9.5	10.1	80.4	2398
Very Strong	6.6	13.3	80.1	1554	5.4	4.8	89.8	792
Fairly Strong	10.2	20.3	69.5	1122	10.1	10.8	79.1	1185
Not Very Strong	18.3	24.6	57.1	142	12.8	15.9	71.3	327
Not At All Strong	11.3	18.9	69.8	53	23.4	25.5	51.1	94

Table 1.13   *A future Labour/Conservative government should/should not spend money to get rid of poverty (%)*

Partisanship	Labour				Conservative			
	Should	Doesn't matter	Should not	N	Should	Doesn't matter	Should not	N
All	98.0	0.9	1.1	2870	80.3	8.4	11.3	2351
Very Strong	98.6	0.8	0.6	1559	73.2	10.8	16.0	770
Fairly Strong	97.6	1.0	1.4	1116	82.9	7.6	9.5	1164
Not Very Strong	97.2	0.0	2.8	142	86.7	5.3	8.0	323
Not At All Strong	94.3	3.8	1.9	53	84.0	8.5	7.5	94

Table 1.14   *A future Labour/Conservative government should/should not encourage the growth of private medicine (%)*

Partisanship	Labour				Conservative			
	Should	Doesn't matter	Should not	N	Should	Doesn't matter	Should not	N
All	3.8	4.7	91.5	2863	52.0	15.8	32.2	2362
Very Strong	2.8	4.1	93.1	1553	62.4	14.9	22.7	777
Fairly Strong	4.0	4.9	91.1	1116	50.3	15.9	33.8	1167
Not Very Strong	7.1	9.9	83.0	141	40.2	18.4	41.4	326
Not At All Strong	17.0	5.7	77.3	53	28.3	13.0	58.7	92

Table 1.15   *A future Labour/Conservative government should/should not put more money into the National Health Service (%)*

Partisanship	Labour				Conservative			
	Should	Doesn't matter	Should not	N	Should	Doesn't matter	Should not	N
All	98.0	0.7	1.3	2875	79.3	7.4	13.3	2368
Very Strong	98.8	0.4	0.8	1560	70.6	9.5	19.9	775
Fairly Strong	97.3	0.7	2.0	1119	81.9	7.2	10.9	1173
Not Very Strong	95.8	2.8	1.4	142	88.0	4.3	7.7	326
Not At All Strong	94.4	1.9	3.7	54	89.4	3.2	7.4	94

Table 1.16   *A future Labour/Conservative government should/should not reduce spending in general (%)*

Partisanship	Labour					Conservative			
	Should	Doesn't matter	Should not	N		Should	Doesn't matter	Should not	N
All	19.6	7.3	73.1	2829		60.6	8.9	30.5	2348
Very Strong	17.6	6.3	76.1	1527		64.5	7.8	27.7	770
Fairly Strong	20.9	8.6	70.5	1110		61.0	8.3	30.7	1163
Not Very Strong	28.1	7.9	64.0	139		53.3	12.7	34.0	323
Not At All Strong	28.3	7.5	64.2	53		46.7	10.9	42.4	92

Table 1.17   *A future Labour/Conservative government should/should not introduce stricter laws to regulate the trade unions (%)*

Partisanship	Labour					Conservative			
	Should	Doesn't matter	Should not	N		Should	Doesn't matter	Should not	N
All	10.1	14.8	75.1	2839		66.4	12.2	21.4	2375
Very Strong	8.7	12.1	79.2	1536		76.6	9.5	13.9	786
Fairly Strong	11.0	17.6	71.4	1111		64.8	13.6	21.6	1168
Not Very Strong	12.3	21.7	66.0	138		57.4	12.3	30.3	326
Not At All Strong	27.8	14.8	57.4	54		31.6	15.8	52.6	95

Table 1.18   *A future Labour/Conservative government should/should not give workers more say in the places where they work (%)*

Partisanship	Labour					Conservative			
	Should	Doesn't matter	Should not	N		Should	Doesn't matter	Should not	N
All	91.2	5.7	3.1	2866		63.8	13.4	22.8	2382
Very Strong	92.4	4.8	2.8	1558		58.3	13.9	27.8	784
Fairly Strong	90.4	6.1	3.5	1113		64.9	13.6	21.5	1180
Not Very Strong	88.7	8.5	2.8	142		70.7	11.4	17.9	324
Not At All Strong	77.4	13.2	9.4	53		72.3	13.8	13.9	94

Table 1.19   A future Labour/Conservative government should/should not spend less on defence (%)

Partisanship	Labour				Conservative			
	Should	Doesn't matter	Should not	N	Should	Doesn't matter	Should not	N
All	82.7	4.7	12.6	2868	44.1	4.9	51.0	2369
Very Strong	83.9	3.6	12.5	1557	34.7	5.0	60.3	779
Fairly Strong	81.7	5.7	12.6	1116	45.6	5.0	49.4	1172
Not Very Strong	79.6	8.5	11.9	142	57.7	4.9	37.4	324
Not At All Strong	75.5	3.8	20.7	53	57.4	3.2	39.4	94

Table 1.20   Should a future Labour/Conservative government :
(A) Reduce taxes & spend less on health, education & social benefits ?
(B) Keep taxes/spending on these services at the same levels as now ?
(C) Increase taxes & spend more on health, education & social benefits ?

Partisanship	Labour				Conservative			
	A	B	C	N	A	B	C	N
All	2.7	6.4	90.9	2869	6.8	67.1	26.1	2366
Very Strong	2.8	4.9	92.3	1556	10.8	72.9	16.3	771
Fairly Strong	2.5	6.7	90.8	1120	5.3	68.2	26.5	1178
Not Very Strong	2.8	16.9	80.3	142	4.0	56.9	39.1	325
Not At All Strong	2.0	17.6	80.4	51	3.3	41.3	55.4	92

Table 1.21   On joining the Labour/Conservative party did the member approach the party (MA) or did the party approach the member (PA) ? (%)

Partisanship	Labour				Conservative			
	MA	Don't Know	PA	N	MA	Don't Know	PA	N
All	77.4	20.1	2.5	2901	34.4	50.2	15.4	2420
Very Strong	80.5	17.6	1.9	1576	43.0	42.8	14.2	795
Fairly Strong	73.5	23.4	3.1	1126	31.9	53.4	14.7	1206
Not Very Strong	71.2	23.3	5.5	146	25.5	56.6	17.9	325
Not At All Strong	83.0	15.1	1.9	53	24.5	48.9	26.6	94

Table 1.22 How often has the member attended a party meeting in the last 12 months ? (%)

Partisanship	Labour				Conservative			
	Not at all	Occas- ionally	Frequ- ently	N	Not at all	Occas- ionally	Frequ- ently	N
All	41.6	30.6	27.8	2915	66.0	22.1	11.9	2435
Very Strong	32.6	29.5	37.9	1581	53.1	24.6	22.3	796
Fairly Strong	49.2	32.9	17.9	1133	67.4	24.1	8.5	1213
Not Very Strong	66.7	28.6	4.7	147	85.2	11.5	3.3	331
Not At All Strong	75.9	16.7	7.4	54	88.4	11.6	0.0	95

Table 1.23 Is the member more or less politically active than 5 years ago ? (%)

Partisanship	Labour				Conservative			
	More active	About same	Less active	N	More active	About same	Less active	N
All	12.9	38.4	48.7	2874	9.3	62.8	27.9	2045
Very Strong	16.2	38.7	45.1	1558	14.0	54.3	31.7	709
Fairly Strong	9.5	38.9	51.6	1120	7.8	65.4	26.8	1023
Not Very Strong	5.6	34.3	60.1	143	4.5	73.1	22.4	242
Not At All Strong	7.5	28.3	64.2	53	0.0	74.6	25.4	71

Table 1.24 Does the member hold any office within the Labour/Conservative Party ? (%)

Partisanship	Labour			Conservative		
	Yes	No	N	Yes	No	N
All	15.9	84.1	2861	8.4	91.6	2397
Very Strong	19.8	80.2	1549	14.2	85.8	786
Fairly Strong	12.7	87.3	1119	7.0	93.0	1192
Not Very Strong	2.8	97.2	142	1.5	98.5	330
Not At All Strong	7.8	92.2	51	1.1	98.9	89

Table 1.25   *How much time does the member devote to party activities per month ? (%)*

Partisanship	Labour					Conservative				
	None	Up to 5 hrs	5 to 10 hrs	Over 10 hrs	N	None	Up to 5 hrs	5 to 10 hrs	Over 10 hrs	N
All	51.2	29.6	9.4	9.8	2871	76.1	15.2	4.5	4.2	2386
Very Strong	42.0	30.5	12.3	15.2	1547	65.1	18.0	7.8	9.1	783
Fairly Strong	58.9	30.2	6.8	4.1	1124	77.8	16.3	3.6	2.3	1184
Not Very Strong	78.2	20.4	1.4	0.0	147	90.5	8.3	0.6	0.6	327
Not At All Strong	81.1	13.2	3.8	1.9	53	96.7	2.2	1.1	0.0	92

Table 1.26   *What was the overall financial contribution made by the member in the last year ? (%)*

Partisanship	Labour				Conservative			
	0 to £10	£10 to £20	Over £20	N	0 to £10	£10 to £20	Over £20	N
All	24.4	19.6	56.0	2560	34.1	21.2	44.7	1797
Very Strong	20.1	18.5	61.4	1413	24.3	18.9	56.8	613
Fairly Strong	27.4	19.8	52.8	983	34.3	22.2	43.5	877
Not Very Strong	36.4	28.0	35.6	118	49.2	25.6	25.2	242
Not At All Strong	63.0	23.9	13.1	46	66.2	12.3	21.5	65

Table 1.27   *Is the member a local Labour/Conservative councillor ? (%)*

Partisanship	Labour			Conservative		
	Yes	No	N	Yes	No	N
All	7.9	92.1	2886	2.3	97.7	2412
Very Strong	11.7	88.3	1560	4.2	95.8	788
Fairly Strong	4.0	96.0	1128	1.7	98.3	1201
Not Very Strong	0.0	100.0	145	0.6	99.4	330
Not At All Strong	0.0	100.0	53	0.0	100.0	93

Table 1.28   The Labour/Conservative leader should be elected by a system of one party member/one vote (%)

Partisanship	Labour					Conservative			
	Agree	Neith-er	Dis-agree	N		Agree	Neith-er	Dis-agree	N
All	86.0	5.3	8.7	2882		50.0	14.3	35.7	2349
Very Strong	86.6	4.3	9.1	1565		46.9	12.9	40.2	770
Fairly Strong	86.0	5.8	8.2	1122		52.3	13.5	34.2	1169
Not Very Strong	81.1	10.5	8.4	143		45.8	18.8	35.4	319
Not At All Strong	80.8	9.6	9.6	52		61.5	22.0	16.5	91

Table 1.29   People like me can have a real influence in politics if they are prepared to get involved (%)

Partisanship	Labour					Conservative			
	Agree	Neith-er	Dis-agree	N		Agree	Neith-er	Dis-agree	N
All	65.9	16.1	18.0	2871		56.4	20.2	23.4	2361
Very Strong	73.0	12.8	14.2	1561		65.2	17.9	16.9	770
Fairly Strong	59.6	19.7	20.7	1115		55.5	20.2	24.3	1172
Not Very Strong	46.9	20.3	32.8	143		41.8	24.9	33.3	325
Not At All Strong	40.4	23.1	36.5	52		46.8	21.3	31.9	94

Table 1.30   Attending party meetings can be pretty tiring after a hard days work (%)

Partisanship	Labour					Conservative			
	Agree	Neith-er	Dis-agree	N		Agree	Neith-er	Dis-agree	N
All	77.1	11.4	11.5	2874		69.1	19.2	11.7	2339
Very Strong	77.1	10.2	12.7	1557		66.2	16.2	17.6	760
Fairly Strong	77.0	12.4	10.6	1120		71.1	20.0	8.9	1166
Not Very Strong	77.1	14.6	8.3	144		67.8	25.0	7.2	320
Not At All Strong	81.1	15.1	3.8	53		73.1	21.5	5.4	93

Table 1.31   Someone like me could do a good job of being a local councillor (%)

Partisanship	Labour				Conservative			
	Agree	Neith-er	Dis-agree	N	Agree	Neith-er	Dis-agree	N
All	48.7	21.9	29.4	2849	27.5	24.5	48.0	2326
Very Strong	57.1	20.4	22.5	1541	36.4	23.4	40.2	755
Fairly Strong	40.4	23.2	36.4	1115	26.2	25.5	48.3	1157
Not Very Strong	27.7	27.7	44.6	141	13.7	23.1	63.2	321
Not At All Strong	34.6	23.1	42.3	52	19.4	25.8	54.8	93

Table 1.32   Being an active party member is a good way of meeting interesting people (%)

Partisanship	Labour				Conservative			
	Agree	Neith-er	Dis-agree	N	Agree	Neith-er	Dis-agree	N
All	64.7	21.9	13.4	2871	59.5	29.9	10.6	2332
Very Strong	70.7	18.0	11.3	1558	71.4	20.1	8.5	762
Fairly Strong	59.4	26.3	14.3	1118	59.6	30.9	9.5	1160
Not Very Strong	45.1	29.6	25.3	142	38.2	46.1	15.7	317
Not At All Strong	52.8	20.8	26.4	53	34.4	41.9	23.7	93

Table 1.33   The only way to be really educated about politics is to be a party activist (%)

Partisanship	Labour				Conservative			
	Agree	Neith-er	Dis-agree	N	Agree	Neith-er	Dis-agree	N
All	41.9	11.2	46.9	2879	35.7	17.2	47.1	2336
Very Strong	45.0	10.7	44.3	1565	41.8	15.1	43.1	764
Fairly Strong	37.9	11.7	50.4	1120	33.1	17.6	49.3	1160
Not Very Strong	38.7	13.4	47.9	142	31.8	20.2	48.0	321
Not At All Strong	44.2	9.6	46.2	52	33.0	19.8	47.2	91

Table 1.34   *The party leadership does not pay a lot of attention to ordinary party members (%)*

Partisanship	Labour				Conservative			
	Agree	Neith-er	Dis-agree	N	Agree	Neith-er	Dis-agree	N
All	47.0	18.8	34.2	2878	42.2	23.9	33.9	2348
Very Strong	47.8	15.8	36.4	1560	36.5	20.4	43.1	770
Fairly Strong	44.5	22.5	33.0	1122	43.9	23.7	32.4	1167
Not Very Strong	52.1	22.2	25.7	144	47.0	30.4	22.6	319
Not At All Strong	61.5	19.2	19.3	52	53.3	33.7	13.0	92

Table 1.35   *Party activity often takes time away from one's family (%)*

Partisanship	Labour				Conservative			
	Agree	Neith-er	Dis-agree	N	Agree	Neith-er	Dis-agree	N
All	85.1	10.3	4.6	2871	67.0	25.5	7.5	2315
Very Strong	86.7	8.6	4.7	1559	68.9	21.6	9.5	756
Fairly Strong	83.2	12.2	4.6	1115	67.4	25.8	6.8	1153
Not Very Strong	83.4	13.9	2.7	144	61.7	33.9	4.4	316
Not At All Strong	83.0	11.3	5.7	53	65.6	25.6	8.8	90

Table 1.36   *The Labour/Conservative party would be more successful if people like me were elected to parliament (%)*

Partisanship	Labour				Conservative			
	Agree	Neith-er	Dis-agree	N	Agree	Neith-er	Dis-agree	N
All	33.7	34.2	32.1	2849	21.2	31.6	47.2	2304
Very Strong	39.3	34.1	26.6	1538	27.3	30.8	41.9	751
Fairly Strong	26.9	35.1	38.0	1116	18.9	32.1	49.0	1144
Not Very Strong	27.3	27.3	45.4	143	13.5	32.3	54.2	319
Not At All Strong	34.6	36.5	28.9	52	27.8	30.0	42.2	90

Table 1.37 *During the last 5 years, how often has the member displayed an election poster in his/her window ? (%)*

Partisanship	Labour				Conservative			
	Not at all	Occas- ionally	Freq- uently	N	Not at all	Occas- ionally	Freq- uently	N
All	9.6	21.7	68.7	2856	49.0	31.7	19.3	2299
Very Strong	6.7	17.3	76.0	1548	40.1	29.3	30.6	751
Fairly Strong	12.3	26.4	61.3	1113	47.6	36.5	15.9	1140
Not Very Strong	11.9	35.0	53.1	143	66.4	24.6	9.0	321
Not At All Strong	28.8	17.3	53.9	52	80.5	16.1	3.4	87

Table 1.38 *During the last 5 years, how often has the member donated money to party funds ? (%)*

Partisanship	Labour				Conservative			
	Not at all	Occas- ionally	Freq- uently	N	Not at all	Occas- ionally	Freq- uently	N
All	9.7	50.9	39.4	2851	15.0	55.2	29.8	2349
Very Strong	6.8	44.2	49.0	1549	8.7	43.1	48.2	772
Fairly Strong	11.3	59.5	29.2	1110	14.3	60.9	24.8	1164
Not Very Strong	19.7	62.7	17.6	142	26.0	63.5	10.5	323
Not At All Strong	34.0	38.0	28.0	50	38.9	55.6	5.5	90

Table 1.39 *During the last 5 years, how often has the member delivered party leaflets ? (%)*

Partisanship	Labour				Conservative			
	Not at all	Occas- ionally	Freq- uently	N	Not at all	Occas- ionally	Freq- uently	N
All	17.6	27.2	55.2	2802	61.0	16.9	22.1	2244
Very Strong	14.0	20.5	65.5	1523	46.2	17.2	36.6	723
Fairly Strong	20.7	34.7	44.6	1089	63.0	18.8	18.2	1120
Not Very Strong	28.4	41.1	30.5	141	81.4	11.4	7.2	317
Not At All Strong	30.6	26.5	42.9	49	84.5	10.7	4.8	84

Table 1.40   *During the last 5 years, how often has the member attended a party meeting ? (%)*

Partisanship	Labour				Conservative			
	Not at all	Occas-ionally	Freq-uently	N	Not at all	Occas-ionally	Freq-uently	N
All	21.5	40.8	37.7	2806	50.7	32.6	16.7	2274
Very Strong	16.5	34.8	48.7	1523	38.6	30.0	31.4	743
Fairly Strong	26.1	47.8	26.1	1093	50.5	38.0	11.5	1131
Not Very Strong	34.3	53.6	12.1	140	71.1	24.4	4.5	311
Not At All Strong	38.0	34.0	28.0	50	84.3	13.5	2.2	89

Table 1.41   *During the last 5 years, how often has the member canvassed voters on behalf of the party ? (%)*

Partisanship	Labour				Conservative			
	Not at all	Occas-ionally	Freq-uently	N	Not at all	Occas-ionally	Freq-uently	N
All	37.0	31.2	31.8	2782	74.8	14.8	10.4	2236
Very Strong	28.7	29.0	42.3	1506	61.0	17.4	21.6	729
Fairly Strong	45.5	34.3	20.2	1086	76.7	16.7	6.6	1105
Not Very Strong	54.3	35.0	10.7	140	93.0	6.0	1.0	315
Not At All Strong	52.0	18.0	30.0	50	98.9	1.1	0.0	87

Table 1.42   *Where would you place yourself on a Left/Right scale within the Labour/Conservative party ? (%)*

Partisanship	Labour				Conservative			
	Left	Centre	Right	N	Left	Centre	Right	N
All	57.3	20.7	22.0	2882	13.3	25.9	60.8	2384
Very Strong	63.3	19.8	16.9	1568	4.3	15.4	80.3	788
Fairly Strong	51.1	22.0	26.9	1120	12.5	29.5	58.0	1185
Not Very Strong	42.3	22.5	35.2	142	30.3	37.5	32.2	317
Not At All Strong	51.9	13.5	34.6	52	41.5	30.9	27.6	94

Table 1.43   *Where would you place yourself on a Left/Right scale within British Politics ? (%)*

Partisanship	Labour				Conservative			
	Left	Centre	Right	N	Left	Centre	Right	N
All	79.9	10.4	9.7	2880	3.7	18.2	78.1	2378
Very Strong	81.7	8.6	9.7	1565	1.9	8.8	89.3	784
Fairly Strong	78.8	11.7	9.5	1121	3.2	18.8	78.0	1180
Not Very Strong	75.4	16.2	8.4	142	6.9	33.1	60.0	320
Not At All Strong	59.6	21.2	19.2	52	12.8	38.3	48.9	94

Table 1.44   *What thermometer rating would the Labour/Conservative member give the Conservative Party ? (%)*

Partisanship	Labour					Conservative				
	Cd	Cl	W	H	M	Cd	Cl	W	H	M
All	76.0	20.4	3.0	0.6	14.8	0.2	3.6	33.6	62.6	80.9
Very Strong	80.5	17.1	2.0	0.4	12.3	0.0	1.2	18.1	80.7	87.3
Fairly Strong	72.3	22.8	4.0	0.9	17.0	0.2	2.6	37.7	59.5	80.0
Not Very Strong	61.3	32.1	5.1	1.5	21.3	0.0	4.6	54.2	41.2	74.0
Not At All Strong	61.5	32.7	3.8	2.0	20.1	2.2	34.1	40.7	23.0	61.6

Table 1.45   *What thermometer rating would the Labour/Conservative member give the Labour Party ? (%)*

Partisanship	Labour					Conservative				
	Cd	Cl	W	H	M	Cd	Cl	W	H	M
All	0.9	3.8	24.7	70.6	82.7	50.1	43.3	6.1	0.5	26.7
Very Strong	0.6	2.1	16.7	80.6	86.9	62.8	33.4	3.5	0.3	21.6
Fairly Strong	0.9	3.7	32.4	63.0	79.4	47.8	45.2	6.6	0.4	27.5
Not Very Strong	0.7	13.3	46.9	39.1	70.6	36.5	55.5	7.4	0.6	32.3
Not At All Strong	11.3	30.2	35.8	22.7	58.2	24.4	55.6	17.8	2.2	38.6

Table 1.46   *What thermometer rating would the Labour/Conservative member*
give the Liberal Democratic Party ? (%)

Partisanship	Labour					Conservative				
	Cd	Cl	W	H	M	Cd	Cl	W	H	M
All	33.0	44.3	20.9	1.8	36.9	32.7	50.8	15.3	1.2	36.2
Very Strong	39.7	41.6	17.3	1.4	33.4	46.7	44.8	7.7	0.8	29.6
Fairly Strong	25.4	47.0	25.2	2.4	41.1	27.7	53.3	17.9	1.1	38.3
Not Very Strong	19.9	52.9	25.0	2.2	42.2	20.9	55.9	20.6	2.6	42.3
Not At All Strong	30.8	42.3	23.1	3.8	36.6	20.0	50.0	26.7	3.3	43.2

Table 1.47   *What thermometer rating would the Labour/Conservative member*
give the Scottish Nationalist Party ? (%)

Partisanship	Labour					Conservative				
	Cd	Cl	W	H	M	Cd	Cl	W	H	M
All	43.8	37.3	16.0	2.9	32.2	68.9	26.7	4.0	0.4	19.1
Very Strong	48.1	34.1	14.2	3.6	30.5	77.9	19.4	2.4	0.3	15.0
Fairly Strong	39.2	41.0	17.8	2.0	33.9	64.7	30.0	5.1	0.2	20.8
Not Very Strong	28.7	48.1	20.4	2.8	39.3	63.8	32.1	3.7	0.4	22.1
Not At All Strong	50.0	26.1	21.7	2.2	28.8	58.6	34.5	6.9	0.0	23.7

Table 1.48   *What thermometer rating would the Labour/Conservative member*
give Plaid Cymru ? (%)

Partisanship	Labour					Conservative				
	Cd	Cl	W	H	M	Cd	Cl	W	H	M
All	47.5	37.8	12.9	1.8	29.6	82.6	16.0	1.1	0.3	12.9
Very Strong	52.0	33.7	12.2	2.1	28.0	87.9	11.9	0.2	0.0	9.6
Fairly Strong	41.9	42.6	13.6	1.9	31.7	81.0	16.7	1.9	0.4	14.1
Not Very Strong	40.6	44.6	14.8	0.0	32.1	78.2	21.3	0.0	0.5	15.9
Not At All Strong	45.7	41.3	13.0	0.0	28.9	66.0	30.2	3.8	0.0	19.4

Table 1.49   What thermometer rating would the Labour/Conservative member give the Green Party ? (%)

Partisanship	Labour					Conservative				
	Cd	Cl	W	H	M	Cd	Cl	W	H	M
All	33.3	35.9	25.7	5.1	39.4	70.2	24.3	5.0	0.5	19.5
Very Strong	37.8	35.0	22.7	4.5	36.8	79.3	17.5	3.0	0.2	14.7
Fairly Strong	27.9	36.8	29.7	5.6	42.4	68.1	25.4	5.7	0.8	20.8
Not Very Strong	26.9	36.9	27.7	8.5	44.1	59.0	34.3	6.3	0.4	24.8
Not At All Strong	30.6	36.7	24.5	8.2	40.6	53.7	35.8	9.0	1.5	25.9

Table 1.50   What thermometer rating would the Labour/Conservative member give the BBC ? (%)

Partisanship	Labour					Conservative				
	Cd	Cl	W	H	M	Cd	Cl	W	H	M
All	9.4	26.3	39.8	24.5	60.3	8.4	30.5	40.5	20.6	59.3
Very Strong	10.1	28.1	37.9	23.9	59.6	13.8	36.6	32.1	17.5	54.5
Fairly Strong	8.1	24.1	42.7	25.1	61.5	5.7	27.6	45.2	21.5	61.4
Not Very Strong	9.6	22.2	42.2	26.0	60.7	6.4	26.6	43.9	23.1	62.0
Not At All Strong	17.6	29.4	27.5	25.5	54.5	4.5	27.0	41.6	26.9	64.5

Table 1.51   What thermometer rating would the Labour/Conservative member give the European Community ? (%)

Partisanship	Labour					Conservative				
	Cd	Cl	W	H	M	Cd	Cl	W	H	M
All	11.1	32.4	41.8	14.7	55.5	14.2	40.8	35.6	9.4	50.8
Very Strong	10.7	30.7	42.3	16.3	56.7	18.8	39.6	31.4	10.2	48.5
Fairly Strong	11.1	34.5	41.8	12.6	54.5	11.0	42.3	38.2	8.5	52.1
Not Very Strong	10.3	38.8	37.9	13.0	54.3	12.0	38.9	39.7	9.4	52.9
Not At All Strong	28.9	24.4	37.8	8.9	45.0	23.9	38.8	23.9	13.4	47.0

Table 1.52   *What thermometer rating would the Labour/Conservative member*
               give the Trade Union Congress ? (%)

Partisanship	Labour					Conservative				
	Cd	Cl	W	H	M	Cd	Cl	W	H	M
All	5.6	29.1	47.5	17.8	60.0	53.6	39.9	5.6	0.9	26.3
Very Strong	4.2	24.3	48.2	23.3	63.2	62.4	32.9	3.9	0.8	22.0
Fairly Strong	6.0	34.4	48.7	10.9	57.1	50.9	42.2	6.2	0.7	27.7
Not Very Strong	11.3	40.3	38.7	9.7	52.8	46.2	45.7	7.2	0.9	29.8
Not At All Strong	27.7	36.2	23.4	12.7	44.0	35.5	51.6	8.1	4.8	34.6

Table 1.53   *What thermometer rating would the Labour/Conservative member*
               give the Police ? (%)

Partisanship	Labour					Conservative				
	Cd	Cl	W	H	M	Cd	Cl	W	H	M
All	17.7	44.4	28.4	9.5	48.1	1.4	12.5	39.9	46.2	73.0
Very Strong	18.0	42.7	29.6	9.7	48.2	1.5	9.8	33.9	54.8	75.9
Fairly Strong	17.0	46.2	27.6	9.2	48.3	1.4	11.5	43.1	44.0	72.4
Not Very Strong	16.4	51.5	23.9	8.2	47.6	1.3	19.2	41.7	37.8	69.2
Not At All Strong	25.5	37.3	25.5	11.7	46.0	1.1	23.3	43.3	32.3	68.4

Table 1.54   *What thermometer rating would the Labour/Conservative member*
               give the House of Commons ? (%)

Partisanship	Labour					Conservative				
	Cd	Cl	W	H	M	Cd	Cl	W	H	M
All	10.1	33.7	38.1	18.1	56.8	2.4	17.0	49.1	31.5	68.4
Very Strong	10.0	32.5	37.1	20.4	57.8	1.8	10.7	44.4	43.1	72.7
Fairly Strong	9.0	34.7	40.3	16.0	56.8	2.0	17.6	51.8	28.6	67.7
Not Very Strong	13.6	41.6	36.0	8.8	50.1	4.8	26.0	53.6	15.6	61.4
Not At All Strong	28.0	28.0	30.0	14.0	43.1	3.6	33.3	40.5	22.6	62.4

Table 1.55   What thermometer rating would the Labour/Conservative member give the CBI ? (%)

Partisanship	Labour					Conservative				
	Cd	Cl	W	H	M	Cd	Cl	W	H	M
All	44.7	41.8	11.4	2.1	31.0	5.4	29.7	49.1	15.8	59.7
Very Strong	49.9	37.5	10.2	2.4	28.8	5.1	25.1	47.9	21.9	62.1
Fairly Strong	37.4	47.7	13.1	1.8	34.2	4.4	30.4	51.7	13.5	59.8
Not Very Strong	39.6	47.2	13.1	0.1	32.9	8.8	34.3	47.5	9.4	55.2
Not At All Strong	55.8	32.6	11.6	0.0	25.5	10.0	48.0	30.0	12.0	50.3

Table 1.56   What thermometer rating would the Labour/Conservative member give the Queen ? (%)

Partisanship	Labour					Conservative				
	Cd	Cl	W	H	M	Cd	Cl	W	H	M
All	34.6	29.2	19.3	16.9	43.4	0.9	4.6	15.9	78.6	86.4
Very Strong	38.4	27.7	16.8	17.1	41.8	0.8	2.9	11.1	85.2	90.0
Fairly Strong	29.2	31.7	22.0	17.1	45.9	0.9	3.9	17.0	78.2	86.0
Not Very Strong	32.4	27.3	23.7	16.6	44.8	0.9	9.5	24.7	64.9	80.9
Not At All Strong	43.4	26.4	22.6	7.6	37.0	2.2	12.4	11.2	74.2	81.0

Table 1.57   What thermometer rating would the Labour/Conservative member give Judges ? (%)

Partisanship	Labour					Conservative				
	Cd	Cl	W	H	M	Cd	Cl	W	H	M
All	38.0	43.4	14.9	3.7	35.0	4.5	30.9	45.6	19.0	60.5
Very Strong	41.4	40.8	14.0	3.8	33.4	4.6	29.6	44.5	21.3	61.4
Fairly Strong	33.3	47.0	16.2	3.5	37.1	4.0	28.9	49.1	18.0	61.0
Not Very Strong	35.3	45.1	16.5	3.1	38.1	5.6	37.8	39.3	17.3	57.9
Not At All Strong	44.9	38.8	12.2	4.1	30.7	6.6	44.7	31.6	17.1	56.2

2   Social Class

Table 2.1   *The Labour/Conservative party should try to capture the middle ground in politics (%)*

Social Class	Labour				Conservative			
	Agree	Neith-er	Dis-agree	N	Agree	Neith-er	Dis-agree	N
All	50.0	12.2	37.8	2658	68.2	13.9	17.9	1983
Salariat	45.8	14.2	40.0	1554	66.1	13.5	20.4	1108
Routine Non-Manual	49.5	9.8	40.7	396	66.0	16.6	17.4	350
Petty Bourgeoisie	50.7	11.6	37.7	69	74.0	10.0	16.0	269
Foreman/Technician	58.7	7.8	33.5	155	73.0	17.1	9.9	111
Working Class	61.0	9.5	29.5	484	75.9	14.5	9.7	145

Table 2.2   *A Labour/Conservative government should introduce a prices and incomes policy as a means of controlling inflation (%)*

Social Class	Labour				Conservative			
	Agree	Neith-er	Dis-agree	N	Agree	Neith-er	Dis-agree	N
All	56.3	19.3	24.4	2656	40.1	11.9	48.0	2025
Salariat	51.7	21.7	26.6	1554	32.9	11.2	55.9	1125
Routine Non-Manual	57.9	20.0	22.1	390	50.8	13.0	36.2	356
Petty Bourgeoisie	63.2	23.5	13.3	68	42.9	13.1	44.0	273
Foreman/Technician	66.5	13.2	20.3	158	50.0	14.2	35.8	120
Working Class	65.4	12.6	22.0	486	56.3	9.3	34.4	151

Table 2.3   *Income and wealth should be re-distributed towards ordinary working people (%)*

Social Class	Labour				Conservative			
	Agree	Neith-er	Dis-agree	N	Agree	Neith-er	Dis-agree	N
All	86.0	9.1	4.9	2685	24.7	20.9	54.4	2024
Salariat	88.2	7.8	4.0	1570	21.8	22.6	55.6	1126
Routine Non-Manual	81.4	10.8	7.8	398	26.5	19.7	53.8	355
Petty Bourgeoisie	87.0	4.3	8.7	69	22.8	15.8	61.4	272
Foreman/Technician	80.3	15.3	4.4	157	36.1	19.4	44.5	119
Working Class	84.3	10.4	5.3	491	36.2	21.0	42.8	152

Table 2.4   *The Labour/Conservative Party should always stand by its principles even if this should lose it an election (%)*

Social Class	Labour				Conservative			
	Agree	Neith-er	Dis-agree	N	Agree	Neith-er	Dis-agree	N
All	67.4	11.9	20.7	2682	80.6	8.6	10.8	2058
Salariat	63.8	14.0	22.2	1562	80.4	8.9	10.7	1141
Routine Non-Manual	71.4	9.4	19.2	402	82.0	8.4	9.6	366
Petty Bourgeoisie	73.9	4.4	21.7	69	78.1	7.5	14.4	278
Foreman/Technician	72.2	10.7	17.1	158	82.5	7.5	10.0	120
Working Class	73.5	8.4	18.1	491	81.7	9.2	9.1	153

Table 2.5   *Further nuclear energy development is essential for the future prosperity of Britain (%)*

Social Class	Labour				Conservative			
	Agree	Neith-er	Dis-agree	N	Agree	Neith-er	Dis-agree	N
All	13.6	12.0	74.4	2677	60.0	17.0	23.0	2040
Salariat	11.5	11.7	76.8	1564	63.0	15.7	21.3	1131
Routine Non-Manual	11.8	13.0	75.2	399	54.3	23.4	22.3	359
Petty Bourgeoisie	8.8	7.4	83.8	68	60.3	13.3	26.4	277
Foreman/Technician	22.8	12.0	65.2	158	53.7	17.4	28.9	121
Working Class	19.5	12.7	67.8	488	56.6	17.1	26.3	152

Table 2.6   *A future Labour/Conservative government should not agree to a single European currency (%)*

Social Class	Labour				Conservative			
	Agree	Neith-er	Dis-agree	N	Agree	Neith-er	Dis-agree	N
All	24.0	19.2	56.8	2663	56.6	12.3	31.1	2044
Salariat	19.3	20.1	60.6	1552	55.4	11.4	33.2	1137
Routine Non-Manual	28.5	19.9	51.6	397	58.1	14.9	27.0	363
Petty Bourgeoisie	24.6	21.8	53.6	69	58.0	9.9	32.1	274
Foreman/Technician	30.4	16.2	53.4	161	55.2	18.9	25.9	116
Working Class	32.9	16.7	50.4	484	60.4	11.7	27.9	154

Table 2.7   *High income tax makes people less willing to work hard (%)*

Social Class	Labour				Conservative			
	Agree	Neith-er	Dis-agree	N	Agree	Neith-er	Dis-agree	N
All	25.4	10.8	63.8	2691	81.8	6.0	12.2	2062
Salariat	17.2	10.7	72.1	1568	81.9	6.7	11.4	1143
Routine Non-Manual	28.0	12.0	60.0	403	80.5	5.8	13.7	364
Petty Bourgeoisie	34.8	13.0	52.2	69	84.9	2.6	12.5	279
Foreman/Technician	36.7	15.2	48.1	158	80.2	7.4	12.4	121
Working Class	44.2	8.5	47.3	493	79.4	6.4	14.2	155

Table 2.8   *Britain's electoral system should be replaced by a system of proportional representation (%)*

Social Class	Labour				Conservative			
	Agree	Neith-er	Dis-agree	N	Agree	Neith-er	Dis-agree	N
All	58.4	12.7	28.9	2686	21.0	11.6	67.4	2035
Salariat	63.7	12.1	24.2	1568	21.0	10.8	68.2	1136
Routine Non-Manual	50.1	17.0	32.9	401	18.6	14.5	66.9	360
Petty Bourgeoisie	55.9	10.3	33.8	68	23.0	7.7	69.3	270
Foreman/Technician	52.8	12.0	35.2	159	20.3	17.8	61.9	118
Working Class	50.2	12.0	37.8	490	24.5	12.6	62.9	151

Table 2.9   *Further moves towards integration within the European Community*
should be resisted (%)

Social Class	Labour				Conservative			
	Agree	Neith-er	Dis-agree	N	Agree	Neith-er	Dis-agree	N
All	20.6	12.7	66.7	2676	52.1	16.0	31.9	2045
Salariat	17.9	11.3	70.8	1569	49.5	15.3	35.2	1140
Routine Non-Manual	22.5	15.9	61.6	396	53.6	20.4	26.0	362
Petty Bourgeoisie	18.9	24.6	56.5	69	52.9	13.3	33.8	272
Foreman/Technician	26.1	10.8	63.1	157	59.2	15.8	25.0	120
Working Class	26.0	14.0	60.0	485	60.9	15.3	23.8	151

Table 2.10   *There is no need for a Bill of Rights in this country (%)*

Social Class	Labour				Conservative			
	Agree	Neith-er	Dis-agree	N	Agree	Neith-er	Dis-agree	N
All	10.8	9.4	79.8	2670	39.4	26.9	33.7	1985
Salariat	9.0	8.2	82.8	1562	42.9	25.8	31.3	1111
Routine Non-Manual	11.6	14.1	74.3	397	36.4	31.5	32.1	349
Petty Bourgeoisie	16.4	7.5	76.1	67	36.1	28.6	35.3	266
Foreman/Technician	11.5	8.2	80.3	157	28.1	23.7	48.2	114
Working Class	15.0	10.3	74.7	487	34.5	24.8	40.7	145

Table 2.11   *A future Labour/Conservative government should introduce a directly elected Scottish Assembly with taxing powers (%)*

Social Class	Labour				Conservative			
	Agree	Neith-er	Dis-agree	N	Agree	Neith-er	Dis-agree	N
All	61.6	22.0	16.4	2689	22.0	26.5	51.5	2024
Salariat	63.3	21.1	15.6	1566	21.0	24.9	54.1	1129
Routine Non-Manual	57.0	24.8	18.2	400	21.6	33.5	44.9	361
Petty Bourgeoisie	57.1	30.0	12.9	70	23.7	24.4	51.9	270
Foreman/Technician	54.3	26.5	19.2	162	28.2	24.8	47.0	117
Working Class	62.7	20.2	17.1	491	22.0	26.5	51.5	148

Table 2.12   *Coalition governments are the best form of government for Britain (%)*

Social Class	Labour				Conservative			
	Agree	Neith-er	Dis-agree	N	Agree	Neith-er	Dis-agree	N
All	8.4	17.0	74.6	2680	8.6	9.8	81.6	2065
Salariat	7.7	19.2	73.1	1564	7.6	10.5	81.9	1145
Routine Non-Manual	10.3	15.4	74.3	397	8.4	12.0	79.6	367
Petty Bourgeoisie	5.8	18.8	75.4	69	7.9	6.4	85.7	279
Foreman/Technician	6.3	8.8	84.9	159	12.6	5.9	81.5	119
Working Class	10.2	13.6	76.2	491	13.5	9.1	77.4	155

Table 2.13   *A future Labour/Conservative government should/should not spend money to get rid of poverty (%)*

Social Class	Labour				Conservative			
	Should	Doesn't matter	Should not	N	Should	Doesn't matter	Should not	N
All	98.1	0.9	1.0	2680	79.8	8.5	11.7	2034
Salariat	98.3	0.7	1.0	1560	78.7	8.9	12.4	1127
Routine Non-Manual	97.6	1.2	1.2	403	82.9	7.7	9.4	362
Petty Bourgeoisie	95.6	2.9	1.5	68	80.9	6.1	13.0	277
Foreman/Technician	97.6	1.2	1.2	161	82.4	9.2	8.4	119
Working Class	98.6	0.8	0.6	488	76.5	12.1	11.4	149

Table 2.14   *A future Labour/Conservative government should/should not encourage the growth of private medicine (%)*

Social Class	Labour				Conservative			
	Should	Doesn't matter	Should not	N	Should	Doesn't matter	Should not	N
All	3.3	4.5	92.2	2677	51.8	16.0	32.2	2040
Salariat	2.1	3.7	94.2	1558	53.2	16.6	30.2	1133
Routine Non-Manual	3.7	4.5	91.8	401	44.9	19.4	35.7	361
Petty Bourgeoisie	0.0	10.1	89.9	69	58.8	13.1	28.1	274
Foreman/Technician	5.6	5.6	88.8	161	48.7	11.0	40.3	119
Working Class	7.0	5.7	87.3	488	47.1	13.7	39.2	153

Table 2.15   A future Labour/Conservative government should/should not put
more money into the National Health Service (%)

Social Class	Labour				Conservative			
	Should	Doesn't matter	Should not	N	Should	Doesn't matter	Should not	N
All	98.1	0.7	1.2	2684	79.0	7.3	13.7	2040
Salariat	97.8	0.9	1.3	1562	77.1	8.1	14.8	1128
Routine Non-Manual	98.0	0.8	1.2	404	83.0	6.3	10.7	364
Petty Bourgeoisie	98.6	0.0	1.4	69	78.0	6.8	15.2	277
Foreman/Technician	98.8	0.6	0.6	161	86.7	4.1	9.2	120
Working Class	98.6	0.4	1.0	488	79.5	7.3	13.2	151

Table 2.16   A future Labour/Conservative government should/should not reduce
spending in general (%)

Social Class	Labour				Conservative			
	Should	Doesn't matter	Should not	N	Should	Doesn't matter	Should not	N
All	18.8	7.3	73.9	2648	60.0	8.9	31.1	2036
Salariat	15.3	5.7	79.0	1546	61.2	8.7	30.1	1133
Routine Non-Manual	22.0	9.1	68.9	395	56.0	9.1	34.9	361
Petty Bourgeoisie	23.5	8.9	67.6	68	60.1	7.2	32.7	276
Foreman/Technician	19.1	8.9	72.0	157	66.1	6.1	27.8	115
Working Class	27.0	10.0	63.0	482	56.3	15.2	28.5	151

Table 2.17   *A future Labour/Conservative government should/should not introduce stricter laws to regulate the trade unions (%)*

Social Class	Labour				Conservative			
	Should	Doesn't matter	Should not	N	Should	Doesn't matter	Should not	N
All	9.6	14.3	76.1	2656	65.3	12.4	22.3	2049
Salariat	8.2	14.3	77.5	1546	62.7	13.6	23.7	1141
Routine Non-Manual	10.8	13.8	75.4	398	71.7	10.4	17.9	364
Petty Bourgeoisie	11.6	14.5	73.9	69	69.3	9.5	21.2	274
Foreman/Technician	12.0	19.6	68.4	158	70.6	11.8	17.6	119
Working Class	12.4	12.8	74.8	485	58.9	12.6	28.5	151

Table 2.18   *A future Labour/Conservative government should/should not give workers more say in the places where they work (%)*

Social Class	Labour				Conservative			
	Should	Doesn't matter	Should not	N	Should	Doesn't matter	Should not	N
All	91.4	5.4	3.2	2678	62.7	13.7	23.6	2053
Salariat	91.5	4.9	3.6	1559	61.1	14.2	24.7	1140
Routine Non-Manual	91.3	5.7	3.0	402	70.5	13.7	15.8	366
Petty Bourgeoisie	88.4	11.6	0.0	69	57.3	12.4	30.3	274
Foreman/Technician	88.1	9.4	2.5	160	62.5	11.7	25.8	120
Working Class	92.8	4.7	2.5	488	66.7	13.7	19.6	153

Table 2.19   *A future Labour/Conservative government should/should not spend less on defence (%)*

Social Class	Labour				Conservative			
	Should	Doesn't matter	Should not	N	Should	Doesn't matter	Should not	N
All	83.2	4.6	12.2	2680	44.3	5.0	50.7	2046
Salariat	86.9	2.5	10.6	1563	45.6	4.6	49.8	1137
Routine Non-Manual	80.9	6.2	12.9	403	41.8	4.1	54.1	366
Petty Bourgeoisie	84.1	8.7	7.2	69	44.7	4.8	50.5	273
Foreman/Technician	73.9	7.5	18.6	161	47.9	5.0	47.1	119
Working Class	76.2	8.3	15.5	484	37.1	10.6	52.3	151

Table 2.20   *Should a future Labour/Conservative government :*
(A) Reduce taxes & spend less on health, education & social benefits ?
(B) Keep taxes & spending on these services at the same levels as now ?
(C) Increase taxes & spend more on health, education & social benefits ?

Social Class	Labour				Conservative			
	A	B	C	N	A	B	C	N
All	2.5	6.2	91.3	2677	6.5	67.8	25.7	2037
Salariat	1.9	5.7	92.4	1556	7.9	68.3	23.8	1128
Routine Non-Manual	2.7	4.8	92.5	401	3.8	67.5	28.7	363
Petty Bourgeoisie	2.9	7.1	90.0	70	7.7	67.8	24.5	273
Foreman/Technician	3.8	8.2	88.0	158	5.0	65.8	29.2	120
Working Class	3.9	7.7	88.4	492	1.3	66.7	32.0	153

Table 2.21   *On joining the Labour/Conservative party did the member approach the party (MA) or did the party approach the member (PA) ? (%)*

Social Class	Labour				Conservative			
	MA	Don't Know	PA	N	MA	Don't Know	PA	N
All	77.8	19.8	2.4	2703	35.0	50.9	14.1	2069
Salariat	79.1	18.2	2.7	1574	36.7	50.3	13.0	1146
Routine Non-Manual	76.6	21.4	2.0	402	32.5	52.7	14.8	366
Petty Bourgeoisie	79.7	18.8	1.5	69	32.3	53.8	13.9	279
Foreman/Technician	73.9	24.2	1.9	161	34.2	47.5	18.3	120
Working Class	75.9	21.9	2.2	497	34.2	49.4	16.4	158

Table 2.22   *How often has the member attended a party meeting in the last 12 months ? (%)*

Social Class	Labour				Conservative			
	Not at all	Occasionally	Frequently	N	Not at all	Occasionally	Frequently	N
All	41.5	30.6	27.9	2713	66.1	21.8	12.1	2083
Salariat	43.1	30.9	26.0	1578	63.6	23.9	12.5	1153
Routine Non-Manual	45.8	25.9	28.3	406	64.7	21.3	14.0	371
Petty Bourgeoisie	37.1	35.7	27.2	70	72.3	16.9	10.8	278
Foreman/Technician	41.4	32.1	26.5	162	77.0	13.9	9.1	122
Working Class	33.8	32.0	34.2	497	68.6	22.0	9.4	159

Table 2.23   Is the member more or less politically active than 5 years ago ? (%)

Social Class	Labour				Conservative			
	More active	About same	Less active	N	More active	About same	Less active	N
All	13.2	38.2	48.6	2683	9.9	63.7	26.4	1756
Salariat	12.7	37.9	49.4	1562	11.4	61.2	27.4	988
Routine Non-Manual	15.2	41.0	43.8	402	8.8	67.1	24.1	316
Petty Bourgeoisie	20.0	34.3	45.7	70	10.8	65.0	24.2	223
Foreman/Technician	8.8	36.5	54.7	159	3.0	67.0	30.0	100
Working Class	13.4	38.0	48.6	490	5.4	69.8	24.8	129

Table 2.24   Does the member hold any office within the Labour/Conservative Party ? (%)

Social Class	Labour			Conservative		
	Yes	No	N	Yes	No	N
All	16.3	83.7	2673	8.7	91.3	2051
Salariat	18.2	81.8	1553	9.4	90.6	1138
Routine Non-Manual	12.2	87.8	400	9.4	90.6	361
Petty Bourgeoisie	18.8	81.2	69	6.5	93.5	275
Foreman/Technician	17.3	82.7	162	6.7	93.3	120
Working Class	13.3	86.7	489	7.0	93.0	157

Table 2.25 *How much time does the member devote to party activities per month ? (%)*

Social Class	Labour					Conservative				
	None	Up to 5 hrs	5 to 10 hrs	Over 10 hrs	N	None	Up to 5 hrs	5 to 10 hrs	Over 10 hrs	N
All	50.8	29.8	9.2	10.2	2686	75.4	15.9	4.4	4.3	2050
Salariat	50.1	31.4	9.3	9.2	1564	74.2	15.7	4.9	5.2	1142
Routine Non-Manual	55.1	24.3	9.7	10.9	403	72.3	20.1	4.7	2.9	364
Petty Bourgeoisie	51.4	28.6	4.3	15.7	70	80.1	13.3	3.3	3.3	271
Foreman/Technician	54.4	30.0	7.5	8.1	160	83.1	11.9	2.5	2.5	118
Working Class	48.3	29.4	9.6	12.7	489	77.4	15.5	3.2	3.9	155

Table 2.26 *What was the overall financial contribution made by the member in the last year ? (%)*

Social Class	Labour				Conservative			
	0 to £10	£10 to £20	Over £20	N	0 to £10	£10 to £20	Over £20	N
All	23.2	19.6	57.2	2400	33.9	21.1	45.0	1596
Salariat	16.9	17.7	65.4	1415	30.7	20.3	49.0	927
Routine Non-Manual	32.7	21.3	46.0	346	37.4	24.8	37.8	278
Petty Bourgeoisie	23.7	18.7	57.6	59	34.3	22.6	43.1	204
Foreman/Technician	30.4	25.7	43.9	148	45.3	19.8	34.9	86
Working Class	33.8	22.2	44.0	432	42.6	16.8	40.6	101

Table 2.27   *Is the member a local Labour/Conservative councillor ? (%)*

Social Class	Labour			Conservative		
	Yes	No	N	Yes	No	N
All	8.1	91.9	2698	2.4	97.6	2070
Salariat	7.7	92.3	1575	2.7	97.3	1149
Routine Non-Manual	7.7	92.3	402	0.8	99.2	368
Petty Bourgeoisie	10.0	90.0	70	2.9	97.1	277
Foreman/Technician	7.5	92.5	161	1.7	98.3	120
Working Class	9.6	90.4	490	3.2	96.8	156

Table 2.28   *The Labour/Conservative leader should be elected by a system of one party member/one vote (%)*

Social Class	Labour				Conservative			
	Agree	Neith-er	Dis-agree	N	Agree	Neith-er	Dis-agree	N
All	85.8	5.3	8.9	2691	49.3	14.7	36.0	2029
Salariat	84.8	6.1	9.1	1562	44.7	15.8	39.5	1128
Routine Non-Manual	87.8	4.5	7.7	403	53.7	13.0	33.3	363
Petty Bourgeoisie	85.3	4.4	10.3	68	52.6	14.4	33.0	270
Foreman/Technician	90.1	4.3	5.6	162	54.7	12.8	32.5	117
Working Class	85.7	4.0	10.3	496	62.9	12.6	24.5	151

Table 2.29   *People like me can have a real influence in politics if they are prepared to get involved (%)*

Social Class	Labour				Conservative			
	Agree	Neither	Disagree	N	Agree	Neither	Disagree	N
All	66.0	16.1	17.9	2684	56.9	19.9	23.2	2043
Salariat	63.5	16.9	19.6	1564	59.1	19.7	21.2	1139
Routine Non-Manual	66.9	16.1	17.0	399	50.7	21.3	28.0	361
Petty Bourgeoisie	63.8	20.3	15.9	69	60.4	18.9	20.7	275
Foreman/Technician	65.8	15.6	18.6	161	53.0	20.5	26.5	117
Working Class	73.5	13.3	13.2	491	51.7	20.5	27.8	151

Table 2.30   *Attending party meetings can be pretty tiring after a hard days work (%)*

Social Class	Labour				Conservative			
	Agree	Neither	Disagree	N	Agree	Neither	Disagree	N
All	77.4	11.3	11.3	2693	69.2	19.4	11.4	2028
Salariat	81.5	9.3	9.2	1568	70.5	19.8	9.7	1129
Routine Non-Manual	74.7	13.9	11.4	403	65.7	19.8	14.5	359
Petty Bourgeoisie	60.9	15.9	23.2	69	70.6	16.2	13.2	272
Foreman/Technician	65.6	17.5	16.9	160	64.7	24.1	11.2	116
Working Class	72.8	12.8	14.4	493	69.1	18.4	12.5	152

Table 2.31   Someone like me could do a good job of being a local councillor (%)

Social Class	Labour				Conservative			
	Agree	Neith-er	Dis-agree	N	Agree	Neith-er	Dis-agree	N
All	49.4	21.7	28.9	2670	29.0	24.5	46.5	2025
Salariat	51.9	20.9	27.2	1558	34.2	25.3	40.5	1136
Routine Non-Manual	39.1	26.1	34.8	396	16.4	21.9	61.7	360
Petty Bourgeoisie	52.9	17.7	29.4	68	29.7	24.6	45.7	269
Foreman/Technician	45.6	24.4	30.0	160	16.0	21.2	62.8	113
Working Class	50.2	20.3	29.5	488	27.9	27.2	44.9	147

Table 2.32   Being an active party member is a good way of meeting interesting people (%)

Social Class	Labour				Conservative			
	Agree	Neith-er	Dis-agree	N	Agree	Neith-er	Dis-agree	N
All	64.1	21.9	14.0	2688	58.2	31.1	10.7	2021
Salariat	57.5	25.8	16.7	1563	57.0	32.4	10.6	1128
Routine Non-Manual	69.0	18.7	12.3	402	66.3	24.2	9.5	359
Petty Bourgeoisie	63.8	20.3	15.9	69	51.9	35.8	12.3	268
Foreman/Technician	75.0	16.9	8.1	160	56.1	32.5	11.4	114
Working Class	77.3	14.4	8.3	494	61.2	28.9	9.9	152

Table 2.33 *The only way to be really educated about politics is to be a party activist (%)*

Social Class	Labour				Conservative			
	Agree	Neith-er	Dis-agree	N	Agree	Neith-er	Dis-agree	N
All	41.2	11.4	47.4	2691	33.8	17.9	48.3	2026
Salariat	34.8	11.5	53.7	1567	29.4	19.9	50.7	1132
Routine Non-Manual	44.5	12.2	43.3	402	39.8	13.7	46.5	357
Petty Bourgeoisie	39.1	8.7	52.2	69	37.4	16.3	46.3	270
Foreman/Technician	52.8	10.7	36.5	159	43.1	17.2	39.7	116
Working Class	55.7	10.7	33.6	494	39.1	16.5	44.4	151

Table 2.34 *The party leadership does not pay a lot of attention to ordinary party members (%)*

Social Class	Labour				Conservative			
	Agree	Neith-er	Dis-agree	N	Agree	Neith-er	Dis-agree	N
All	46.7	19.3	34.0	2691	41.3	24.6	34.1	2032
Salariat	44.4	20.5	35.1	1567	40.9	24.5	34.6	1133
Routine Non-Manual	48.3	20.1	31.6	402	40.3	23.9	35.8	360
Petty Bourgeoisie	44.9	18.9	36.2	69	43.0	24.6	32.4	272
Foreman/Technician	43.5	25.4	31.1	161	46.1	21.7	32.2	115
Working Class	54.1	12.8	33.1	492	40.1	29.6	30.3	152

Table 2.35   Party activity often takes time away from one's family (%)

Social Class	Labour				Conservative			
	Agree	Neith-er	Dis-agree	N	Agree	Neith-er	Dis-agree	N
All	85.5	10.1	4.4	2689	66.7	25.6	7.7	2008
Salariat	84.5	10.9	4.6	1566	66.8	25.9	7.3	1125
Routine Non-Manual	87.6	9.0	3.4	402	66.9	22.5	10.6	356
Petty Bourgeoisie	82.6	10.1	7.3	69	63.4	30.2	6.4	262
Foreman/Technician	88.8	8.7	2.5	161	68.4	23.7	7.9	114
Working Class	86.4	8.8	4.8	491	70.9	25.2	3.9	151

Table 2.36   The Labour/Conservative party would be more successful if people like me were elected to parliament (%)

Social Class	Labour				Conservative			
	Agree	Neith-er	Dis-agree	N	Agree	Neith-er	Dis-agree	N
All	33.5	34.1	32.4	2669	21.5	32.1	46.4	2004
Salariat	33.8	34.9	31.3	1551	22.6	34.6	42.8	1120
Routine Non-Manual	27.2	35.9	36.9	401	13.8	30.8	55.4	354
Petty Bourgeoisie	33.3	36.2	30.5	69	27.5	27.5	45.0	269
Foreman/Technician	34.4	31.8	33.8	160	16.5	26.1	57.4	115
Working Class	37.1	30.3	32.6	488	24.0	30.1	45.9	146

Table 2.37   *During the last 5 years, how often has the member displayed an election poster in his/her window ? (%)*

Social Class	Labour				Conservative			
	Not at all	Occasionally	Frequently	N	Not at all	Occasionally	Frequently	N
All	9.4	21.7	68.9	2671	48.5	31.8	19.7	1984
Salariat	9.5	21.5	69.0	1560	46.8	32.1	21.1	1095
Routine Non-Manual	8.7	23.6	67.7	402	48.6	33.4	18.0	350
Petty Bourgeoisie	1.4	26.1	72.5	69	50.9	30.1	19.0	269
Foreman/Technician	9.0	20.5	70.5	156	54.2	24.6	21.2	118
Working Class	10.7	20.5	68.8	484	52.0	34.2	13.8	152

Table 2.38   *During the last 5 years, how often has the member donated money to party funds ? (%)*

Social Class	Labour				Conservative			
	Not at all	Occasionally	Frequently	N	Not at all	Occasionally	Frequently	N
All	9.3	51.1	39.6	2664	15.1	56.0	28.9	2023
Salariat	8.1	49.4	42.5	1559	14.2	53.8	32.0	1131
Routine Non-Manual	13.7	53.8	32.5	394	15.4	58.7	25.9	351
Petty Bourgeoisie	10.1	43.5	46.4	69	13.5	60.6	25.9	274
Foreman/Technician	7.4	60.5	32.1	162	19.8	59.5	20.7	116
Working Class	10.6	52.1	37.3	480	20.5	55.0	24.5	151

Table 2.39   *During the last 5 years, how often has the member delivered party leaflets ? (%)*

Social Class	Labour				Conservative			
	Not at all	Occas-ionally	Freq-uently	N	Not at all	Occas-ionally	Freq-uently	N
All	17.0	27.1	55.9	2622	60.1	17.3	22.6	1948
Salariat	14.9	28.2	56.9	1540	58.3	17.7	24.0	1079
Routine Non-Manual	21.4	27.6	51.0	388	56.2	20.0	23.8	345
Petty Bourgeoisie	17.4	27.5	55.1	69	67.5	12.5	20.0	265
Foreman/Technician	22.4	26.3	51.3	156	63.7	22.1	14.2	113
Working Class	18.8	23.0	58.2	469	66.5	13.0	20.5	146

Table 2.40   *During the last 5 years, how often has the member attended a party meeting ? (%)*

Social Class	Labour				Conservative			
	Not at all	Occas-ionally	Freq-uently	N	Not at all	Occas-ionally	Freq-uently	N
All	21.3	41.1	37.6	2629	50.8	32.2	17.0	1971
Salariat	20.8	43.6	35.6	1540	46.7	35.7	17.6	1099
Routine Non-Manual	24.5	39.3	36.2	389	54.5	27.2	18.3	345
Petty Bourgeoisie	23.2	37.7	39.1	69	55.6	28.2	16.2	266
Foreman/Technician	22.9	35.7	41.4	157	63.2	24.6	12.2	114
Working Class	19.4	36.9	43.7	474	55.1	30.6	14.3	147

Table 2.41   *During the last 5 years, how often has the member canvassed voters on behalf of the party ? (%)*

Social Class	Labour				Conservative			
	Not at all	Occas-ionally	Freq-uently	N	Not at all	Occas-ionally	Freq-uently	N
All	36.3	31.7	32.0	2609	74.4	15.2	10.4	1950
Salariat	35.1	33.5	31.4	1532	71.3	17.6	11.1	1082
Routine Non-Manual	44.2	29.2	26.6	387	78.7	12.3	9.0	342
Petty Bourgeoisie	33.8	26.5	39.7	68	74.6	12.5	12.9	264
Foreman/Technician	37.2	32.1	30.7	156	85.8	12.4	1.8	113
Working Class	34.1	28.6	37.3	466	77.2	11.4	11.4	149

Table 2.42   *Where would you place yourself on a Left/Right scale within the Labour/Conservative party ? (%)*

Social Class	Labour				Conservative			
	Left	Centre	Right	N	Left	Centre	Right	N
All	58.6	20.1	21.3	2692	14.1	26.1	59.8	2051
Salariat	59.3	19.1	21.6	1568	16.0	23.7	60.3	1144
Routine Non-Manual	58.3	20.7	21.0	405	11.7	28.1	60.2	359
Petty Bourgeoisie	62.3	21.7	15.9	69	11.6	27.3	61.1	275
Foreman/Technician	50.6	24.7	24.7	162	10.0	33.3	56.7	120
Working Class	59.0	21.1	19.9	488	12.4	32.0	55.6	153

Table 2.43   *Where would you place yourself on a Left/Right scale within British Politics ? (%)*

Social Class	Labour				Conservative			
	Left	Centre	Right	N	Left	Centre	Right	N
All	81.6	9.8	8.6	2692	3.9	18.7	77.4	2050
Salariat	87.1	7.3	5.6	1568	4.0	16.2	79.8	1145
Routine Non-Manual	78.7	12.2	9.1	403	4.5	20.7	74.8	357
Petty Bourgeoisie	78.2	8.8	13.0	69	2.9	20.4	76.7	274
Foreman/Technician	70.4	18.5	11.1	162	4.2	23.3	72.5	120
Working Class	70.5	12.9	16.6	490	2.6	26.6	70.8	154

Table 2.44   *What thermometer rating would the Labour/Conservative member give the Conservative Party ? (%)*

Social Class	Labour					Conservative				
	Cd	Cl	W	H	M	Cd	Cl	W	H	M
All	76.7	19.9	2.7	0.7	14.4	0.3	3.6	34.5	61.6	80.6
Salariat	80.8	17.1	1.7	0.4	12.5	0.3	3.5	37.1	59.1	79.7
Routine Non-Manual	76.6	20.7	2.4	0.3	14.7	0.0	1.6	30.3	68.1	83.5
Petty Bourgeoisie	76.9	18.5	3.1	1.5	15.9	0.7	4.0	31.8	63.5	80.2
Foreman/Technician	65.8	28.4	4.5	1.3	18.8	0.0	5.1	29.9	65.0	81.6
Working Class	67.0	25.8	5.8	1.4	18.9	0.0	7.1	33.3	59.6	79.8

Table 2.45   *What thermometer rating would the Labour/Conservative member give the Labour Party ? (%)*

Social Class	Labour					Conservative				
	Cd	Cl	W	H	M	Cd	Cl	W	H	M
All	0.8	3.8	25.3	70.1	82.5	51.0	42.8	5.8	0.4	26.3
Salariat	0.8	4.0	29.7	65.5	80.7	50.0	44.3	5.5	0.2	26.3
Routine Non-Manual	0.9	4.3	22.6	72.2	83.4	50.6	43.8	5.1	0.5	25.9
Petty Bourgeoisie	1.5	2.9	24.6	71.0	83.4	58.8	35.9	4.6	0.7	24.3
Foreman/Technician	0.0	0.6	22.4	77.0	86.1	55.4	36.6	8.0	0.0	26.4
Working Class	1.0	3.8	14.6	80.6	86.3	42.5	45.9	11.0	0.6	31.2

Table 2.46   *What thermometer rating would the Labour/Conservative member give the Liberal Democratic Party ? (%)*

Social Class	Labour					Conservative				
	Cd	Cl	W	H	M	Cd	Cl	W	H	M
All	33.0	44.5	20.7	1.8	36.7	33.5	50.7	14.6	1.2	35.9
Salariat	32.5	46.1	20.5	0.9	36.3	35.3	50.0	13.7	1.0	35.1
Routine Non-Manual	30.9	42.8	23.2	3.1	38.5	29.9	54.5	13.8	1.8	36.5
Petty Bourgeoisie	33.3	34.8	27.3	4.6	40.8	34.0	46.7	17.4	1.9	36.6
Foreman/Technician	33.8	45.2	18.5	2.5	37.6	34.9	51.4	13.7	0.0	34.6
Working Class	36.3	41.7	19.0	3.0	35.8	25.7	54.1	18.9	1.3	40.5

Table 2.47   What thermometer rating would the Labour/Conservative member
              give the Scottish Nationalist Party ? (%)

Social Class	Labour					Conservative				
	Cd	Cl	W	H	M	Cd	Cl	W	H	M
All	43.7	37.3	16.1	2.9	32.3	69.7	26.3	3.7	0.3	18.8
Salariat	41.7	38.9	16.7	2.7	33.0	70.0	26.0	3.6	0.4	18.7
Routine Non-Manual	43.5	36.6	17.1	2.8	31.5	71.0	27.3	1.7	0.0	17.5
Petty Bourgeoisie	55.1	30.6	14.3	0.0	28.7	73.9	21.7	3.4	1.0	17.7
Foreman/Technician	43.1	37.7	14.6	4.6	33.6	67.4	28.3	4.3	0.0	19.3
Working Class	49.0	33.2	13.9	3.9	30.6	58.3	33.3	8.3	0.1	23.9

Table 2.48   What thermometer rating would the Labour/Conservative member
              give Plaid Cymru ? (%)

Social Class	Labour					Conservative				
	Cd	Cl	W	H	M	Cd	Cl	W	H	M
All	47.4	37.7	13.1	1.8	29.6	82.9	15.7	1.1	0.3	12.8
Salariat	44.4	39.1	14.3	2.2	31.2	82.3	16.4	1.1	0.2	13.0
Routine Non-Manual	47.9	37.5	12.0	2.6	29.2	85.0	14.5	0.5	0.0	12.8
Petty Bourgeoisie	59.6	34.0	6.4	0.0	24.7	86.5	12.0	1.0	0.5	10.5
Foreman/Technician	44.5	43.0	12.5	0.0	30.8	82.7	16.0	1.3	0.0	13.0
Working Class	56.0	31.8	10.9	1.3	26.2	76.8	20.2	2.0	1.0	16.3

Table 2.49   *What thermometer rating would the Labour/Conservative member*
                give the Green Party ? (%)

Social Class	Labour					Conservative				
	Cd	Cl	W	H	M	Cd	Cl	W	H	M
All	33.0	35.8	26.1	5.1	39.7	70.5	24.1	4.9	0.5	19.4
Salariat	30.6	35.4	28.2	5.8	41.0	70.3	24.9	4.3	0.5	19.1
Routine Non-Manual	30.5	35.1	27.6	6.8	41.2	69.3	24.5	5.7	0.5	20.1
Petty Bourgeoisie	40.3	37.1	14.5	8.1	36.4	72.0	20.6	6.0	1.4	19.4
Foreman/Technician	37.0	41.1	19.9	2.0	36.9	74.5	21.3	4.2	0.0	18.6
Working Class	40.2	35.4	21.5	2.9	35.6	69.2	25.0	5.8	0.0	19.9

Table 2.50   *What thermometer rating would the Labour/Conservative member*
                give the BBC ? (%)

Social Class	Labour					Conservative				
	Cd	Cl	W	H	M	Cd	Cl	W	H	M
All	8.8	25.7	40.4	25.1	60.8	8.4	30.5	40.4	20.7	59.4
Salariat	6.8	21.7	43.2	28.3	63.3	8.4	30.6	40.7	20.3	59.0
Routine Non-Manual	9.7	27.7	40.5	22.1	59.2	6.8	26.4	42.8	24.0	62.3
Petty Bourgeoisie	10.4	28.4	32.8	28.4	61.2	9.8	33.2	38.1	18.9	57.7
Foreman/Technician	8.3	35.7	31.2	24.8	58.7	10.3	30.2	36.2	23.3	59.9
Working Class	15.0	33.1	35.4	16.5	54.5	7.8	35.2	39.4	17.6	58.8

Table 2.51 *What thermometer rating would the Labour/Conservative member give the European Community ? (%)*

Social Class	Labour					Conservative				
	Cd	Cl	W	H	M	Cd	Cl	W	H	M
All	10.6	32.6	42.3	14.5	55.8	14.3	41.2	35.2	9.3	50.7
Salariat	9.1	32.3	45.0	13.6	56.6	14.4	39.8	36.1	9.7	50.8
Routine Non-Manual	15.3	33.5	39.6	11.6	52.4	14.5	45.3	34.6	5.6	49.6
Petty Bourgeoisie	21.3	29.5	36.1	13.1	51.8	12.9	40.6	35.9	10.6	51.6
Foreman/Technician	6.4	31.2	43.3	19.1	58.8	15.4	39.7	35.9	9.0	51.4
Working Class	12.3	33.7	35.4	18.6	55.6	15.0	46.0	27.4	11.6	49.9

Table 2.52 *What thermometer rating would the Labour/Conservative member give the Trade Union Congress ? (%)*

Social Class	Labour					Conservative				
	Cd	Cl	W	H	M	Cd	Cl	W	H	M
All	5.5	29.4	48.0	17.1	59.9	53.8	39.7	5.7	0.8	26.3
Salariat	5.5	31.1	49.5	13.9	58.5	54.5	39.1	5.7	0.7	26.0
Routine Non-Manual	5.0	30.5	47.5	17.0	60.1	58.8	34.6	5.7	0.9	25.3
Petty Bourgeoisie	10.3	35.3	42.6	11.8	56.2	53.7	41.0	4.8	0.5	25.1
Foreman/Technician	3.9	26.1	49.7	20.3	62.5	50.0	41.4	7.1	1.5	27.9
Working Class	6.0	23.1	43.9	27.0	63.9	38.9	52.6	6.3	2.2	32.2

Table 2.53 *What thermometer rating would the Labour/Conservative member give the Police ? (%)*

Social Class	Labour					Conservative				
	Cd	Cl	W	H	M	Cd	Cl	W	H	M
All	18.0	45.0	28.1	8.9	47.7	1.5	12.7	40.5	45.3	72.7
Salariat	19.0	49.0	26.7	5.3	45.4	1.4	12.5	44.4	41.7	71.6
Routine Non-Manual	17.5	44.2	27.4	10.9	49.0	2.0	9.4	36.5	52.1	74.7
Petty Bourgeoisie	20.3	37.7	26.1	15.9	50.6	2.0	17.0	34.8	46.2	71.5
Foreman/Technician	9.7	41.9	35.5	12.9	53.0	0.0	15.9	31.9	52.2	75.5
Working Class	17.8	34.7	31.1	16.4	52.3	0.7	12.1	36.9	50.3	75.4

Table 2.54 *What thermometer rating would the Labour/Conservative member give the House of Commons ? (%)*

Social Class	Labour					Conservative				
	Cd	Cl	W	H	M	Cd	Cl	W	H	M
All	10.3	33.5	38.3	17.9	56.7	2.4	17.0	49.6	31.0	68.2
Salariat	10.4	33.9	40.2	15.5	55.8	2.6	16.8	52.3	28.3	67.4
Routine Non-Manual	9.4	37.0	37.2	16.4	56.5	2.2	13.4	49.7	34.7	70.1
Petty Bourgeoisie	10.4	29.9	31.3	28.4	60.4	0.8	20.5	46.6	32.1	68.2
Foreman/Technician	9.3	32.7	34.0	24.0	59.5	2.9	23.8	39.0	34.3	67.3
Working Class	11.1	30.3	35.7	22.9	58.3	3.8	15.0	42.1	39.1	70.2

Table 2.55   *What thermometer rating would the Labour/Conservative member give the CBI ? (%)*

Social Class	Labour					Conservative				
	Cd	Cl	W	H	M	Cd	Cl	W	H	M
All	45.1	41.9	11.0	2.0	30.7	5.5	29.7	49.0	15.8	59.5
Salariat	46.4	43.1	9.3	1.2	29.7	4.9	30.8	50.5	13.8	58.8
Routine Non-Manual	41.5	43.0	13.7	1.8	32.1	5.7	29.9	43.7	20.7	60.6
Petty Bourgeoisie	46.6	36.2	13.8	3.4	32.8	4.9	26.2	50.0	18.9	60.9
Foreman/Technician	38.1	45.5	13.4	3.0	34.9	11.4	24.3	51.4	12.9	58.6
Working Class	45.8	36.4	13.5	4.3	31.5	8.1	29.7	41.9	20.3	59.4

Table 2.56   *What thermometer rating would the Labour/Conservative member give the Queen ? (%)*

Social Class	Labour					Conservative				
	Cd	Cl	W	H	M	Cd	Cl	W	H	M
All	35.4	29.9	19.0	15.7	42.3	0.9	4.9	16.5	77.7	86.0
Salariat	39.3	32.6	17.4	10.7	37.9	0.8	4.9	18.1	76.2	85.5
Routine Non-Manual	34.0	26.0	21.4	18.6	44.8	0.6	4.5	11.9	83.0	88.4
Petty Bourgeoisie	35.8	25.4	23.9	14.9	44.5	2.5	6.3	19.2	72.0	82.8
Foreman/Technician	19.0	32.3	25.9	22.8	53.5	0.9	3.4	12.9	82.8	87.4
Working Class	29.6	24.2	19.1	27.1	50.3	0.0	4.6	12.6	82.8	88.6

Table 2.57   *What thermometer rating would the Labour/Conservative member give Judges ? (%)*

Social Class	Labour					Conservative				
	Cd	Cl	W	H	M	Cd	Cl	W	H	M
All	38.2	43.9	14.6	3.3	34.7	4.4	31.5	45.7	18.4	60.3
Salariat	40.4	44.1	13.5	2.0	33.2	3.5	28.7	48.3	19.5	61.4
Routine Non-Manual	36.7	45.3	14.8	3.2	35.0	5.9	33.2	42.2	18.7	59.4
Petty Bourgeoisie	36.4	37.9	18.1	7.6	38.1	6.5	35.6	43.7	14.2	57.9
Foreman/Technician	26.8	47.1	18.5	7.6	41.6	6.2	33.0	40.2	20.6	59.0
Working Class	36.7	41.7	16.1	5.5	36.4	3.1	40.3	41.1	15.5	59.3

3   Market Research Grading

Table 3.1   *The Labour/Conservative party should try to capture the middle ground in politics (%)*

Market Research Grading	Labour				Conservative			
	Agree	Neith-er	Dis-agree	N	Agree	Neith-er	Dis-agree	N
All	51.0	12.1	36.9	2631	68.2	13.9	17.9	1983
A	50.0	12.8	37.2	282	64.9	12.4	22.7	242
B	50.4	12.1	37.5	1161	68.4	12.7	18.9	916
C1	50.9	13.9	35.2	446	66.6	17.3	16.1	542
C2	53.4	10.0	36.6	350	77.3	12.9	9.8	132
D	51.7	11.3	37.0	300	72.8	13.2	14.0	114
E	52.2	10.9	36.9	92	62.2	8.1	29.7	37

Table 3.2   *A Labour/Conservative government should introduce a prices and Incomes policy as a means of controlling inflation (%)*

Market Research Grading	Labour				Conservative			
	Agree	Neith-er	Dis-agree	N	Agree	Neith-er	Dis-agree	N
All	57.4	19.1	23.5	2638	40.1	11.8	48.1	2025
A	59.5	17.9	22.6	279	29.2	13.6	57.2	243
B	56.9	20.2	22.9	1166	36.1	11.9	52.0	933
C1	54.7	18.2	27.1	450	44.6	12.4	43.0	556
C2	62.1	18.2	19.7	351	57.1	10.7	32.2	140
D	55.2	20.7	24.1	299	47.0	7.0	46.0	115
E	58.1	12.9	29.0	93	60.5	7.9	31.6	38

Table 3.3   *Income and wealth should be re-distributed towards ordinary working people (%)*

Market Research Grading	Labour				Conservative			
	Agree	Neith-er	Dis-agree	N	Agree	Neith-er	Dis-agree	N
All	85.8	9.0	5.2	2663	24.7	20.8	54.5	2024
A	84.8	9.2	6.0	283	24.2	21.7	54.1	244
B	86.2	9.3	4.5	1177	21.8	22.3	55.9	930
C1	86.8	7.7	5.5	454	23.6	20.0	56.4	554
C2	87.6	8.7	3.7	355	37.9	15.0	47.1	140
D	83.0	9.3	7.7	300	30.5	20.3	49.2	118
E	81.9	11.7	6.4	94	47.4	15.8	36.8	38

Table 3.4   *The Labour/Conservative Party should always stand by its principles even if this should lose it an election (%)*

Market Research Grading	Labour				Conservative			
	Agree	Neith-er	Dis-agree	N	Agree	Neith-er	Dis-agree	N
All	68.1	11.7	20.2	2660	80.6	8.6	10.8	2058
A	66.5	14.8	18.7	284	78.8	8.4	12.8	250
B	67.1	12.0	20.9	1175	80.5	8.9	10.6	942
C1	67.7	11.3	21.0	452	80.2	9.0	10.8	565
C2	69.8	10.5	19.7	354	81.0	9.2	9.8	142
D	70.8	9.6	19.6	301	83.3	5.8	10.9	120
E	71.3	10.6	18.1	94	89.7	2.6	7.7	39

Table 3.5   *Further nuclear energy development is essential for the future*
                 prosperity of Britain (%)

Market Research Grading	Labour				Conservative			
	Agree	Neith-er	Dis-agree	N	Agree	Neith-er	Dis-agree	N
All	14.3	11.7	74.0	2651	60.0	17.0	23.0	2040
A	13.8	9.9	76.3	282	68.2	15.1	16.7	245
B	14.1	11.4	74.5	1173	60.3	15.9	23.8	938
C1	14.3	11.3	74.4	453	57.6	19.5	22.9	559
C2	13.4	12.3	74.3	350	55.7	15.7	28.6	140
D	16.0	13.7	70.3	300	52.9	21.0	26.1	119
E	16.1	14.0	69.9	93	74.4	10.3	15.3	39

Table 3.6   *A future Labour/Conservative government should not agree to a*
                 single European currency (%)

Market Research Grading	Labour				Conservative			
	Agree	Neith-er	Dis-agree	N	Agree	Neith-er	Dis-agree	N
All	25.4	18.9	55.7	2638	56.6	12.3	31.1	2044
A	25.6	17.1	57.3	281	54.3	8.1	37.6	247
B	24.1	19.2	56.7	1169	56.6	12.2	31.2	938
C1	26.5	20.5	53.0	453	57.4	14.1	28.5	559
C2	29.2	15.6	55.2	346	60.7	10.0	29.3	140
D	23.5	22.1	54.4	298	51.2	18.2	30.6	121
E	28.6	14.3	57.1	91	61.5	5.1	33.4	39

Table 3.7　　*High Income tax makes people less willing to work hard (%)*

Market Research Grading	Labour				Conservative			
	Agree	Neith-er	Dis-agree	N	Agree	Neith-er	Dis-agree	N
All	26.6	10.8	62.6	2665	81.8	6.0	12.2	2062
A	24.8	11.7	63.5	282	79.8	7.3	12.9	247
B	25.7	11.1	63.2	1182	82.0	5.9	12.1	947
C1	26.4	11.2	62.4	454	82.0	5.7	12.3	566
C2	29.5	9.9	60.6	353	81.7	4.9	13.4	142
D	28.7	10.0	61.3	300	81.8	7.4	10.8	121
E	25.5	8.5	66.0	94	84.6	5.1	10.3	39

Table 3.8　　*Britain's electoral system should be replaced by a system of proportional representation (%)*

Market Research Grading	Labour				Conservative			
	Agree	Neith-er	Dis-agree	N	Agree	Neith-er	Dis-agree	N
All	57.9	13.1	29.0	2658	21.0	11.6	67.4	2035
A	55.1	12.5	32.4	287	22.7	8.5	68.8	247
B	58.2	13.2	28.6	1175	20.1	11.1	68.8	931
C1	59.5	11.8	28.7	452	20.3	12.6	67.1	562
C2	61.5	11.6	26.9	353	23.2	13.0	63.8	138
D	54.0	17.4	28.6	298	23.5	15.1	61.4	119
E	54.8	11.8	33.4	93	28.9	13.2	57.9	38

Table 3.9   *Further moves towards integration within the European Community*
               should be resisted (%)

Market Research Grading	Labour				Conservative			
	Agree	Neith-er	Dis-agree	N	Agree	Neith-er	Dis-agree	N
All	21.9	12.9	65.2	2652	52.1	16.0	31.9	2045
A	21.6	11.3	67.1	283	48.8	13.7	37.5	248
B	21.2	12.5	66.3	1172	50.8	16.1	33.1	937
C1	19.2	14.3	66.5	453	52.6	17.6	29.8	563
C2	25.4	14.4	60.2	354	63.3	14.4	22.3	139
D	24.4	12.4	63.2	299	52.1	16.0	31.9	119
E	24.2	9.9	65.9	91	56.4	10.3	33.3	39

Table 3.10   *There is no need for a Bill of Rights in this country (%)*

Market Research Grading	Labour				Conservative			
	Agree	Neith-er	Dis-agree	N	Agree	Neith-er	Dis-agree	N
All	11.4	10.0	78.6	2638	39.4	27.0	33.6	1985
A	13.6	11.2	75.2	286	40.7	28.0	31.3	243
B	10.9	9.7	79.4	1170	41.8	26.2	32.0	912
C1	8.7	10.0	81.3	450	38.3	29.2	32.5	545
C2	13.5	8.0	78.5	349	30.3	24.2	45.5	132
D	11.7	12.0	76.3	291	33.6	23.3	43.1	116
E	17.4	12.0	70.6	92	37.8	27.0	35.2	37

Table 3.11   *A future Labour/Conservative government should introduce a directly elected Scottish Assembly with taxing powers (%)*

Market Research Grading	Labour				Conservative			
	Agree	Neith-er	Dis-agree	N	Agree	Neith-er	Dis-agree	N
All	61.3	22.0	16.7	2659	22.0	26.5	51.5	2024
A	62.7	21.1	16.2	284	20.7	23.2	56.1	246
B	63.0	20.6	16.4	1171	20.6	26.9	52.5	927
C1	60.6	24.2	15.2	454	23.7	29.6	46.7	561
C2	60.2	23.0	16.8	357	23.0	24.4	52.6	135
D	60.3	21.5	18.2	302	24.6	19.5	55.9	118
E	47.3	29.7	23.0	91	27.0	21.6	51.4	37

Table 3.12   *Coalition governments are the best form of government for Britain (%)*

Market Research Grading	Labour				Conservative			
	Agree	Neith-er	Dis-agree	N	Agree	Neith-er	Dis-agree	N
All	8.7	16.8	74.5	2655	8.5	9.8	81.7	2065
A	7.3	14.3	78.4	287	8.8	8.4	82.8	250
B	8.4	18.3	73.3	1171	7.4	10.5	82.1	945
C1	9.3	18.7	72.0	450	8.1	10.2	81.7	571
C2	11.0	14.2	74.8	353	16.2	8.5	75.3	142
D	6.0	15.9	78.1	302	10.1	8.4	81.5	119
E	13.0	8.7	78.3	92	7.9	7.9	84.2	38

Table 3.13   *A future Labour/Conservative government should/should not spend money to get rid of poverty (%)*

Market Research Grading	Labour				Conservative			
	Should	Doesn't matter	Should not	N	Should	Doesn't matter	Should not	N
All	98.1	0.9	1.0	2658	79.8	8.6	11.6	2034
A	97.9	1.8	0.3	283	81.1	9.0	9.9	244
B	98.0	0.8	1.2	1178	79.1	8.2	12.7	937
C1	98.5	0.2	1.3	454	81.4	7.5	11.1	559
C2	99.4	0.6	0.0	351	77.5	10.9	11.6	138
D	97.7	1.0	1.3	298	76.5	11.8	11.7	119
E	95.7	2.1	2.2	94	83.8	10.8	5.4	37

Table 3.14   *A future Labour/Conservative government should/should not encourage the growth of private medicine (%)*

Market Research Grading	Labour				Conservative			
	Should	Doesn't matter	Should not	N	Should	Doesn't matter	Should not	N
All	3.8	4.6	91.6	2651	51.8	16.1	32.1	2040
A	4.0	5.4	90.6	278	50.8	17.1	32.1	246
B	3.3	3.9	92.8	1175	53.5	16.0	30.5	934
C1	3.5	4.8	91.7	456	52.1	15.1	32.8	562
C2	2.3	6.6	91.1	351	47.1	15.0	37.9	140
D	5.7	4.4	89.9	297	47.9	19.3	32.8	119
E	9.6	4.3	86.1	94	38.5	20.5	41.0	39

Table 3.15   *A future Labour/Conservative government should/should not put*
more money into the National Health Service (%)

Market Research Grading	Labour				Conservative			
	Should	Doesn't matter	Should not	N	Should	Doesn't matter	Should not	N
All	98.0	0.7	1.3	2662	79.0	7.3	13.7	2040
A	96.5	1.8	1.7	282	74.7	6.5	18.8	245
B	98.2	0.6	1.2	1180	78.4	8.3	13.3	935
C1	97.4	0.9	1.7	454	80.8	6.2	13.0	563
C2	98.0	0.6	1.4	353	81.4	7.1	11.5	140
D	99.3	0.0	0.7	298	80.3	6.0	13.7	117
E	97.9	1.1	1.0	95	82.5	7.5	10.0	40

Table 3.16   *A future Labour/Conservative government should/should not reduce*
spending in general (%)

Market Research Grading	Labour				Conservative			
	Should	Doesn't matter	Should not	N	Should	Doesn't matter	Should not	N
All	19.3	7.4	73.3	2620	60.0	8.9	31.1	2036
A	18.1	11.9	70.0	277	63.1	7.8	29.1	244
B	19.0	7.2	73.8	1161	59.4	8.6	32.0	939
C1	19.5	7.2	73.3	446	58.3	7.9	33.8	556
C2	19.8	6.0	74.2	349	57.2	15.9	26.9	138
D	21.4	7.8	70.8	295	66.7	10.8	22.5	120
E	16.3	2.2	81.5	92	69.2	7.7	23.1	39

Table 3.17   *A future Labour/Conservative government should/should not introduce stricter laws to regulate the trade unions (%)*

Market Research Grading	Labour				Conservative			
	Should	Doesn't matter	Should not	N	Should	Doesn't matter	Should not	N
All	10.3	14.8	74.9	2627	65.3	12.3	22.4	2049
A	11.4	13.9	74.7	281	58.9	13.4	27.7	246
B	9.5	13.6	76.9	1159	64.9	13.1	22.0	945
C1	8.9	16.5	74.6	449	69.3	11.2	19.5	561
C2	11.4	14.2	74.4	351	61.2	12.2	26.6	139
D	12.2	19.0	68.8	294	71.7	6.7	21.6	120
E	12.9	11.8	75.3	93	55.3	21.1	23.6	38

Table 3.18   *A future Labour/Conservative government should/should not give workers more say in the places where they work (%)*

Market Research Grading	Labour				Conservative			
	Should	Doesn't matter	Should not	N	Should	Doesn't matter	Should not	N
All	91.3	5.5	3.2	2653	62.7	13.7	23.6	2053
A	89.7	7.1	3.2	282	56.2	12.4	31.4	249
B	91.8	4.9	3.3	1178	61.1	13.7	25.2	939
C1	93.2	4.6	2.2	453	67.2	13.8	19.0	564
C2	90.0	6.8	3.2	351	65.5	12.0	22.5	142
D	91.2	6.4	2.4	296	63.3	15.8	20.9	120
E	87.1	4.3	8.6	93	66.7	17.9	15.4	39

Table 3.19   *A future Labour/Conservative government should/should not spend less on defence (%)*

Market Research Grading	Labour				Conservative			
	Should	Doesn't matter	Should not	N	Should	Doesn't matter	Should not	N
All	82.8	4.6	12.6	2656	44.3	5.0	50.7	2046
A	83.3	3.9	12.8	282	47.6	4.9	47.5	246
B	84.1	4.1	11.8	1178	45.2	4.8	50.0	939
C1	81.7	5.5	12.8	454	41.9	4.4	53.7	563
C2	81.2	4.8	14.0	351	43.9	7.9	48.2	139
D	82.9	5.0	12.1	298	44.2	8.3	47.5	120
E	76.3	7.5	16.2	93	38.5	0.0	61.5	39

Table 3.20   *Should a future Labour/Conservative government:*
(A) Reduce taxes & spend less on health, education & social benefits ?
(B) Keep taxes & spending on these services at the same levels as now ?
(C) Increase taxes & spend more on health, education & social benefits ?

Market Research Grading	Labour				Conservative			
	A	B	C	N	A	B	C	N
All	2.6	6.3	91.1	2657	6.5	67.8	25.7	2037
A	2.5	8.8	88.7	283	7.3	68.2	24.5	245
B	2.3	5.7	92.0	1168	7.5	68.2	24.3	931
C1	2.4	6.4	91.2	454	4.6	67.5	27.9	563
C2	3.4	7.6	89.0	353	1.4	71.1	27.5	142
D	3.9	4.6	91.5	305	9.2	62.2	28.6	119
E	1.1	6.4	92.5	94	13.5	64.9	21.6	37

Table 3.21   *On joining the Labour/Conservative party did the member approach*
                 the party (MA) or did the party approach the member (PA) ? (%)

Market Research Grading	Labour				Conservative			
	MA	Don't Know	PA	N	MA	Don't Know	PA	N
All	77.4	20.0	2.6	2684	35.0	50.9	14.1	2069
A	76.4	19.4	4.2	288	38.3	47.6	14.1	248
B	77.6	19.8	2.6	1185	35.3	51.2	13.5	949
C1	76.5	20.8	2.7	456	31.3	54.1	14.6	566
C2	77.5	20.0	2.5	355	35.9	47.6	16.5	145
D	79.7	19.0	1.3	305	36.1	50.0	13.9	122
E	74.7	24.2	1.1	95	56.4	35.9	7.7	39

Table 3.22   *How often has the member attended a party meeting in the last*
                 12 months ? (%)

Market Research Grading	Labour				Conservative			
	Not at all	Occas- ionally	Frequ- ently	N	Not at all	Occas- ionally	Frequ- ently	N
All	41.6	30.5	27.9	2897	66.1	21.8	12.1	2083
A	42.1	31.0	26.9	290	63.7	22.3	14.0	251
B	43.7	31.2	25.1	1193	65.1	21.8	13.1	953
C1	42.0	29.5	28.5	457	68.9	20.7	10.4	569
C2	39.3	29.8	30.9	356	65.8	24.7	9.5	146
D	37.3	31.0	31.7	306	66.9	20.2	12.9	124
E	35.8	26.3	37.9	95	65.0	27.5	7.5	40

Table 3.23   *Is the member more or less politically active than 5 years ago ? (%)*

Market Research Grading	Labour				Conservative			
	More active	About same	Less active	N	More active	About same	Less active	N
All	13.0	38.5	48.5	2659	9.9	63.7	26.4	1756
A	15.5	40.3	44.2	283	13.1	59.5	27.4	222
B	12.3	37.7	50.0	1180	11.4	61.9	26.7	800
C1	11.8	39.9	48.3	451	7.5	67.8	24.7	481
C2	12.6	36.5	50.9	348	5.8	65.3	28.9	121
D	14.2	39.9	45.9	303	6.9	67.3	25.8	101
E	17.0	39.4	43.6	94	12.9	61.3	25.8	31

Table 3.24   *Does the member hold any office within the Labour/Conservative Party ? (%)*

Market Research Grading	Labour			Conservative		
	Yes	No	N	Yes	No	N
All	15.9	84.1	2648	8.7	91.3	2051
A	13.1	86.9	282	10.8	89.2	249
B	14.7	85.3	1173	9.0	91.0	942
C1	18.2	81.8	450	8.2	91.8	559
C2	16.3	83.7	350	7.0	93.0	143
D	18.5	81.5	298	5.8	94.2	121
E	18.9	81.1	95	8.1	91.9	37

Table 3.25   *How much time does the member devote to party activities per month ? (%)*

Market Research Grading	Labour					Conservative				
	None	Up to 5 hrs	5 to 10 hrs	Over 10 hrs	N	None	Up to 5 hrs	5 to 10 hrs	Over 10 hrs	N
All	51.0	29.5	9.6	9.9	2654	75.4	15.9	4.4	4.3	2050
A	50.3	30.4	10.1	9.2	286	72.8	15.6	6.8	4.8	250
B	53.5	28.8	9.0	8.7	1178	74.8	16.1	4.1	5.0	945
C1	49.9	29.2	11.0	9.9	445	77.2	16.0	3.8	3.0	556
C2	51.0	28.0	7.4	13.6	349	76.4	17.1	3.6	2.9	140
D	45.8	32.9	11.0	10.3	301	75.4	14.8	6.6	3.2	122
E	44.2	31.6	13.7	10.5	95	75.7	10.8	2.7	10.8	37

Table 3.26   *What was the overall financial contribution made by the member in the last year ? (%)*

Market Research Grading	Labour				Conservative			
	0 to £10	£10 to £20	Over £20	N	0 to £10	£10 to £20	Over £20	N
All	24.3	19.8	55.9	2367	33.9	21.1	45.0	1596
A	20.7	22.3	57.0	251	29.4	24.3	46.3	218
B	25.5	20.6	53.9	1063	32.7	20.2	47.1	734
C1	22.8	17.3	59.9	404	35.2	23.0	41.8	435
C2	25.6	18.9	55.5	312	45.4	15.5	39.1	97
D	21.7	18.3	60.0	263	31.4	18.6	50.0	86
E	29.7	23.0	47.3	74	50.0	19.2	30.8	26

Table 3.27   Is the member a local Labour/Conservative councillor ? (%)

Market Research Grading	Labour			Conservative		
	Yes	No	N	Yes	No	N
All	7.5	92.5	2669	2.4	97.6	2070
A	9.1	90.9	285	2.4	97.6	248
B	6.5	93.5	1182	2.7	97.3	954
C1	8.0	92.0	451	1.2	98.8	568
C2	6.8	93.2	353	3.5	96.5	143
D	8.9	91.1	303	3.4	96.6	117
E	11.6	88.4	95	2.5	97.5	40

Table 3.28   The Labour/Conservative leader should be elected by a system of one party member/one vote (%)

Market Research Grading	Labour				Conservative			
	Agree	Neither	Disagree	N	Agree	Neither	Disagree	N
All	85.7	5.3	9.0	2666	49.3	14.7	36.0	2029
A	85.1	4.5	10.4	288	40.6	19.3	40.1	244
B	86.3	5.4	8.3	1176	45.8	16.2	38.0	927
C1	85.1	4.9	10.0	451	51.5	12.8	35.7	563
C2	87.9	3.7	8.4	354	60.4	10.8	28.8	139
D	82.5	7.9	9.6	303	65.5	8.4	26.1	119
E	86.2	5.3	8.5	94	64.9	10.8	24.3	37

Table 3.29   *People like me can have a real influence in politics if they are*
                 prepared to get involved (%)

Market Research Grading	Labour				Conservative			
	Agree	Neith-er	Dis-agree	N	Agree	Neith-er	Dis-agree	N
All	66.1	15.9	18.0	2655	56.9	20.0	23.1	2043
A	66.3	18.6	15.1	285	62.6	17.5	19.9	246
B	64.1	16.6	19.3	1174	57.9	20.4	21.7	940
C1	66.2	16.4	17.4	452	56.0	19.6	24.4	562
C2	68.0	14.3	17.7	350	48.6	23.2	28.2	138
D	69.7	11.3	19.0	300	52.1	18.5	29.4	119
E	71.3	16.0	12.7	94	52.6	23.7	23.7	38

Table 3.30   *Attending party meetings can be pretty tiring after a hard days*
                 work (%)

Market Research Grading	Labour				Conservative			
	Agree	Neith-er	Dis-agree	N	Agree	Neith-er	Dis-agree	N
All	76.7	11.6	11.7	2659	69.2	19.4	11.4	2028
A	78.7	9.6	11.7	282	67.5	22.6	9.9	243
B	76.7	12.4	10.9	1179	70.1	18.8	11.1	932
C1	76.5	13.1	10.4	452	68.0	20.1	11.9	557
C2	76.0	13.3	10.7	354	69.1	17.3	13.6	139
D	76.5	8.4	15.1	298	73.7	16.1	10.2	118
E	75.5	5.3	19.2	94	64.1	23.1	12.8	39

Table 3.31   *Someone like me could do a good job of being a local councillor (%)*

Market Research Grading	Labour				Conservative			
	Agree	Neith-er	Dis-agree	N	Agree	Neith-er	Dis-agree	N
All	48.3	22.1	29.6	2636	29.0	24.5	46.5	2025
A	42.5	27.1	30.4	280	37.3	24.2	38.5	244
B	48.8	21.4	29.8	1173	31.2	25.3	43.5	936
C1	50.7	23.1	26.2	446	21.6	23.1	55.3	555
C2	49.0	18.7	32.3	347	27.6	25.4	47.0	134
D	46.6	21.8	31.6	298	29.7	22.9	47.4	118
E	48.9	23.9	27.2	92	31.6	28.9	39.5	38

Table 3.32   *Being an active party member is a good way of meeting interesting people (%)*

Market Research Grading	Labour				Conservative			
	Agree	Neith-er	Dis-agree	N	Agree	Neith-er	Dis-agree	N
All	65.8	21.6	12.6	2656	58.2	31.1	10.7	2021
A	64.3	24.3	11.4	280	54.7	35.9	9.4	245
B	62.0	23.5	14.5	1177	57.0	32.3	10.7	932
C1	69.2	17.4	13.4	454	59.6	29.7	10.7	549
C2	63.3	21.0	15.7	353	59.4	29.7	10.9	138
D	38.5	20.1	41.4	298	67.2	21.8	11.0	119
E	70.2	16.0	13.8	94	60.5	26.3	13.2	38

Table 3.33   *The only way to be really educated about politics is to be a party activist (%)*

Market Research Grading	Labour				Conservative			
	Agree	Neith-er	Dis-agree	N	Agree	Neith-er	Dis-agree	N
All	41.9	10.9	47.2	2663	33.8	17.9	48.3	2026
A	40.0	10.9	49.1	285	27.3	18.4	54.3	245
B	40.6	11.0	48.4	1179	31.4	20.4	48.2	932
C1	43.4	10.9	45.7	449	38.1	14.1	47.8	554
C2	42.7	11.2	46.1	356	40.4	16.9	42.7	136
D	46.3	11.0	42.7	300	40.8	16.7	42.5	120
E	39.4	6.4	54.2	94	25.6	17.9	56.5	39

Table 3.34   *The party leadership does not pay a lot of attention to ordinary party members (%)*

Market Research Grading	Labour				Conservative			
	Agree	Neith-er	Dis-agree	N	Agree	Neith-er	Dis-agree	N
All	47.5	18.7	33.8	2664	41.3	24.7	34.0	2032
A	47.9	16.1	36.0	286	39.7	23.1	37.2	247
B	45.8	21.0	33.2	1176	41.6	24.5	33.9	936
C1	50.3	17.7	32.0	453	38.7	25.5	35.8	556
C2	47.3	17.0	35.7	353	43.8	25.5	30.7	137
D	49.0	15.6	35.4	302	50.0	25.4	24.6	118
E	48.9	18.1	33.0	94	47.4	21.1	31.5	38

Table 3.35   Party activity often takes time away from one's family (%)

Market Research Grading	Labour				Conservative			
	Agree	Neith-er	Dis-agree	N	Agree	Neith-er	Dis-agree	N
All	85.1	10.3	4.6	2657	66.7	25.6	7.7	2008
A	83.5	11.0	5.5	281	67.8	22.9	9.3	245
B	85.4	11.7	2.9	1178	65.4	27.3	7.3	922
C1	85.9	10.6	3.5	452	66.1	25.9	8.0	548
C2	86.1	8.8	5.1	353	72.3	20.4	7.3	137
D	87.3	6.0	6.7	299	72.6	23.9	3.5	117
E	88.2	8.5	3.3	94	64.1	23.1	12.8	39

Table 3.36   The Labour/Conservative party would be more successful if people like me were elected to parliament (%)

Market Research Grading	Labour				Conservative			
	Agree	Neith-er	Dis-agree	N	Agree	Neith-er	Dis-agree	N
All	33.5	34.4	32.1	2637	21.5	32.2	46.3	2004
A	28.7	39.4	31.9	279	24.0	36.2	39.8	246
B	32.8	34.8	32.4	1172	23.1	31.7	45.2	922
C1	34.7	36.9	28.4	447	14.9	33.4	51.7	545
C2	34.8	29.9	35.3	351	27.4	26.7	45.9	135
D	34.5	33.1	32.4	296	26.5	27.4	46.1	117
E	42.4	23.9	33.7	92	23.1	35.9	41.0	39

Table 3.37   *During the last 5 years, how often has the member displayed an election poster in his/her window ? (%)*

Market Research Grading	Labour				Conservative			
	Not at all	Occas- ionally	Freq- uently	N	Not at all	Occas- ionally	Freq- uently	N
All	9.8	21.7	68.5	2647	48.5	31.8	19.7	1984
A	10.6	20.9	68.5	282	48.3	31.5	20.2	238
B	9.2	21.3	69.5	1174	48.2	31.2	20.6	908
C1	10.3	21.9	67.8	447	50.0	32.1	17.9	542
C2	9.9	22.9	67.2	353	48.6	33.6	17.8	140
D	10.3	22.3	67.4	300	47.5	30.5	22.0	118
E	11.0	20.9	68.1	91	39.5	42.1	18.4	38

Table 3.38   *During the last 5 years, how often has the member donated money to party funds ? (%)*

Market Research Grading	Labour				Conservative			
	Not at all	Occas- ionally	Freq- uently	N	Not at all	Occas- ionally	Freq- uently	N
All	9.8	50.9	39.3	2639	15.1	56.0	28.9	2023
A	7.7	52.8	39.5	284	13.1	50.8	36.1	244
B	11.2	50.0	38.8	1165	14.5	56.7	28.8	938
C1	9.1	51.9	39.0	453	15.0	57.3	27.7	546
C2	9.2	52.6	38.2	348	17.9	52.9	29.2	140
D	9.1	48.7	42.2	298	18.5	58.0	23.5	119
E	7.7	52.7	39.6	91	25.0	55.6	19.4	36

Table 3.39   *During the last 5 years, how often has the member delivered party leaflets ? (%)*

Market Research Grading	Labour				Conservative			
	Not at all	Occas-ionally	Freq-uently	N	Not at all	Occas-ionally	Freq-uently	N
All	17.5	27.1	55.4	2596	60.1	17.3	22.6	1948
A	20.8	27.2	52.0	279	59.2	17.2	23.6	233
B	17.1	27.6	55.3	1151	60.2	15.8	24.0	896
C1	17.2	26.3	56.5	441	59.6	19.9	20.5	534
C2	14.4	20.6	65.0	340	62.2	17.0	20.8	135
D	18.4	22.5	59.1	293	58.8	16.7	24.5	114
E	22.8	26.1	51.1	92	69.4	19.4	11.2	36

Table 3.40   *During the last 5 years, how often has the member attended a party meeting ? (%)*

Market Research Grading	Labour				Conservative			
	Not at all	Occas-ionally	Freq-uently	N	Not at all	Occas-ionally	Freq-uently	N
All	21.7	40.5	37.8	2598	50.8	32.2	17.0	1971
A	20.5	44.2	35.3	278	44.9	37.3	17.8	236
B	24.0	41.0	35.0	1151	48.9	33.3	17.8	916
C1	20.8	41.6	37.6	437	55.8	27.7	16.5	534
C2	18.7	38.5	42.8	343	54.1	32.6	13.3	135
D	19.5	37.7	42.8	297	49.6	33.6	16.8	113
E	19.6	34.8	45.6	92	56.8	29.7	13.5	37

Table 3.41 *During the last 5 years, how often has the member canvassed voters on behalf of the party ? (%)*

Market Research Grading	Labour				Conservative			
	Not at all	Occas-ionally	Freq-uently	N	Not at all	Occas-ionally	Freq-uently	N
All	37.4	31.4	31.2	2575	74.4	15.2	10.4	1950
A	41.1	30.9	28.0	275	72.5	17.2	10.3	233
B	38.6	31.4	30.0	1136	72.1	15.8	12.1	901
C1	37.2	29.4	33.4	436	78.2	13.4	8.4	528
C2	31.9	35.4	32.7	342	76.8	13.0	10.2	138
D	36.1	31.6	32.3	294	74.6	14.9	10.5	114
E	37.0	26.1	36.9	92	75.0	22.2	2.8	36

Table 3.42 *Where would you place yourself on a Left/Right scale within the Labour/Conservative party ? (%)*

Market Research Grading	Labour				Conservative			
	Left	Centre	Right	N	Left	Centre	Right	N
All	57.7	20.2	22.1	2667	14.0	26.1	59.9	2051
A	57.0	20.1	22.9	284	14.5	26.9	58.6	249
B	58.7	20.4	20.9	1174	15.2	24.3	60.5	948
C1	58.4	21.4	20.2	457	13.0	26.8	60.2	560
C2	55.6	18.8	25.6	356	13.4	34.5	52.1	142
D	59.0	21.3	19.7	305	9.2	28.6	62.2	119
E	59.4	14.3	26.3	91	15.2	18.2	66.6	33

Table 3.43   *Where would you place yourself on a Left/Right scale within*
British Politics ? (%)

Market Research Grading	Labour				Conservative			
	Left	Centre	Right	N	Left	Centre	Right	N
All	80.9	10.4	8.7	2664	3.9	18.7	77.4	2050
A	79.2	13.4	7.4	284	2.8	20.9	76.3	249
B	82.3	9.1	8.6	1171	4.1	16.7	79.2	948
C1	79.9	10.3	9.8	458	3.8	18.8	77.4	558
C2	75.5	12.4	12.1	356	2.1	30.1	67.8	143
D	77.6	10.5	11.9	304	6.7	19.3	74.0	119
E	75.9	9.9	14.2	91	3.0	9.1	87.9	33

Table 3.44   *What thermometer rating would the Labour/Conservative member*
give the Party ? (%)

Market Research Grading	Labour					Conservative				
	Cd	Cl	W	H	M	Cd	Cl	W	H	M
All	76.1	20.2	3.1	0.6	14.8	0.2	3.6	34.5	61.7	80.5
A	74.7	20.4	4.5	0.4	15.4	0.0	3.6	38.1	58.3	79.2
B	77.7	18.9	2.6	0.8	13.9	0.4	3.1	35.3	61.2	80.2
C1	74.3	21.1	3.9	0.7	15.4	0.2	3.4	32.4	64.0	81.9
C2	78.9	18.5	2.6	0.0	13.5	0.0	6.3	35.0	58.7	79.7
D	71.0	25.2	3.1	0.7	17.4	0.0	4.2	29.2	66.6	81.5
E	75.3	22.6	2.1	0.0	15.7	0.0	7.9	39.5	52.6	77.4

Table 3.45   *What thermometer rating would the Labour/Conservative member give the Labour Party ? (%)*

Market Research Grading	Labour					Conservative				
	Cd	Cl	W	H	M	Cd	Cl	W	H	M
All	0.9	3.8	24.8	70.5	82.6	51.0	42.8	5.8	0.4	26.3
A	1.1	3.5	24.0	71.4	82.8	46.1	47.3	6.2	0.4	28.1
B	0.9	4.1	25.5	69.5	82.0	51.7	42.7	5.4	0.2	25.6
C1	0.4	4.6	24.5	70.5	82.8	53.1	41.4	4.9	0.6	25.5
C2	1.4	2.8	25.1	70.7	83.2	46.6	42.1	10.5	0.8	30.3
D	0.7	1.7	24.4	73.2	83.7	49.6	43.5	6.1	0.8	27.0
E	1.1	7.4	21.1	70.4	82.6	57.1	31.4	11.4	0.1	25.7

Table 3.46   *What thermometer rating would the Labour/Conservative member give the Liberal Democratic Party ? (%)*

Market Research Grading	Labour					Conservative				
	Cd	Cl	W	H	M	Cd	Cl	W	H	M
All	33.0	44.2	21.0	1.8	36.8	33.5	50.7	14.6	1.2	35.8
A	31.6	45.2	21.7	1.5	35.9	36.8	51.2	11.2	0.8	33.6
B	33.3	43.3	21.7	1.7	36.9	34.0	49.7	15.2	1.1	35.9
C1	33.4	44.4	20.6	1.6	37.9	31.6	53.1	13.5	1.8	35.7
C2	33.6	46.7	18.5	1.2	35.1	27.6	55.2	16.4	0.8	38.9
D	32.1	44.4	21.5	2.0	37.3	35.7	47.8	14.8	1.7	36.7
E	31.9	42.6	21.3	4.2	38.4	38.9	27.8	33.3	0.0	38.9

Table 3.47   *What thermometer rating would the Labour/Conservative member give the Scottish Nationalist Party ? (%)*

Market Research Grading	Labour					Conservative				
	Cd	Cl	W	H	M	Cd	Cl	W	H	M
All	44.0	37.1	16.2	2.7	32.0	69.7	26.3	3.7	0.3	18.7
A	43.2	35.8	17.5	3.5	33.3	72.4	23.4	3.1	1.1	18.4
B	45.0	36.4	16.4	2.2	31.5	70.2	25.5	4.0	0.3	18.7
Cl	40.7	41.2	14.8	3.3	33.7	70.3	27.0	2.5	0.2	18.1
C2	50.0	32.2	15.8	2.0	28.8	60.4	31.7	7.9	0.0	23.0
D	39.9	40.3	16.7	3.1	33.6	64.4	32.2	3.4	0.0	19.5
E	42.1	35.5	18.4	4.0	34.2	80.0	16.7	3.3	0.0	15.3

Table 3.48   *What thermometer rating would the Labour/Conservative member give Plaid Cymru ? (%)*

Market Research Grading	Labour					Conservative				
	Cd	Cl	W	H	M	Cd	Cl	W	H	M
All	47.8	37.7	12.8	1.7	29.5	82.9	15.7	1.1	0.3	12.8
A	47.5	35.3	14.5	2.7	30.5	83.3	15.6	1.1	0.0	12.7
B	48.9	36.1	13.7	1.3	29.0	82.9	16.2	0.6	0.3	12.4
Cl	43.3	44.4	9.9	2.4	31.1	83.7	15.2	0.8	0.3	12.9
C2	53.2	33.5	11.5	1.8	26.9	78.3	17.4	3.3	1.0	16.1
D	43.9	41.9	13.4	0.8	30.7	81.3	16.3	2.4	0.0	13.5
E	50.0	31.9	15.3	2.8	29.9	89.3	7.1	3.6	0.0	9.7

Table 3.49   *What thermometer rating would the Labour/Conservative member give the Green Party ? (%)*

Market Research Grading	Labour						Conservative				
	Cd	Cl	W	H	M		Cd	Cl	W	H	M
All	33.6	35.5	25.7	5.2	39.4		70.5	24.1	4.9	0.5	19.3
A	32.3	36.1	24.1	7.5	40.7		71.1	24.6	3.8	0.5	18.2
B	34.0	34.9	24.1	7.0	39.1		70.0	24.1	5.0	0.9	19.8
Cl	34.0	34.9	26.3	4.8	41.3		70.9	24.2	4.7	0.2	19.0
C2	39.0	35.3	19.9	5.8	36.2		74.1	21.3	4.6	0.0	19.1
D	31.3	35.9	28.1	4.7	40.3		66.3	26.3	7.4	0.0	20.2
E	34.1	40.9	22.7	2.3	37.6		74.2	19.4	6.4	0.0	17.8

Table 3.50   *What thermometer rating would the Labour/Conservative member give the BBC ? (%)*

Market Research Grading	Labour						Conservative				
	Cd	Cl	W	H	M		Cd	Cl	W	H	M
All	9.2	26.5	39.5	24.8	60.4		8.4	30.5	40.4	20.7	59.4
A	8.7	24.5	40.4	26.4	61.6		7.3	26.9	41.6	24.2	60.6
B	8.8	26.8	38.1	26.3	60.9		8.5	33.0	38.8	19.7	58.6
Cl	7.7	23.8	38.1	30.4	61.4		7.4	27.6	42.8	22.2	61.0
C2	11.6	28.2	36.6	23.6	58.0		10.5	30.1	39.8	19.6	58.6
D	10.1	27.6	40.4	21.9	59.1		9.8	32.1	39.3	18.8	58.2
E	10.2	33.0	36.4	20.4	57.7		13.2	34.2	39.5	13.1	52.6

Table 3.51   *What thermometer rating would the Labour/Conservative member give the European Community ? (%)*

Market Research Grading	Labour					Conservative				
	Cd	Cl	W	H	M	Cd	Cl	W	H	M
All	10.6	33.1	41.7	14.6	55.7	14.3	41.2	35.2	9.3	50.7
A	9.9	30.6	44.0	15.5	57.1	17.8	36.2	37.6	8.4	49.8
B	10.8	32.4	42.0	14.8	55.3	13.1	41.1	35.5	10.3	51.2
C1	8.3	33.7	43.2	14.8	56.8	12.7	42.6	37.4	7.3	51.3
C2	13.9	33.5	37.7	14.9	53.8	16.7	43.1	30.4	9.8	49.6
D	10.6	36.0	41.3	12.1	55.1	17.1	48.8	24.4	9.7	48.6
E	7.4	37.0	39.5	16.1	59.3	26.5	32.4	29.4	11.7	45.8

Table 3.52   *What thermometer rating would the Labour/Conservative member give the Trade Union Congress ? (%)*

Market Research Grading	Labour					Conservative				
	Cd	Cl	W	H	M	Cd	Cl	W	H	M
All	5.6	29.2	47.4	17.8	60.1	53.8	39.7	5.7	0.8	26.2
A	4.9	31.2	47.0	16.9	59.6	53.6	39.3	7.1	0.0	26.6
B	6.7	29.5	45.3	18.5	59.3	54.5	39.4	5.1	1.0	25.7
C1	4.2	28.9	49.1	17.8	61.2	53.0	40.8	5.4	0.8	26.4
C2	5.7	26.1	49.5	18.7	60.4	41.9	52.3	5.8	0.0	30.4
D	4.5	29.5	51.0	15.0	60.9	62.2	28.4	6.8	2.6	24.7
E	3.5	31.4	45.3	19.8	61.6	61.3	29.0	9.7	0.0	23.3

Table 3.53   *What thermometer rating would the Labour/Conservative member give the Police ? (%)*

Market Research Grading	Labour					Conservative				
	Cd	Cl	W	H	M	Cd	Cl	W	H	M
All	17.5	44.8	28.3	9.4	48.1	1.5	12.7	40.5	45.3	72.6
A	18.4	42.6	27.9	11.1	47.9	2.4	8.1	48.4	41.1	72.7
B	18.7	45.7	26.8	8.8	47.1	1.4	14.2	41.0	43.4	71.5
C1	13.8	44.4	32.4	9.4	49.9	1.5	11.8	36.6	50.1	73.9
C2	18.8	47.4	24.3	9.5	47.4	0.0	14.4	39.6	46.0	74.5
D	15.0	41.5	33.3	10.2	50.6	2.7	11.7	40.5	45.1	73.2
E	20.2	42.7	28.1	9.0	47.7	0.0	16.2	35.1	48.7	71.8

Table 3.54   *What thermometer rating would the Labour/Conservative member give the House of Commons ? (%)*

Market Research Grading	Labour					Conservative				
	Cd	Cl	W	H	M	Cd	Cl	W	H	M
All	9.8	33.9	38.2	18.1	56.9	2.9	14.9	52.3	29.9	68.1
A	10.4	35.1	36.6	17.9	56.0	2.9	14.9	52.3	29.9	68.3
B	10.6	33.9	37.6	17.9	56.4	2.4	17.6	50.8	29.2	67.5
C1	9.1	33.5	39.9	17.5	57.5	1.4	17.0	48.1	33.5	69.1
C2	8.7	34.0	38.0	19.3	57.6	4.0	17.6	43.2	35.2	68.7
D	7.6	33.6	41.5	17.3	58.6	3.8	16.0	47.2	33.0	68.7
E	13.5	31.5	33.7	21.3	55.7	6.1	15.2	54.5	24.2	65.6

Table 3.55   *What thermometer rating would the Labour/Conservative member give the CBI ? (%)*

Market Research Grading	Labour						Conservative				
	Cd	Cl	W	H	M		Cd	Cl	W	H	M
All	45.0	41.7	11.2	2.1	30.8		5.5	29.7	49.0	15.8	59.4
A	43.5	43.0	11.4	2.1	30.6		4.3	30.8	51.9	13.0	58.3
B	47.4	41.1	9.5	2.0	29.5		4.9	30.4	49.0	15.7	59.7
C1	42.9	42.9	11.7	2.5	32.2		4.6	28.1	50.7	16.6	60.7
C2	49.1	36.5	12.3	2.1	29.5		9.6	31.5	39.7	19.2	58.3
D	37.1	44.7	15.6	2.6	35.6		12.9	21.0	46.8	19.3	57.8
E	41.3	47.5	10.0	1.2	31.9		11.5	38.5	42.3	7.7	52.8

Table 3.56   *What thermometer rating would the Labour/Conservative member give the Queen ? (%)*

Market Research Grading	Labour						Conservative				
	Cd	Cl	W	H	M		Cd	Cl	W	H	M
All	34.6	29.5	19.1	16.8	43.3		0.9	4.9	16.5	77.7	86.0
A	30.8	28.9	23.8	16.5	45.4		0.4	4.9	20.5	74.2	84.2
B	35.6	30.4	17.7	16.3	42.0		1.4	5.3	18.6	74.7	85.0
C1	34.4	31.7	19.0	14.9	42.0		0.5	3.3	12.9	83.3	88.4
C2	37.9	24.7	17.0	20.4	43.3		0.0	5.7	11.4	82.9	87.6
D	32.5	24.9	23.5	19.1	48.4		0.9	7.0	13.9	78.2	85.7
E	26.7	43.3	15.6	14.4	44.1		2.7	10.8	16.2	70.3	80.9

Table 3.57   *What thermometer rating would the Labour/Conservative member give Judges ? (%)*

Market Research Grading	Labour					Conservative				
	Cd	Cl	W	H	M	Cd	Cl	W	H	M
All	38.2	43.5	14.6	3.7	34.8	4.4	31.5	45.7	18.4	60.3
A	36.5	47.5	12.2	3.8	35.1	1.7	24.7	54.5	19.1	62.8
B	39.4	43.4	14.0	3.2	34.1	4.3	31.6	45.9	18.2	59.1
Cl	37.8	44.4	14.0	3.8	34.4	5.3	33.2	42.3	19.2	59.7
C2	38.7	39.3	18.5	3.5	35.5	5.1	43.2	35.6	16.1	58.0
D	34.9	43.4	16.7	5.0	37.5	5.2	26.0	51.0	17.8	60.2
E	40.4	46.1	12.4	1.1	32.4	8.8	23.5	47.1	20.6	61.3

4   Subjective Class

Table 4.1   *The Labour/Conservative party should try to capture the middle ground in politics (%)*

Subjective Class	Labour				Conservative			
	Agree	Neith-er	Dis-agree	N	Agree	Neith-er	Dis-agree	N
All	51.6	11.5	36.9	2053	71.0	12.8	16.2	1459
Middle Class	42.8	15.7	41.5	670	70.8	12.8	16.4	1188
Working Class	56.9	9.1	34.0	1325	72.5	13.1	14.4	244
Other	32.8	17.2	50.0	58	66.7	11.1	22.2	27

Table 4.2   *A Labour/Conservative government should introduce a prices and incomes policy as a means of controlling inflation (%)*

Subjective Class	Labour				Conservative			
	Agree	Neith-er	Dis-agree	N	Agree	Neith-er	Dis-agree	N
All	57.9	18.4	23.7	2058	42.1	11.2	46.7	1497
Middle Class	48.4	26.8	24.8	668	39.0	11.2	49.8	1209
Working Class	62.9	13.7	23.4	1331	58.6	11.9	29.5	261
Other	52.5	30.5	17.0	59	22.2	7.4	70.4	27

Table 4.3   *Income and wealth should be re-distributed towards ordinary working people (%)*

Subjective Class	Labour				Conservative			
	Agree	Neith-er	Dis-agree	N	Agree	Neith-er	Dis-agree	N
All	87.9	7.6	4.5	2081	24.8	19.1	56.1	1495
Middle Class	89.9	6.2	3.9	682	20.7	19.8	59.5	1205
Working Class	86.9	8.4	4.7	1339	43.7	15.2	41.1	263
Other	90.0	6.7	3.3	60	25.9	22.2	51.9	27

Table 4.4 *The Labour/Conservative Party should always stand by its principles even if this should lose it an election (%)*

Subjective Class	Labour				Conservative			
	Agree	Neith-er	Dis-agree	N	Agree	Neith-er	Dis-agree	N
All	68.1	11.5	20.4	2079	80.9	7.5	11.6	1528
Middle Class	58.2	17.8	24.0	679	80.8	7.6	11.6	1235
Working Class	72.8	8.4	18.8	1341	82.3	6.4	11.3	266
Other	74.6	11.9	13.5	59	70.4	14.8	14.8	27

Table 4.5 *Further nuclear energy development is essential for the future prosperity of Britain (%)*

Subjective Class	Labour				Conservative			
	Agree	Neith-er	Dis-agree	N	Agree	Neith-er	Dis-agree	N
All	13.8	10.9	75.3	2064	62.0	15.6	22.4	1509
Middle Class	9.9	10.6	79.5	679	64.5	14.8	20.7	1213
Working Class	16.2	10.7	73.1	1325	52.4	18.2	29.4	269
Other	5.0	16.7	78.3	60	44.4	25.9	29.7	27

Table 4.6 *A future Labour/Conservative government should not agree to a single European currency (%)*

Subjective Class	Labour				Conservative			
	Agree	Neith-er	Dis-agree	N	Agree	Neith-er	Dis-agree	N
All	25.7	18.9	55.4	2057	57.6	10.6	31.8	1516
Middle Class	16.8	19.5	63.7	673	57.9	10.6	31.5	1222
Working Class	30.6	18.1	51.3	1326	59.6	10.1	30.3	267
Other	15.5	29.3	55.2	58	22.2	14.8	63.0	27

Table 4.7 High income tax makes people less willing to work hard (%)

Subjective Class	Labour				Conservative			
	Agree	Neith-er	Dis-agree	N	Agree	Neith-er	Dis-agree	N
All	26.8	11.3	61.9	2080	83.2	5.6	11.2	1533
Middle Class	14.1	11.8	74.1	679	82.8	5.9	11.3	1236
Working Class	33.5	10.9	55.6	1341	84.8	3.7	11.5	270
Other	21.7	15.0	63.3	60	81.5	11.1	7.4	27

Table 4.8 Britain's electoral system should be replaced by a system of proportional representation (%)

Subjective Class	Labour				Conservative			
	Agree	Neith-er	Dis-agree	N	Agree	Neith-er	Dis-agree	N
All	57.7	13.4	28.9	2073	22.4	11.5	66.1	1503
Middle Class	70.3	12.1	17.6	680	20.7	11.3	68.0	1215
Working Class	50.7	14.2	35.1	1334	28.4	12.6	59.0	261
Other	71.2	10.2	18.6	59	37.0	11.1	51.9	27

Table 4.9 Further moves towards integration within the European Community should be resisted (%)

Subjective Class	Labour				Conservative			
	Agree	Neith-er	Dis-agree	N	Agree	Neith-er	Dis-agree	N
All	22.9	13.4	63.7	2067	54.5	15.0	30.5	1515
Middle Class	16.2	10.9	72.9	680	54.1	14.9	31.0	1221
Working Class	26.7	14.5	58.8	1327	59.6	14.2	26.2	267
Other	16.6	16.7	66.7	60	18.5	25.9	55.6	27

Table 4.10   There is no need for a Bill of Rights in this country (%)

Subjective Class	Labour				Conservative			
	Agree	Neith-er	Dis-agree	N	Agree	Neith-er	Dis-agree	N
All	11.3	9.8	78.9	2050	40.4	25.2	34.4	1459
Middle Class	7.7	8.4	83.9	678	42.8	25.0	32.2	1174
Working Class	13.3	10.6	76.1	1313	29.1	26.0	44.9	258
Other	10.2	8.5	81.3	59	40.7	25.9	33.4	27

Table 4.11   A future Labour/Conservative government should introduce a directly elected Scottish Assembly with taxing powers (%)

Subjective Class	Labour				Conservative			
	Agree	Neith-er	Dis-agree	N	Agree	Neith-er	Dis-agree	N
All	62.5	21.2	16.3	2075	23.6	25.7	50.7	1486
Middle Class	64.8	22.6	12.6	682	21.7	25.7	52.6	1199
Working Class	60.9	20.4	18.7	1333	32.7	25.8	41.5	260
Other	70.0	23.3	6.7	60	22.2	25.9	51.9	27

Table 4.12   Coalition governments are the best form of government for Britain (%)

Subjective Class	Labour				Conservative			
	Agree	Neith-er	Dis-agree	N	Agree	Neith-er	Dis-agree	N
All	8.3	16.2	75.5	2072	9.9	9.9	80.2	1531
Middle Class	9.9	22.7	67.4	679	8.7	9.1	82.2	1236
Working Class	7.5	12.3	80.2	1335	15.7	12.3	72.0	268
Other	10.3	31.0	58.7	58	7.4	22.2	70.4	27

Table 4.13   *A future Labour/Conservative government should/should not spend money to get rid of poverty (%)*

Subjective Class	Labour				Conservative			
	Should	Doesn't matter	Should not	N	Should	Doesn't matter	Should not	N
All	98.0	1.0	1.0	2073	80.9	7.7	11.4	1510
Middle Class	98.5	0.7	0.8	676	80.1	7.9	12.0	1215
Working Class	97.8	1.0	1.2	1339	85.1	6.3	8.6	269
Other	96.6	3.4	0.0	58	73.1	11.5	15.4	26

Table 4.14   *A future Labour/Conservative government should/should not encourage the growth of private medicine (%)*

Subjective Class	Labour				Conservative			
	Should	Doesn't matter	Should not	N	Should	Doesn't matter	Should not	N
All	3.7	4.7	91.6	2068	54.3	14.7	31.0	1516
Middle Class	2.4	3.1	94.5	677	55.3	15.1	29.6	1219
Working Class	4.4	5.7	89.9	1333	49.6	13.7	36.7	270
Other	1.7	0.0	98.3	58	55.6	7.4	37.0	27

Table 4.15   *A future Labour/Conservative government should/should not put more money into the National Health Service (%)*

Subjective Class	Labour				Conservative			
	Should	Doesn't matter	Should not	N	Should	Doesn't matter	Should not	N
All	98.2	0.6	1.2	2077	79.3	6.6	14.1	1523
Middle Class	97.8	0.6	1.6	676	78.1	6.7	15.2	1223
Working Class	98.5	0.4	1.1	1343	84.7	6.2	9.1	274
Other	94.8	5.2	0.0	58	80.8	3.8	15.4	26

Table 4.16   *A future Labour/Conservative government should/should not reduce spending in general (%)*

Subjective Class	Labour				Conservative			
	Should	Doesn't matter	Should not	N	Should	Doesn't matter	Should not	N
All	19.3	6.7	74.0	2047	60.2	8.7	31.1	1508
Middle Class	12.7	3.7	83.6	677	60.0	8.7	31.3	1213
Working Class	22.9	7.9	69.2	1312	61.9	9.0	29.1	268
Other	15.5	15.5	69.0	58	51.9	7.4	40.7	27

Table 4.17   *A future Labour/Conservative government should/should not introduce stricter laws to regulate the trade unions (%)*

Subjective Class	Labour				Conservative			
	Should	Doesn't matter	Should not	N	Should	Doesn't matter	Should not	N
All	9.7	13.7	76.6	2056	69.4	10.2	20.4	1523
Middle Class	8.6	15.1	76.3	674	70.9	10.5	18.6	1225
Working Class	10.3	12.6	77.1	1324	64.6	8.1	27.3	271
Other	6.9	20.7	72.4	58	48.1	14.8	37.1	27

Table 4.18   *A future Labour/Conservative government should/should not give workers more say in the places where they work (%)*

Subjective Class	Labour				Conservative			
	Should	Doesn't matter	Should not	N	Should	Doesn't matter	Should not	N
All	92.4	5.0	2.6	2068	64.6	13.1	22.3	2354
Middle Class	92.3	4.9	2.8	676	62.9	13.5	23.6	1227
Working Class	92.6	5.0	2.4	1334	71.7	12.1	16.2	272
Other	89.7	5.2	5.1	58	70.4	3.7	25.9	27

Table 4.19   *A future Labour/Conservative government should/should not spend*
less on defence (%)

Subjective Class	Labour				Conservative			
	Should	Doesn't matter	Should not	N	Should	Doesn't matter	Should not	N
All	83.1	4.1	12.8	2068	44.9	4.3	50.8	1520
Middle Class	88.9	2.5	8.6	677	44.8	4.1	51.1	1223
Working Class	79.7	5.0	15.3	1333	45.2	5.6	49.2	270
Other	93.1	0.0	6.9	58	48.1	3.7	48.2	27

Table 4.20   *Should a future Labour/Conservative government :*
(A) Reduce taxes & spend less on health, education & social benefits ?
(B) Keep taxes & spending on these services at the same levels as now ?
(C) Increase taxes & spend more on health, education & social benefits ?

Subjective Class	Labour				Conservative			
	A	B	C	N	A	B	C	N
All	2.7	6.6	90.7	2070	7.6	66.4	26.0	1522
Middle Class	1.0	5.2	93.8	676	7.9	67.8	24.3	1227
Working Class	3.6	7.2	89.2	1335	5.9	59.5	34.6	269
Other	0.0	8.5	91.5	59	7.7	69.2	23.1	26

Table 4.21   *On joining the Labour/Conservative party did the member approach*
the party (MA) or did the party approach the member (PA) ? (%)

Subjective Class	Labour				Conservative			
	MA	Don't Know	PA	N	MA	Don't Know	PA	N
All	78.8	19.4	1.8	2092	35.1	49.4	15.5	1543
Middle Class	81.4	14.3	4.3	683	32.3	51.6	16.1	1245
Working Class	76.2	22.0	1.8	1351	48.0	38.7	13.3	271
Other	77.6	19.0	3.4	58	37.0	59.3	3.7	27

Table 4.22 *How often has the member attended a party meeting in the last 12 months ? (%)*

Subjective Class	Labour				Conservative			
	Not at all	Occas- ionally	Frequ- ently	N	Not at all	Occas- ionally	Frequ- ently	N
All	41.7	30.7	27.6	2104	65.8	22.6	11.6	1551
Middle Class	49.0	31.4	19.6	684	63.4	24.2	12.4	1249
Working Class	38.0	30.4	31.6	1360	77.1	14.9	8.0	275
Other	41.7	28.3	30.0	60	63.0	25.9	11.1	27

Table 4.23 *Is the member more or less politically active than 5 years ago ? (%)*

Subjective Class	Labour				Conservative			
	More active	About same	Less active	N	More active	About same	Less active	N
All	13.4	38.4	48.2	2077	9.4	61.6	29.0	1307
Middle Class	13.7	37.7	48.6	679	9.2	59.9	30.9	1086
Working Class	13.1	38.9	48.0	1339	10.4	69.7	19.9	201
Other	16.9	33.9	49.2	59	10.0	70.0	20.0	20

Table 4.24 *Does the member hold any office within the Labour/Conservative Party ? (%)*

Subjective Class	Labour			Conservative		
	Yes	No	N	Yes	No	N
All	15.7	84.3	2069	8.5	91.5	1525
Middle Class	16.1	83.9	670	8.8	91.2	1229
Working Class	15.7	84.3	1339	6.3	93.7	270
Other	10.0	90.0	60	15.4	84.6	26

Table 4.25   *How much time does the member devote to party activities per month ? (%)*

Subjective Class	Labour					Conservative				
	None	Up to 5 hrs	5 to 10 hrs	Over 10 hrs	N	None	Up to 5 hrs	5 to 10 hrs	Over 10 hrs	N
All	51.4	28.8	9.2	10.6	2076	77.3	14.3	4.4	4.0	1523
Middle Class	54.5	30.6	6.8	8.1	679	76.0	15.3	4.3	4.4	1230
Working Class	50.4	27.6	10.1	11.9	1339	83.6	9.0	5.2	2.2	268
Other	39.7	36.2	15.5	8.6	58	76.0	24.0	0.0	0.0	25

Table 4.26   *What was the overall financial contribution made by the member in the last year ? (%)*

Subjective Class	Labour				Conservative			
	0 to £10	£10 to £20	Over £20	N	0 to £10	£10 to £20	Over £20	N
All	24.9	19.1	56.0	1851	32.8	22.1	45.1	1163
Middle Class	15.4	18.5	66.1	623	29.9	23.0	47.1	962
Working Class	30.1	19.9	50.0	1176	47.2	19.9	32.9	176
Other	21.2	7.7	71.1	52	44.0	4.0	52.0	25

Table 4.27   *Is the member a local Labour/Conservative councillor ? (%)*

Subjective Class	Labour			Conservative		
	Yes	No	N	Yes	No	N
All	7.8	92.2	2086	2.1	97.9	1534
Middle Class	4.4	95.6	681	2.3	97.7	1236
Working Class	9.4	90.6	1345	1.1	98.9	271
Other	10.0	90.0	60	0.0	100.0	27

Table 4.28 *The Labour/Conservative leader should be elected by a system of one party member/one vote (%)*

Subjective Class	Labour				Conservative			
	Agree	Neith-er	Dis-agree	N	Agree	Neith-er	Dis-agree	N
All	84.8	5.6	9.6	2077	49.2	14.0	36.8	1500
Middle Class	81.0	8.0	11.0	675	46.9	13.7	39.4	1208
Working Class	86.9	4.3	8.8	1342	62.3	14.0	23.7	265
Other	80.0	6.7	13.3	60	25.9	29.6	44.5	27

Table 4.29 *People like me can have a real influence in politics if they are prepared to get involved (%)*

Subjective Class	Labour				Conservative			
	Agree	Neith-er	Dis-agree	N	Agree	Neith-er	Dis-agree	N
All	67.3	15.5	17.2	2074	55.6	20.4	24.0	1500
Middle Class	60.9	17.6	21.5	680	55.6	21.2	23.2	1212
Working Class	70.9	14.4	14.7	1336	55.2	17.2	27.6	261
Other	60.3	17.2	22.5	58	59.3	14.8	25.9	27

Table 4.30 *Attending party meetings can be pretty tiring after a hard days work (%)*

Subjective Class	Labour				Conservative			
	Agree	Neith-er	Dis-agree	N	Agree	Neith-er	Dis-agree	N
All	78.3	10.8	10.9	2072	71.3	18.5	10.2	1487
Middle Class	82.6	9.5	7.9	677	71.5	18.5	10.0	1197
Working Class	76.4	11.3	12.3	1338	68.1	20.5	11.4	263
Other	71.9	15.8	12.3	57	92.6	0.0	7.4	27

Table 4.31   Someone like me could do a good job of being a local councillor (%)

Subjective Class	Labour				Conservative			
	Agree	Neith-er	Dis-agree	N	Agree	Neith-er	Dis-agree	N
All	50.5	20.8	28.7	2052	27.0	24.3	48.7	1480
Middle Class	51.0	19.7	29.3	675	28.1	24.5	47.4	1197
Working Class	49.9	21.1	29.0	1319	22.3	22.7	55.0	256
Other	58.6	27.6	13.8	58	25.9	29.6	44.5	27

Table 4.32   Being an active party member is a good way of meeting interesting people (%)

Subjective Class	Labour				Conservative			
	Agree	Neith-er	Dis-agree	N	Agree	Neith-er	Dis-agree	N
All	65.3	21.3	13.4	2069	60.1	29.4	10.5	1492
Middle Class	54.8	26.6	18.6	677	60.8	29.2	10.0	1203
Working Class	71.1	18.7	10.2	1334	58.0	30.2	11.8	262
Other	53.5	19.0	27.5	58	48.1	29.6	22.3	27

Table 4.33   The only way to be really educated about politics is to be a party activist (%)

Subjective Class	Labour				Conservative			
	Agree	Neith-er	Dis-agree	N	Agree	Neith-er	Dis-agree	N
All	43.5	10.6	45.9	2076	37.0	16.8	46.2	1486
Middle Class	29.7	10.7	59.6	680	36.1	17.3	46.6	1198
Working Class	50.8	10.6	38.6	1340	42.1	14.2	43.7	261
Other	35.7	8.9	55.4	56	29.6	22.2	48.2	27

Table 4.34   *The party leadership does not pay a lot of attention to ordinary party members (%)*

Subjective Class	Labour				Conservative			
	Agree	Neith-er	Dis-agree	N	Agree	Neith-er	Dis-agree	N
All	48.8	17.8	33.4	2078	43.5	23.8	32.7	1499
Middle Class	42.1	22.9	35.0	680	43.1	24.5	32.4	1206
Working Class	52.1	15.2	32.7	1340	45.5	21.1	33.4	266
Other	51.7	17.2	31.1	58	40.7	22.2	37.1	27

Table 4.35   *Party activity often takes time away from one's family (%)*

Subjective Class	Labour				Conservative			
	Agree	Neith-er	Dis-agree	N	Agree	Neith-er	Dis-agree	N
All	85.3	10.2	4.5	2071	68.1	24.5	7.4	1481
Middle Class	81.5	13.6	4.9	675	69.0	23.5	7.5	1192
Working Class	87.8	7.9	4.3	1338	64.1	29.0	6.9	262
Other	69.0	24.1	6.9	58	66.7	25.9	7.4	27

Table 4.36   *The Labour/Conservative party would be more successful if people like me were elected to parliament (%)*

Subjective Class	Labour				Conservative			
	Agree	Neith-er	Dis-agree	N	Agree	Neith-er	Dis-agree	N
All	34.3	33.3	32.4	2054	22.3	30.0	47.7	1472
Middle Class	31.0	36.2	32.8	672	22.7	29.8	47.5	1183
Working Class	36.2	31.4	32.4	1324	21.0	30.2	48.8	262
Other	31.0	43.1	25.9	58	18.5	33.3	48.2	27

Table 4.37   During the last 5 years, how often has the member displayed an election poster in his/her window ? (%)

Subjective Class	Labour				Conservative			
	Not at all	Occas-ionally	Freq-uently	N	Not at all	Occas-ionally	Freq-uently	N
All	8.5	21.7	69.8	2068	47.7	33.0	19.3	1466
Middle Class	9.5	24.5	66.0	677	45.9	33.8	20.3	1178
Working Class	7.6	20.6	71.8	1332	55.0	29.4	15.6	262
Other	16.9	13.6	69.5	59	53.8	34.6	11.6	26

Table 4.38   During the last 5 years, how often has the member donated money to party funds ? (%)

Subjective Class	Labour				Conservative			
	Not at all	Occas-ionally	Freq-uently	N	Not at all	Occas-ionally	Freq-uently	N
All	9.7	50.2	40.1	2063	13.7	55.1	31.2	1506
Middle Class	8.4	52.1	39.5	679	12.3	54.5	33.2	1218
Working Class	10.5	49.6	39.9	1325	19.5	58.2	22.3	261
Other	6.8	40.7	52.5	59	22.2	51.9	25.9	27

Table 4.39   During the last 5 years, how often has the member delivered party leaflets ? (%)

Subjective Class	Labour				Conservative			
	Not at all	Occas-ionally	Freq-uently	N	Not at all	Occas-ionally	Freq-uently	N
All	16.7	27.3	56.0	2034	61.1	17.4	21.5	1426
Middle Class	13.3	33.4	53.3	667	58.7	17.9	23.4	1144
Working Class	18.7	24.2	57.1	1308	69.9	16.4	13.7	256
Other	11.9	27.1	61.0	59	80.8	3.8	15.4	26

Table 4.40   *During the last 5 years, how often has the member attended a party meeting ? (%)*

Subjective Class	Labour				Conservative			
	Not at all	Occas-ionally	Freq-uently	N	Not at all	Occas-ionally	Freq-uently	N
All	21.3	40.6	38.1	2038	49.4	34.4	16.2	1447
Middle Class	23.3	46.3	30.4	665	45.8	36.6	17.6	1166
Working Class	20.1	38.1	41.8	1313	64.7	24.7	10.6	255
Other	26.7	33.3	40.0	60	61.5	30.8	7.7	26

Table 4.41   *During the last 5 years, how often has the member canvassed voters on behalf of the party ? (%)*

Subjective Class	Labour				Conservative			
	Not at all	Occas-ionally	Freq-uently	N	Not at all	Occas-ionally	Freq-uently	N
All	35.9	31.8	32.3	2020	73.7	15.7	10.6	1423
Middle Class	39.2	34.9	25.9	665	71.6	17.2	11.2	1144
Working Class	34.2	30.2	35.6	1297	81.8	9.9	8.3	253
Other	36.2	32.8	31.0	58	88.5	7.7	3.8	26

Table 4.42   *Where would you place yourself on a Left/Right scale within the Labour/Conservative party ? (%)*

Subjective Class	Labour				Conservative			
	Left	Centre	Right	N	Left	Centre	Right	N
All	59.7	19.4	20.9	2080	13.8	21.6	64.6	1230
Middle Class	58.7	17.1	24.2	683	12.8	21.6	65.6	1230
Working Class	60.3	20.3	19.4	1337	16.0	28.2	55.8	262
Other	58.4	25.0	16.6	60	37.0	29.6	33.4	27

Table 4.43   *Where would you place yourself on a Left/Right scale within British Politics ? (%)*

Subjective Class	Labour				Conservative			
	Left	Centre	Right	N	Left	Centre	Right	N
All	79.9	10.2	9.9	2077	4.0	16.5	79.5	1512
Middle Class	90.7	4.3	5.0	681	3.4	14.1	82.5	1225
Working Class	74.0	13.5	12.5	1336	5.8	27.7	66.5	260
Other	88.3	5.0	6.7	60	11.1	18.5	70.4	27

Table 4.44   *What thermometer rating would the Labour/Conservative member give the Conservative Party ? (%)*

Subjective Class	Labour					Conservative				
	Cd	Cl	W	H	M	Cd	Cl	W	H	M
All	76.4	19.9	3.1	0.6	14.4	0.3	3.6	32.2	63.9	81.5
Middle Class	83.2	15.1	1.5	0.2	11.5	0.3	3.0	31.3	65.4	81.4
Working Class	72.6	22.6	4.0	0.8	16.1	0.0	6.6	33.2	60.2	80.3
Other	82.5	15.8	1.7	0.0	10.8	0.0	3.7	59.3	37.0	74.0

Table 4.45   *What thermometer rating would the Labour/Conservative member give the Labour Party ? (%)*

Subjective Class	Labour					Conservative				
	Cd	Cl	W	H	M	Cd	Cl	W	H	M
All	1.1	3.8	25.1	70.0	82.6	51.1	42.6	5.8	0.5	26.2
Middle Class	0.6	4.1	37.4	57.9	78.4	52.7	42.0	5.0	0.3	25.2
Working Class	1.2	3.4	18.7	76.7	85.0	43.8	45.3	9.4	1.5	30.4
Other	3.4	6.8	28.8	61.0	78.4	51.9	40.7	7.4	0.0	27.9

Table 4.46 *What thermometer rating would the Labour/Conservative member give the Liberal Democratic Party ? (%)*

Subjective Class	Labour					Conservative				
	Cd	Cl	W	H	M	Cd	Cl	W	H	M
All	33.7	44.6	20.0	1.7	36.4	33.5	50.1	15.0	1.4	35.9
Middle Class	29.1	47.3	22.9	0.7	37.7	34.4	50.5	14.1	1.0	35.2
Working Class	36.2	43.2	18.5	2.1	35.6	28.3	49.0	19.5	3.2	39.4
Other	31.6	45.6	21.1	1.7	37.8	40.7	44.4	11.1	3.8	34.7

Table 4.47 *What thermometer rating would the Labour/Conservative member give the Scottish Nationalist Party ? (%)*

Subjective Class	Labour					Conservative				
	Cd	Cl	W	H	M	Cd	Cl	W	H	M
All	44.0	37.6	15.8	2.6	32.0	70.3	25.2	4.1	0.4	18.6
Middle Class	39.5	41.2	17.2	2.1	33.9	72.1	23.9	3.8	0.2	17.8
Working Class	46.7	35.7	14.8	2.8	30.8	63.1	30.3	5.6	1.0	21.4
Other	36.0	36.0	24.0	4.0	37.6	61.1	33.3	5.6	0.0	26.3

Table 4.48 *What thermometer rating would the Labour/Conservative member give Plaid Cymru ? (%)*

Subjective Class	Labour					Conservative				
	Cd	Cl	W	H	M	Cd	Cl	W	H	M
All	47.3	37.3	13.7	1.7	29.6	83.5	15.2	1.2	0.1	12.3
Middle Class	41.1	39.7	16.6	2.6	32.9	84.7	14.2	0.8	0.3	11.6
Working Class	50.6	36.1	12.0	1.3	27.8	78.5	18.6	2.8	0.1	15.3
Other	44.2	34.9	18.6	2.3	33.3	72.2	27.8	0.0	0.0	18.3

Table 4.49   *What thermometer rating would the Labour/Conservative member*
give the Green Party ? (%)

Subjective Class	Labour					Conservative				
	Cd	Cl	W	H	M	Cd	Cl	W	H	M
All	32.8	37.0	25.3	4.9	39.4	70.5	24.4	4.5	0.6	19.2
Middle Class	23.7	36.3	33.3	6.7	44.5	72.5	23.3	3.7	0.5	18.3
Working Class	38.2	37.3	20.9	3.6	36.3	62.7	27.8	8.6	0.9	22.8
Other	20.7	39.7	29.3	10.3	47.6	55.0	45.0	0.0	0.0	24.2

Table 4.50   *What thermometer rating would the Labour/Conservative member*
give the BBC ? (%)

Subjective Class	Labour					Conservative				
	Cd	Cl	W	H	M	Cd	Cl	W	H	M
All	10.2	26.9	38.5	24.4	59.8	8.9	30.0	39.0	22.1	59.4
Middle Class	3.7	17.5	45.4	33.4	67.0	8.7	28.8	41.0	21.5	59.6
Working Class	13.8	32.3	34.4	19.5	55.8	10.5	35.0	30.0	24.5	58.0
Other	5.1	16.9	50.8	27.2	64.8	0.0	33.3	37.0	29.7	65.5

Table 4.51   *What thermometer rating would the Labour/Conservative member*
give the European Community ? (%)

Subjective Class	Labour					Conservative				
	Cd	Cl	W	H	M	Cd	Cl	W	H	M
All	12.2	32.8	40.0	15.0	55.0	13.7	41.0	35.5	9.8	51.2
Middle Class	8.5	30.5	47.4	13.6	56.9	14.1	40.2	36.7	9.0	51.1
Working Class	14.5	33.6	35.8	16.1	53.8	12.6	46.4	27.9	13.1	50.9
Other	6.9	41.4	41.4	10.3	56.2	8.7	30.4	43.5	17.4	58.4

Table 4.52 *What thermometer rating would the Labour/Conservative member give the Trade Union Congress ? (%)*

Subjective Class	Labour					Conservative				
	Cd	Cl	W	H	M	Cd	Cl	W	H	M
All	5.3	28.2	47.7	18.8	60.6	54.3	39.2	5.6	0.9	26.0
Middle Class	4.5	34.3	50.7	10.5	57.2	56.9	37.8	4.7	0.6	24.7
Working Class	5.7	24.8	46.3	23.2	62.5	41.5	45.1	11.0	2.4	32.6
Other	5.2	34.5	46.6	13.7	56.6	52.4	47.6	0.0	0.0	28.0

Table 4.53 *What thermometer rating would the Labour/Conservative member give the Police ? (%)*

Subjective Class	Labour					Conservative				
	Cd	Cl	W	H	M	Cd	Cl	W	H	M
All	19.4	43.8	27.4	9.4	47.4	1.4	12.7	40.6	45.3	72.9
Middle Class	18.9	52.6	25.1	3.4	43.9	1.3	12.5	42.1	44.1	72.5
Working Class	19.5	39.3	28.5	12.7	49.4	1.6	13.6	32.7	52.1	75.2
Other	22.4	44.8	27.6	5.2	43.6	0.0	11.1	51.9	37.0	72.0

Table 4.54 *What thermometer rating would the Labour/Conservative member give the House of Commons ? (%)*

Subjective Class	Labour					Conservative				
	Cd	Cl	W	H	M	Cd	Cl	W	H	M
All	11.0	33.9	37.4	17.7	56.2	1.9	17.9	48.9	31.3	68.4
Middle Class	8.9	38.7	39.3	13.1	55.1	1.9	17.6	49.2	31.3	68.2
Working Class	12.1	31.3	36.2	20.4	56.8	1.7	19.5	47.6	31.2	68.5
Other	10.5	36.8	42.1	10.6	54.2	0.0	14.8	48.1	37.1	72.0

Table 4.55 *What thermometer rating would the Labour/Conservative member give the CBI ? (%)*

Subjective Class	Labour					Conservative				
	Cd	Cl	W	H	M	Cd	Cl	W	H	M
All	45.8	40.8	11.5	1.9	30.4	4.9	28.7	49.3	17.1	60.5
Middle Class	43.2	46.4	9.3	1.1	30.6	4.6	27.2	51.0	17.2	60.9
Working Class	46.9	37.9	12.9	2.3	30.5	7.1	36.5	38.1	18.3	57.9
Other	51.9	37.0	9.3	1.8	26.6	0.0	35.0	55.0	10.0	59.0

Table 4.56 *What thermometer rating would the Labour/Conservative member give the Queen ? (%)*

Subjective Class	Labour					Conservative				
	Cd	Cl	W	H	M	Cd	Cl	W	H	M
All	36.0	29.2	18.8	16.0	42.0	0.7	4.9	15.2	79.2	86.7
Middle Class	38.7	35.2	18.1	8.0	37.1	0.7	4.6	14.9	79.8	87.1
Working Class	34.4	25.8	19.3	20.5	44.8	0.4	6.2	17.3	76.1	85.4
Other	38.6	35.1	15.8	10.5	36.8	3.8	7.7	11.5	77.0	82.4

Table 4.57 *What thermometer rating would the Labour/Conservative member give Judges ? (%)*

Subjective Class	Labour					Conservative				
	Cd	Cl	W	H	M	Cd	Cl	W	H	M
All	39.3	43.5	13.8	3.4	37.8	4.6	28.9	46.7	19.8	61.1
Middle Class	37.5	48.3	14.2	0.0	39.2	4.0	27.6	48.3	20.1	61.8
Working Class	40.1	41.0	14.8	4.1	32.8	8.0	34.8	37.9	19.3	57.8
Other	42.9	42.9	12.5	1.7	32.6	0.0	32.0	56.0	12.0	59.6

5   Completion of Education

Table 5.1   *The Labour/Conservative party should try to capture the middle ground in politics (%)*

Completion of Education	Labour				Conservative			
	Agree	Neith-er	Dis-agree	N	Agree	Neith-er	Dis-agree	N
All	50.8	12.2	37.0	2738	69.5	13.5	17.0	2264
16 and under	66.1	8.8	25.1	1031	75.2	12.3	12.5	1209
17 to 18	46.2	12.4	41.4	823	64.1	15.8	20.1	591
19 and over	37.2	16.1	46.7	884	61.6	13.6	24.8	464

Table 5.2   *A Labour/Conservative government should introduce a prices and incomes policy as a means of controlling inflation (%)*

Completion of Education	Labour				Conservative			
	Agree	Neith-er	Dis-agree	N	Agree	Neith-er	Dis-agree	N
All	57.4	18.7	23.9	2742	41.9	11.6	46.5	2310
16 and under	71.5	10.7	17.8	1038	51.1	11.1	37.8	1250
17 to 18	50.5	21.1	28.4	821	32.6	14.9	52.5	592
19 and over	47.2	25.8	27.0	883	29.1	9.1	61.8	468

Table 5.3   *Income and wealth should be re-distributed towards ordinary working people (%)*

Completion of Education	Labour				Conservative			
	Agree	Neith-er	Dis-agree	N	Agree	Neith-er	Dis-agree	N
All	86.1	9.1	4.8	2769	25.2	20.3	54.5	2304
16 and under	82.8	10.7	6.5	1045	30.2	21.2	48.6	1244
17 to 18	83.2	11.6	5.2	829	20.3	20.1	59.6	596
19 and over	92.5	4.9	2.6	895	18.1	17.9	64.0	464

Table 5.4   *The Labour/Conservative Party should always stand by its principles even if this should lose it an election (%)*

Completion of Education	Labour				Conservative			
	Agree	Neith-er	Dis-agree	N	Agree	Neith-er	Dis-agree	N
All	67.8	11.9	20.3	2767	81.3	8.2	10.5	2363
16 and under	73.3	8.6	18.1	1044	83.3	7.5	9.2	1284
17 to 18	66.4	11.5	22.1	831	81.6	8.1	10.3	604
19 and over	62.7	16.1	21.2	892	75.6	10.3	14.1	475

Table 5.5   *Further nuclear energy development is essential for the future prosperity of Britain (%)*

Completion of Education	Labour				Conservative			
	Agree	Neith-er	Dis-agree	N	Agree	Neith-er	Dis-agree	N
All	14.1	11.8	74.1	2755	60.0	16.9	23.1	2325
16 and under	19.9	12.1	68.0	1031	58.9	15.7	25.4	1262
17 to 18	11.1	12.6	76.3	828	60.0	20.8	19.2	592
19 and over	10.2	10.8	79.0	896	63.1	15.5	21.4	471

Table 5.6   *A future Labour/Conservative government should not agree to a single European currency (%)*

Completion of Education	Labour				Conservative			
	Agree	Neith-er	Dis-agree	N	Agree	Neith-er	Dis-agree	N
All	25.3	18.8	55.9	2747	57.7	12.0	30.3	2342
16 and under	34.1	16.0	49.9	1029	60.7	11.6	27.7	1272
17 to 18	24.4	20.4	55.2	833	56.8	12.2	31.0	597
19 and over	10.2	10.8	79.0	885	51.0	12.6	36.4	473

Table 5.7   *High income tax makes people less willing to work hard (%)*

Completion of Education	Labour				Conservative			
	Agree	Neith-er	Dis-agree	N	Agree	Neith-er	Dis-agree	N
All	26.0	10.9	63.1	2772	81.9	6.0	12.1	2363
16 and under	40.9	12.1	47.0	1044	79.9	6.4	13.7	1283
17 to 18	24.0	8.4	67.6	833	83.4	5.7	10.9	604
19 and over	10.4	11.7	77.9	895	85.3	5.7	9.0	476

Table 5.8   *Britain's electoral system should be replaced by a system of proportional representation (%)*

Completion of Education	Labour				Conservative			
	Agree	Neith-er	Dis-agree	N	Agree	Neith-er	Dis-agree	N
All	57.5	13.2	29.3	2769	21.5	11.8	66.7	2329
16 and under	51.5	11.6	36.9	1038	21.3	13.7	65.0	1255
17 to 18	54.0	14.1	31.9	833	19.7	10.9	69.4	605
19 and over	67.7	14.1	18.2	898	24.3	8.1	67.6	469

Table 5.9   *Further moves towards integration within the European Community should be resisted (%)*

Completion of Education	Labour				Conservative			
	Agree	Neith-er	Dis-agree	N	Agree	Neith-er	Dis-agree	N
All	21.4	13.3	65.3	2761	54.0	15.5	30.5	2342
16 and under	27.1	14.0	58.9	1031	58.8	15.0	26.2	1262
17 to 18	21.4	13.9	64.7	833	51.5	16.8	31.7	608
19 and over	15.1	11.5	73.4	897	44.5	15.2	40.3	472

Table 5.10   There is no need for a Bill of Rights in this country (%)

Completion of Education	Labour				Conservative			
	Agree	Neith-er	Dis-agree	N	Agree	Neith-er	Dis-agree	N
All	11.2	10.0	78.8	2744	40.1	26.3	33.6	2257
16 and under	16.5	11.9	71.6	1020	37.0	25.7	37.3	1220
17 to 18	8.3	10.1	81.6	831	40.6	27.4	32.0	572
19 and over	8.0	7.5	84.5	893	47.7	26.2	26.1	465

Table 5.11   A future Labour/Conservative government should introduce a directly elected Scottish Assembly with taxing powers (%)

Completion of Education	Labour				Conservative			
	Agree	Neith-er	Dis-agree	N	Agree	Neith-er	Dis-agree	N
All	61.0	22.2	16.8	2769	22.7	26.2	51.1	2305
16 and under	57.5	21.0	21.5	1039	24.4	27.2	48.4	1245
17 to 18	60.4	23.1	16.5	834	21.2	25.6	53.2	590
19 and over	65.5	22.8	11.7	896	20.2	24.3	55.5	470

Table 5.12   Coalition governments are the best form of government for Britain (%)

Completion of Education	Labour				Conservative			
	Agree	Neith-er	Dis-agree	N	Agree	Neith-er	Dis-agree	N
All	8.3	16.8	74.9	2767	9.5	10.0	80.5	2368
16 and under	9.3	13.0	77.7	1039	11.6	11.1	77.3	1282
17 to 18	7.0	15.4	77.6	832	7.9	7.5	84.6	609
19 and over	8.5	22.4	69.1	896	6.0	10.1	83.9	477

Table 5.13 *A future Labour/Conservative government should/should not spend money to get rid of poverty (%)*

Completion of Education	Labour				Conservative			
	Should	Doesn't matter	Should not	N	Should	Doesn't matter	Should not	N
All	98.0	0.9	1.1	2766	80.5	8.2	11.3	2323
16 and under	97.6	1.3	1.1	1039	81.1	8.6	10.3	1255
17 to 18	97.7	1.0	1.3	832	81.3	7.3	11.4	599
19 and over	98.8	0.4	0.8	895	77.6	8.3	14.1	469

Table 5.14 *A future Labour/Conservative government should/should not encourage the growth of private medicine (%)*

Completion of Education	Labour				Conservative			
	Should	Doesn't matter	Should not	N	Should	Doesn't matter	Should not	N
All	3.5	4.7	91.8	2758	52.0	15.8	32.2	2332
16 and under	5.4	6.5	88.1	1031	48.7	15.5	35.8	1257
17 to 18	2.7	5.0	92.3	834	57.4	15.0	27.6	601
19 and over	1.9	2.4	95.7	893	53.8	17.7	28.5	474

Table 5.15 *A future Labour/Conservative government should/should not put more money into the National Health Service (%)*

Completion of Education	Labour				Conservative			
	Should	Doesn't matter	Should not	N	Should	Doesn't matter	Should not	N
All	97.9	0.8	1.3	2770	79.3	7.4	13.3	2339
16 and under	98.0	0.7	1.3	1040	82.5	7.0	10.5	1265
17 to 18	98.4	0.8	0.8	835	77.7	8.4	13.9	606
19 and over	97.4	0.8	1.8	895	72.9	7.2	19.9	468

Table 5.16   *A future Labour/Conservative government should/should not reduce spending in general (%)*

Completion of Education	Labour				Conservative			
	Should	Doesn't matter	Should not	N	Should	Doesn't matter	Should not	N
All	19.5	7.4	73.1	2724	60.6	8.9	30.5	2320
16 and under	29.3	9.0	61.7	1009	61.5	10.3	28.2	1250
17 to 18	17.6	7.8	74.7	825	59.4	6.5	34.1	599
19 and over	10.2	5.2	84.6	890	59.9	8.0	32.1	471

Table 5.17   *A future Labour/Conservative government should/should not introduce stricter laws to regulate the trade unions (%)*

Completion of Education	Labour				Conservative			
	Should	Doesn't matter	Should not	N	Should	Doesn't matter	Should not	N
All	10.3	14.6	75.1	2735	66.2	12.2	21.6	2345
16 and under	14.4	15.0	70.6	1023	68.8	10.5	20.7	1268
17 to 18	8.9	13.6	77.5	825	67.1	13.6	19.3	605
19 and over	6.8	15.1	78.1	887	58.1	14.8	27.1	472

Table 5.18   *A future Labour/Conservative government should/should not give workers more say in the places where they work (%)*

Completion of Education	Labour				Conservative			
	Should	Doesn't matter	Should not	N	Should	Doesn't matter	Should not	N
All	91.2	5.6	3.2	2759	63.5	13.5	23.0	2354
16 and under	90.2	6.5	3.3	1034	66.0	13.3	20.7	1273
17 to 18	91.0	5.4	3.6	834	58.6	14.1	27.3	607
19 and over	92.5	4.7	2.8	891	63.1	13.5	23.4	474

Table 5.19   *A future Labour/Conservative government should/should not spend less on defence (%)*

Completion of Education	Labour				Conservative			
	Should	Doesn't matter	Should not	N	Should	Doesn't matter	Should not	N
All	82.7	4.6	12.7	2762	44.3	5.0	50.7	2341
16 and under	76.1	6.2	17.7	1030	44.8	5.0	50.2	1260
17 to 18	84.1	5.3	10.6	836	40.3	4.3	55.4	605
19 and over	89.0	2.1	8.9	896	48.1	5.7	46.2	476

Table 5.20   *Should a future Labour/Conservative government :*
(A) Reduce taxes & spend less on health, education & social benefits ?
(B) Keep taxes & spending on these services at the same levels as now ?
(C) Increase taxes & spend more on health, education & social benefits ?

Completion of Education	Labour				Conservative			
	A	B	C	N	A	B	C	N
All	2.6	6.4	91.0	2763	6.7	67.1	26.2	2335
16 and under	4.2	8.0	87.8	1038	5.4	65.8	28.8	1264
17 to 18	2.8	5.7	91.5	839	8.6	66.7	24.7	600
19 and over	0.7	5.1	94.2	886	7.9	70.9	21.2	471

Table 5.21   *On joining the Labour/Conservative party did the member approach the party (MA) or did the party approach the member (PA) ? (%)*

Completion of Education	Labour				Conservative			
	MA	Don't Know	PA	N	MA	Don't Know	PA	N
All	77.0	20.5	2.5	2792	34.5	50.2	15.3	2377
16 and under	73.7	23.6	2.7	1056	37.3	48.1	14.6	1291
17 to 18	77.2	20.8	2.0	838	30.3	53.7	16.0	613
19 and over	80.8	16.6	2.6	898	32.1	51.4	16.5	473

Table 5.22   *How often has the member attended a party meeting in the last*
                  12 months ? (%)

Completion of Education	Labour				Conservative			
	Not at all	Occas- ionally	Frequ- ently	N	Not at all	Occas- ionally	Frequ- ently	N
All	41.5	30.5	28.0	2803	66.0	22.0	12.0	2395
16 and under	33.6	33.9	32.5	1062	70.0	19.0	11.0	1302
17 to 18	46.4	27.7	25.9	842	61.9	24.5	13.6	617
19 and over	46.2	29.1	24.7	899	60.3	26.9	12.8	476

Table 5.23   *Is the member more or less politically active than 5 years ago ? (%)*

Completion of Education	Labour				Conservative			
	More active	About same	Less active	N	More active	About same	Less active	N
All	12.9	38.4	48.7	2767	9.4	62.7	27.9	2013
16 and under	11.4	39.2	49.4	1040	7.9	65.0	27.1	1057
17 to 18	13.2	37.9	48.9	832	12.1	60.3	27.6	532
19 and over	14.3	38.0	47.7	695	9.7	60.1	30.2	424

Table 5.24   *Does the member hold any office within the Labour/Conservative*
                  Party ? (%)

Completion of Education	Labour			Conservative		
	Yes	No	N	Yes	No	N
All	16.3	83.7	2755	8.5	91.5	2359
16 and under	16.4	83.6	1038	6.9	93.1	1276
17 to 18	14.9	85.1	830	11.2	88.8	609
19 and over	17.5	82.5	887	9.3	90.7	474

Table 5.25   *How much time does the member devote to party activities per month ? (%)*

Completion of Education	Labour					Conservative				
	None	Up to 5 hrs	5 to 10 hrs	Over 10 hrs	N	None	Up to 5 hrs	5 to 10 hrs	Over 10 hrs	N
All	51.3	29.2	9.6	9.9	2764	76.0	15.2	4.6	4.2	2349
16 and under	50.8	27.9	10.8	10.5	1034	78.5	13.7	4.3	3.5	1267
17 to 18	51.6	29.7	9.4	9.3	836	73.0	17.3	4.6	5.1	607
19 and over	51.7	30.3	8.2	9.8	894	73.1	16.8	5.3	4.8	475

Table 5.26   *What was the overall financial contribution made by the member in the last year ? (%)*

Completion of Education	Labour				Conservative			
	0 to £10	£10 to £20	Over £20	N	0 to £10	£10 to £20	Over £20	N
All	23.6	19.8	56.6	2468	33.8	21.4	44.8	1783
16 and under	34.7	21.3	44.0	910	39.9	21.4	38.7	902
17 to 18	21.6	20.1	58.3	746	28.5	21.9	49.6	478
19 and over	12.9	18.0	69.1	812	26.6	20.8	52.6	403

Table 5.27   *Is the member a local Labour/Conservative councillor ? (%)*

Completion of Education	Labour			Conservative		
	Yes	No	N	Yes	No	N
All	8.0	92.0	2778	2.4	97.6	2378
16 and under	8.9	91.1	1040	1.9	98.1	1287
17 to 18	8.3	91.7	839	2.8	97.2	615
19 and over	6.5	93.5	899	2.9	97.1	476

Table 5.28   *The Labour/Conservative leader should be elected by a system of one party member/one vote (%)*

Completion of Education	Labour				Conservative			
	Agree	Neith-er	Dis-agree	N	Agree	Neith-er	Dis-agree	N
All	86.2	5.1	8.7	2776	49.8	14.4	35.8	2321
16 and under	90.5	3.3	6.2	1053	57.5	13.4	29.1	1260
17 to 18	85.6	5.6	8.8	833	43.4	14.7	41.9	590
19 and over	81.7	6.7	11.6	890	37.2	16.5	46.3	471

Table 5.29   *People like me can have a real influence in politics if they are prepared to get involved (%)*

Completion of Education	Labour				Conservative			
	Agree	Neith-er	Dis-agree	N	Agree	Neith-er	Dis-agree	N
All	66.1	16.2	17.7	2764	56.5	20.2	23.3	2331
16 and under	70.1	14.2	15.7	1037	54.2	20.7	25.1	1250
17 to 18	64.4	17.9	17.7	832	56.6	21.2	22.2	604
19 and over	63.0	17.0	20.0	895	62.7	17.6	19.7	477

Table 5.30   *Attending party meetings can be pretty tiring after a hard days work (%)*

Completion of Education	Labour				Conservative			
	Agree	Neith-er	Dis-agree	N	Agree	Neith-er	Dis-agree	N
All	77.5	11.2	11.3	2770	69.2	19.5	11.3	2311
16 and under	72.0	12.7	15.3	1041	67.5	19.6	12.9	1243
17 to 18	79.6	11.6	8.8	834	70.4	21.5	8.1	594
19 and over	81.8	9.2	9.0	895	72.2	16.7	11.1	474

Table 5.31   Someone like me could do a good job of being a local councillor (%)

Completion of Education	Labour					Conservative			
	Agree	Neith-er	Dis-agree	N		Agree	Neith-er	Dis-agree	N
All	48.4	22.1	29.5	2746		27.4	24.6	48.0	2300
16 and under	45.6	23.2	31.2	1026		24.0	24.3	51.7	1231
17 to 18	49.0	23.0	28.0	825		27.7	25.4	46.9	599
19 and over	51.1	20.0	28.9	895		36.2	24.0	39.8	470

Table 5.32   Being an active party member is a good way of meeting interesting people (%)

Completion of Education	Labour					Conservative			
	Agree	Neith-er	Dis-agree	N		Agree	Neith-er	Dis-agree	N
All	65.1	21.6	13.3	2767		59.6	29.9	10.5	2302
16 and under	77.2	14.9	7.9	1045		60.5	29.2	10.3	1236
17 to 18	60.6	23.8	15.6	833		60.3	29.9	9.8	595
19 and over	55.0	27.6	17.4	889		56.1	31.6	12.3	471

Table 5.33   The only way to be really educated about politics is to be a party activist (%)

Completion of Education	Labour					Conservative			
	Agree	Neith-er	Dis-agree	N		Agree	Neith-er	Dis-agree	N
All	42.1	11.1	46.8	2774		35.5	17.1	47.4	2306
16 and under	55.6	11.0	33.4	1045		39.7	17.3	43.0	1239
17 to 18	38.0	10.8	51.2	832		35.4	15.6	49.0	594
19 and over	30.1	11.7	58.2	897		24.7	18.2	57.1	473

Table 5.34   *The party leadership does not pay a lot of attention to ordinary party members (%)*

Completion of Education	Labour				Conservative			
	Agree	Neith-er	Dis-agree	N	Agree	Neith-er	Dis-agree	N
All	46.5	19.0	34.5	2771	42.1	24.0	33.9	2316
16 and under	48.3	14.6	37.1	1044	44.7	22.3	33.0	1247
17 to 18	48.4	20.4	31.2	831	41.4	25.9	32.7	597
19 and over	42.6	22.7	34.7	896	36.0	26.5	37.5	472

Table 5.35   *Party activity often takes time away from one's family (%)*

Completion of Education	Labour				Conservative			
	Agree	Neith-er	Dis-agree	N	Agree	Neith-er	Dis-agree	N
All	85.5	10.1	4.4	2767	67.2	25.4	7.4	2285
16 and under	88.5	7.1	4.4	1042	67.5	24.9	7.6	1226
17 to 18	84.4	10.9	4.7	834	64.6	26.5	8.9	588
19 and over	83.1	12.9	4.0	891	69.4	25.5	5:1	471

Table 5.36   *The Labour/Conservative party would be more successful if people like me were elected to parliament (%)*

Completion of Education	Labour				Conservative			
	Agree	Neith-er	Dis-agree	N	Agree	Neith-er	Dis-agree	N
All	33.5	34.1	32.4	2747	21.4	31.4	47.2	2280
16 and under	34.7	31.7	33.6	1034	21.3	29.6	49.1	1223
17 to 18	33.8	34.4	31.8	826	21.0	33.3	45.7	589
19 and over	31.9	36.8	31.3	887	22.0	33.8	44.2	468

Table 5.37   *During the last 5 years, how often has the member displayed an election poster in his/her window ? (%)*

Completion of Education	Labour				Conservative			
	Not at all	Occas-ionally	Freq-uently	N	Not at all	Occas-ionally	Freq-uently	N
All	9.5	21.4	69.1	2752	48.9	31.8	19.3	2280
16 and under	9.4	20.7	69.9	1029	50.3	31.5	18.2	1232
17 to 18	9.0	23.7	67.3	831	46.7	30.7	22.6	589
19 and over	9.7	20.2	70.1	892	48.1	33.8	18.1	459

Table 5.38   *During the last 5 years, how often has the member donated money to party funds ? (%)*

Completion of Education	Labour				Conservative			
	Not at all	Occas-ionally	Freq-uently	N	Not at all	Occas-ionally	Freq-uently	N
All	9.6	50.5	39.9	2747	14.8	55.3	29.9	2333
16 and under	10.4	50.3	39.3	1015	17.1	56.2	26.7	1259
17 to 18	10.9	50.1	39.0	835	12.8	53.3	33.9	604
19 and over	7.4	51.1	41.5	897	11.1	55.7	33.2	470

Table 5.39   *During the last 5 years, how often has the member delivered party leaflets ? (%)*

Completion of Education	Labour				Conservative			
	Not at all	Occas-ionally	Freq-uently	N	Not at all	Occas-ionally	Freq-uently	N
All	17.6	26.7	55.7	2698	61.0	16.9	22.1	2228
16 and under	21.6	22.2	56.2	990	65.1	16.5	18.4	1205
17 to 18	18.5	26.2	55.3	824	56.3	17.4	26.3	574
19 and over	12.4	32.1	55.5	884	56.1	17.4	26.5	449

Table 5.40   During the last 5 years, how often has the member attended a party meeting ? (%)

Completion of Education	Labour				Conservative			
	Not at all	Occas-ionally	Freq-uently	N	Not at all	Occas-ionally	Freq-uently	N
All	21.5	40.5	38.0	2703	50.8	32.6	16.6	2256
16 and under	19.3	36.8	43.9	995	56.0	28.9	15.1	1213
17 to 18	22.7	40.9	36.4	821	45.6	36.3	18.1	581
19 and over	22.9	44.3	32.8	887	43.7	37.4	18.9	462

Table 5.41   During the last 5 years, how often has the member canvassed voters on behalf of the party ? (%)

Completion of Education	Labour				Conservative			
	Not at all	Occas-ionally	Freq-uently	N	Not at all	Occas-ionally	Freq-uently	N
All	36.7	31.2	32.1	2679	74.8	14.7	10.5	2218
16 and under	37.0	27.0	36.0	974	79.4	11.9	8.7	1192
17 to 18	38.2	30.9	30.9	819	71.1	16.6	12.3	571
19 and over	35.0	36.2	28.8	886	67.7	19.8	12.5	455

Table 5.42   Where would you place yourself on a Left/Right scale within the Labour/Conservative party ? (%)

Completion of Education	Labour				Conservative			
	Left	Centre	Right	N	Left	Centre	Right	N
All	57.6	20.5	21.9	2779	13.3	26.0	60.7	2349
16 and under	52.3	23.9	23.8	1043	11.8	27.6	60.6	1264
17 to 18	62.0	18.7	19.3	843	10.8	23.8	65.4	610
19 and over	59.6	18.3	22.1	893	20.9	24.4	54.7	475

Table 5.43   *Where would you place yourself on a Left/Right scale within British Politics ? (%)*

Completion of Education	Labour				Conservative			
	Left	Centre	Right	N	Left	Centre	Right	N
All	80.1	10.4	9.5	2774	3.6	18.2	78.2	2344
16 and under	64.1	17.0	18.9	1044	4.0	21.3	74.7	1261
17 to 18	85.0	9.8	5.2	838	3.8	14.8	81.4	609
19 and over	94.5	3.1	2.4	892	2.6	14.3	83.1	474

Table 5.44   *What thermometer rating would the Labour/Conservative member give the Conservative Party ? (%)*

Completion of Education	Labour					Conservative				
	Cd	Cl	W	H	M	Cd	Cl	W	H	M
All	76.2	20.3	2.8	0.7	14.7	0.2	3.5	33.7	62.6	80.9
16 and under	65.4	28.8	4.8	1.0	19.7	0.2	4.0	29.7	66.1	82.0
17 to 18	79.9	17.6	2.0	0.5	13.0	0.1	2.7	35.2	62.0	80.9
19 and over	84.6	13.6	1.5	0.3	10.7	0.2	3.2	42.8	53.8	78.0

Table 5.45   *What thermometer rating would the Labour/Conservative member give the Labour Party ? (%)*

Completion of Education	Labour					Conservative				
	Cd	Cl	W	H	M	Cd	Cl	W	H	M
All	1.0	3.7	24.5	70.8	82.8	50.1	43.4	6.1	0.4	26.8
16 and under	1.0	3.0	15.0	81.0	86.9	47.5	44.9	7.1	0.5	28.0
17 to 18	1.0	4.6	24.5	69.9	82.3	54.2	41.0	4.4	0.4	25.0
19 and over	0.9	3.8	35.7	59.6	78.4	51.6	42.5	5.9	0.0	25.8

Table 5.46   *What thermometer rating would the Labour/Conservative member give the Liberal Democratic Party ? (%)*

Completion of Education	Labour					Conservative				
	Cd	Cl	W	H	M	Cd	Cl	W	H	M
All	32.8	44.4	21.0	1.8	37.0	32.7	50.7	15.3	1.3	36.3
16 and under	31.8	44.4	20.3	3.5	38.3	29.5	52.6	16.4	1.5	38.0
17 to 18	35.3	42.5	20.8	1.4	35.9	37.0	49.6	12.0	1.4	33.6
19 and over	31.6	46.2	21.8	0.4	36.5	35.4	47.5	16.6	0.5	35.2

Table 5.47   *What thermometer rating would the Labour/Conservative member give the Scottish Nationalist Party ? (%)*

Completion of Education	Labour					Conservative				
	Cd	Cl	W	H	M	Cd	Cl	W	H	M
All	44.2	36.9	16.0	2.9	32.1	69.1	26.5	4.1	0.3	19.1
16 and under	46.6	35.4	14.2	3.8	31.2	66.2	28.6	4.6	0.6	20.3
17 to 18	47.1	34.6	16.2	2.1	31.0	72.0	24.6	3.4	0.0	17.7
19 and over	39.1	40.6	17.8	2.5	34.0	72.8	23.7	3.5	0.0	17.8

Table 5.48   *What thermometer rating would the Labour/Conservative member give Plaid Cymru ? (%)*

Completion of Education	Labour					Conservative				
	Cd	Cl	W	H	M	Cd	Cl	W	H	M
All	47.7	37.5	12.9	1.9	29.6	82.6	16.0	1.1	0.3	13.0
16 and under	52.5	36.3	10.0	1.2	26.9	82.2	16.1	1.5	0.2	13.4
17 to 18	48.7	36.5	13.4	1.4	28.9	83.4	15.4	0.7	0.5	12.6
19 and over	41.4	39.9	15.5	3.2	33.2	82.5	16.6	0.9	0.0	12.5

Table 5.49   *What thermometer rating would the Labour/Conservative member give the Green Party ? (%)*

Completion of Education	Labour					Conservative				
	Cd	Cl	W	H	M	Cd	Cl	W	H	M
All	33.3	36.0	25.6	5.1	39.4	70.1	24.5	4.8	0.6	19.5
16 and under	41.9	36.9	17.2	4.0	34.2	69.8	24.8	4.6	0.8	19.9
17 to 18	32.6	36.1	27.1	4.2	39.6	71.7	23.3	5.0	0.0	18.7
19 and over	24.6	35.0	33.2	7.2	44.9	69.1	24.9	5.2	0.8	19.5

Table 5.50   *What thermometer rating would the Labour/Conservative member give the BBC ? (%)*

Completion of Education	Labour					Conservative				
	Cd	Cl	W	H	M	Cd	Cl	W	H	M
All	9.3	26.1	40.0	24.6	60.4	8.5	30.3	40.6	20.6	59.3
16 and under	13.0	31.8	36.0	19.2	56.0	8.8	29.8	39.4	22.0	60.0
17 to 18	9.9	26.8	37.1	26.2	60.5	8.5	33.0	40.5	18.0	57.8
19 and over	4.5	19.2	47.1	29.2	65.3	8.0	28.3	43.6	20.1	59.5

Table 5.51   *What thermometer rating would the Labour/Conservative member give the European Community ? (%)*

Completion of Education	Labour					Conservative				
	Cd	Cl	W	H	M	Cd	Cl	W	H	M
All	11.1	32.1	42.3	14.5	55.6	14.3	40.6	35.7	9.4	50.9
16 and under	13.6	30.8	37.4	18.2	55.6	15.2	41.2	33.6	10.0	50.5
17 to 18	12.1	31.9	42.2	13.8	54.9	13.6	39.4	39.0	8.0	50.6
19 and over	7.8	33.5	47.3	11.4	56.3	13.1	40.6	36.3	10.0	52.1

Table 5.52   *What thermometer rating would the Labour/Conservative member give the Trade Union Congress ? (%)*

Completion of Education	Labour					Conservative				
	Cd	Cl	W	H	M	Cd	Cl	W	H	M
All	5.6	28.9	47.7	17.8	60.1	53.6	39.9	5.7	0.8	26.4
16 and under	6.3	23.5	44.0	26.2	63.3	51.2	39.6	7.7	1.5	27.9
17 to 18	6.0	28.4	49.1	16.5	59.8	57.2	38.4	4.4	0.0	24.5
19 and over	4.5	35.5	50.5	9.5	56.8	54.5	42.3	3.0	0.2	25.3

Table 5.53   *What thermometer rating would the Labour/Conservative member give the Police ? (%)*

Completion of Education	Labour					Conservative				
	Cd	Cl	W	H	M	Cd	Cl	W	H	M
All	17.7	43.9	28.8	9.6	48.3	1.5	12.5	39.9	46.1	72.9
16 and under	14.0	33.8	35.5	16.7	54.7	1.3	12.2	36.1	50.4	74.2
17 to 18	21.3	43.2	27.1	8.4	46.4	1.3	11.9	43.3	43.5	72.7
19 and over	18.7	56.0	22.9	2.4	42.8	2.1	14.1	45.3	38.5	69.8

Table 5.54   *What thermometer rating would the Labour/Conservative member give the House of Commons ? (%)*

Completion of Education	Labour					Conservative				
	Cd	Cl	W	H	M	Cd	Cl	W	H	M
All	10.0	33.6	38.4	18.0	56.9	2.3	17.1	49.1	31.5	68.4
16 and under	10.1	27.9	36.9	25.1	60.0	2.9	16.8	45.0	35.3	69.1
17 to 18	10.3	36.3	36.0	17.4	56.1	1.5	16.0	54.1	28.4	68.7
19 and over	9.7	37.3	42.2	10.8	54.3	2.1	19.0	53.1	25.8	66.3

Table 5.55   *What thermometer rating would the Labour/Conservative member give the CBI ? (%)*

Completion of Education	Labour					Conservative				
	Cd	Cl	W	H	M	Cd	Cl	W	H	M
All	44.9	41.8	11.2	2.1	31.0	5.4	29.6	49.2	15.8	59.7
16 and under	41.4	39.5	15.2	3.9	34.3	5.2	30.7	45.3	18.8	60.8
17 to 18	49.1	38.8	10.3	1.8	28.8	5.2	27.9	52.7	14.2	59.6
19 and over	44.8	46.7	8.0	0.5	29.4	5.7	29.5	53.2	11.6	57.7

Table 5.56   *What thermometer rating would the Labour/Conservative member give the Queen ? (%)*

Completion of Education	Labour					Conservative				
	Cd	Cl	W	H	M	Cd	Cl	W	H	M
All	34.4	29.6	19.2	16.8	43.5	0.8	4.6	16.0	78.6	86.5
16 and under	24.5	25.5	21.3	28.7	54.2	0.5	4.7	14.6	80.2	87.1
17 to 18	40.7	26.5	17.8	15.0	39.8	0.7	3.7	15.3	80.3	87.7
19 and over	39.9	37.1	18.1	4.9	34.8	2.0	5.3	20.6	72.1	83.6

Table 5.57   *What thermometer rating would the Labour/Conservative member give Judges ? (%)*

Completion of Education	Labour					Conservative				
	Cd	Cl	W	H	M	Cd	Cl	W	H	M
All	38.0	43.5	14.9	3.6	35.1	4.5	30.9	45.5	19.1	60.6
16 and under	32.9	42.1	19.5	5.5	39.2	5.7	32.6	43.2	18.5	59.6
17 to 18	41.9	42.0	12.9	3.2	32.8	2.6	29.2	48.5	19.7	61.6
19 and over	40.1	46.4	11.6	1.9	32.6	3.7	28.8	47.7	19.8	61.7

6 Annual Income

Table 6.1   *The Labour/Conservative party should try to capture the middle ground in politics (%)*

Annual Income	Labour				Conservative			
	Agree	Neith-er	Dis-agree	N	Agree	Neith-er	Dis-agree	N
All	50.9	12.0	37.1	2810	69.4	13.3	17.3	2166
Under £10,000	64.4	8.2	27.4	922	78.2	12.2	9.6	541
£10,000 - £20,000	45.1	12.6	42.3	949	71.2	12.5	16.3	718
£20,000 - £30,000	43.7	14.0	42.3	542	65.0	11.9	23.1	411
£30,000 - £40,000	43.0	16.0	41.0	263	64.5	14.3	21.2	217
Above £40,000	44.0	17.2	38.8	134	58.1	18.3	23.6	279

Table 6.2   *A Labour/Conservative government should introduce a prices and Incomes policy as a means of controlling inflation (%)*

Annual Income	Labour				Conservative			
	Agree	Neith-er	Dis-agree	N	Agree	Neith-er	Dis-agree	N
All	57.3	18.9	23.8	2810	41.5	11.7	46.8	2201
Under £10,000	75.0	11.2	13.8	936	61.7	12.1	26.2	556
£10,000 - £20,000	52.3	20.9	26.8	947	44.7	12.1	43.2	727
£20,000 - £30,000	45.6	24.4	30.0	533	30.3	13.5	56.2	416
£30,000 - £40,000	40.3	24.0	35.7	258	28.8	10.5	60.7	219
Above £40,000	48.5	25.7	25.8	136	20.1	8.1	71.8	283

Table 6.3 *Income and wealth should be re-distributed towards ordinary working people (%)*

Annual Income	Labour				Conservative			
	Agree	Neith-er	Dis-agree	N	Agree	Neith-er	Dis-agree	N
All	86.0	9.1	4.9	2841	25.3	20.5	54.2	2205
Under £10,000	84.5	9.9	5.6	944	35.4	22.0	42.6	559
£10,000 - £20,000	85.4	9.5	5.1	954	27.1	20.8	52.1	730
£20,000 - £30,000	87.5	8.9	3.6	542	23.3	21.4	55.3	416
£30,000 - £40,000	89.5	6.8	3.7	266	14.0	17.6	68.4	222
Above £40,000	88.1	5.9	6.0	135	11.9	17.6	70.5	278

Table 6.4 *The Labour/Conservative Party should always stand by its principles even if this should lose it an election (%)*

Annual Income	Labour				Conservative			
	Agree	Neith-er	Dis-agree	N	Agree	Neith-er	Dis-agree	N
All	67.9	11.8	20.3	2839	80.9	8.4	10.7	2251
Under £10,000	78.5	7.6	13.9	949	87.1	6.2	6.7	583
£10,000 - £20,000	65.5	12.5	22.0	949	84.5	7.0	8.5	741
£20,000 - £30,000	61.4	15.1	23.5	542	77.7	11.4	10.9	421
£30,000 - £40,000	58.2	16.0	25.8	263	74.9	8.5	16.6	223
Above £40,000	54.4	14.0	31.6	136	68.2	11.7	20.1	283

Table 6.5   *Further nuclear energy development is essential for the future prosperity of Britain (%)*

Annual Income	Labour				Conservative			
	Agree	Neith-er	Dis-agree	N	Agree	Neith-er	Dis-agree	N
All	13.9	11.8	74.3	2827	60.5	16.7	22.8	2215
Under £10,000	18.3	11.9	69.8	928	56.9	17.5	25.6	561
£10,000 - £20,000	12.6	9.8	77.6	955	62.0	15.5	22.5	729
£20,000 - £30,000	10.6	13.5	75.9	547	63.5	15.3	21.2	419
£30,000 - £40,000	10.3	12.5	77.2	263	57.4	17.9	24.7	223
Above £40,000	12.7	17.2	70.1	134	61.8	19.8	18.4	283

Table 6.6   *A future Labour/Conservative government should not agree to a single European currency (%)*

Annual Income	Labour				Conservative			
	Agree	Neith-er	Dis-agree	N	Agree	Neith-er	Dis-agree	N
All	25.0	19.0	56.0	2820	57.1	12.2	30.7	2226
Under £10,000	36.0	16.8	47.2	931	65.0	13.9	21.1	577
£10,000 - £20,000	24.0	20.7	55.3	950	56.7	12.9	30.4	727
£20,000 - £30,000	17.2	20.7	62.1	540	55.2	11.0	33.8	417
£30,000 - £40,000	12.5	19.4	68.1	263	58.3	9.4	32.3	223
Above £40,000	11.8	14.0	74.2	136	44.0	11.0	45.0	282

Table 6.7 *High Income tax makes people less willing to work hard (%)*

Annual Income	Labour				Conservative			
	Agree	Neith-er	Dis-agree	N	Agree	Neith-er	Dis-agree	N
All	25.8	10.9	63.3	2842	81.9	5.8	12.3	2251
Under £10,000	40.2	10.9	48.9	942	80.6	6.3	13.1	583
£10,000 - £20,000	22.6	11.4	66.0	957	80.6	7.0	12.4	739
£20,000 - £30,000	14.4	11.4	74.2	543	81.7	3.8	14.5	421
£30,000 - £40,000	16.7	10.6	72.7	264	84.8	7.1	8.1	224
Above £40,000	12.5	6.6	80.9	136	85.6	3.5	10.9	284

Table 6.8 *Britain's electoral system should be replaced by a system of proportional representation (%)*

Annual Income	Labour				Conservative			
	Agree	Neith-er	Dis-agree	N	Agree	Neith-er	Dis-agree	N
All	57.9	13.1	29.0	2840	22.1	11.8	66.1	2227
Under £10,000	52.8	11.8	35.4	939	23.5	12.8	63.7	570
£10,000 - £20,000	56.9	14.0	29.1	952	23.2	11.8	65.0	729
£20,000 - £30,000	60.8	15.4	23.8	546	18.4	11.6	70.0	423
£30,000 - £40,000	69.7	10.5	19.8	267	19.4	13.1	67.5	222
Above £40,000	65.4	11.8	22.8	136	24.0	9.2	66.8	283

Table 6.9   *Further moves towards integration within the European Community should be resisted (%)*

Annual Income	Labour				Conservative			
	Agree	Neith-er	Dis-agree	N	Agree	Neith-er	Dis-agree	N
All	21.4	13.1	65.5	2834	53.5	15.3	31.2	2231
Under £10,000	30.0	14.2	55.8	937	69.9	10.9	19.2	571
£10,000 - £20,000	20.1	13.7	66.2	951	52.5	17.6	29.9	733
£20,000 - £30,000	16.0	12.8	71.2	545	47.4	16.8	35.8	422
£30,000 - £40,000	11.7	10.2	78.1	266	41.2	19.5	39.3	221
Above £40,000	12.6	8.9	78.5	135	41.5	12.7	45.8	284

Table 6.10   *There is no need for a Bill of Rights in this country (%)*

Annual Income	Labour				Conservative			
	Agree	Neith-er	Dis-agree	N	Agree	Neith-er	Dis-agree	N
All	11.2	9.8	79.0	2818	39.8	26.6	33.6	2158
Under £10,000	16.9	12.3	70.8	927	40.6	25.6	33.8	542
£10,000 - £20,000	8.3	9.5	82.2	947	38.0	27.6	34.4	713
£20,000 - £30,000	7.7	7.0	85.3	543	40.4	28.1	31.5	413
£30,000 - £40,000	7.9	8.7	83.4	265	43.4	23.6	33.0	212
Above £40,000	12.5	7.4	80.1	136	38.8	26.3	34.9	278

Table 6.11   *A future Labour/Conservative government should introduce a directly elected Scottish Assembly with taxing powers (%)*

Annual Income	Labour				Conservative			
	Agree	Neith-er	Dis-agree	N	Agree	Neith-er	Dis-agree	N
All	61.4	22.1	16.5	2840	23.1	26.7	50.2	2201
Under £10,000	60.9	20.6	18.5	942	25.9	25.9	48.2	555
£10,000 - £20,000	61.1	21.5	17.4	952	21.6	27.4	51.0	726
£20,000 - £30,000	64.0	23.9	12.1	544	22.1	30.2	47.7	421
£30,000 - £40,000	56.9	27.7	15.4	267	26.0	20.5	53.5	219
Above £40,000	65.2	18.5	16.3	135	20.7	25.7	53.6	280

Table 6.12   *Coalition governments are the best form of government for Britain (%)*

Annual Income	Labour				Conservative			
	Agree	Neith-er	Dis-agree	N	Agree	Neith-er	Dis-agree	N
All	8.5	16.8	74.7	2839	9.3	9.9	80.8	2254
Under £10,000	12.4	11.8	75.8	944	14.6	11.3	74.1	584
£10,000 - £20,000	6.6	17.4	76.0	951	10.0	8.4	81.6	742
£20,000 - £30,000	6.8	21.5	71.7	545	6.4	10.5	83.1	421
£30,000 - £40,000	6.4	22.6	71.0	265	6.3	9.9	83.8	222
Above £40,000	6.0	17.9	76.1	134	3.2	10.2	86.6	285

Table 6.13   A future Labour/Conservative government should/should not spend money to get rid of poverty (%)

Annual Income	Labour				Conservative			
	Should	Doesn't matter	Should not	N	Should	Doesn't matter	Should not	N
All	98.0	0.9	1.1	2834	80.2	8.4	11.4	2217
Under £10,000	97.4	1.2	1.4	941	80.1	9.2	10.7	574
£10,000 - £20,000	98.4	0.7	0.9	949	78.9	9.1	12.0	726
£20,000 - £30,000	98.2	0.7	1.1	545	80.0	7.2	12.8	419
£30,000 - £40,000	97.7	1.1	1.2	264	83.6	6.8	9.6	220
Above £40,000	99.3	0.7	0.0	135	81.7	7.9	10.4	278

Table 6.14   A future Labour/Conservative government should/should not encourage the growth of private medicine (%)

Annual Income	Labour				Conservative			
	Should	Doesn't matter	Should not	N	Should	Doesn't matter	Should not	N
All	3.6	4.7	91.7	2830	51.6	15.9	32.5	2228
Under £10,000	6.0	5.8	88.2	938	47.7	17.1	35.2	574
£10,000 - £20,000	2.7	4.8	92.5	951	46.4	18.1	35.5	729
£20,000 - £30,000	2.4	2.8	94.8	542	54.5	14.3	31.2	420
£30,000 - £40,000	1.9	4.5	93.6	264	55.7	14.0	30.3	221
Above £40,000	1.5	3.7	94.8	135	65.1	12.0	22.9	284

Table 6.15   A future Labour/Conservative government should/should not put more money into the National Health Service (%)

Annual Income	Labour				Conservative			
	Should	Doesn't matter	Should not	N	Should	Doesn't matter	Should not	N
All	98.0	0.7	1.3	2839	79.1	7.7	13.2	2228
Under £10,000	98.2	0.6	1.2	945	82.0	7.1	10.9	577
£10,000 - £20,000	98.2	0.7	1.1	951	79.9	7.7	12.4	730
£20,000 - £30,000	97.2	0.6	2.2	544	77.3	8.1	14.6	418
£30,000 - £40,000	98.1	0.8	1.1	264	79.6	5.4	15.0	221
Above £40,000	97.8	1.5	0.7	135	73.4	9.9	16.7	282

Table 6.16   A future Labour/Conservative government should/should not reduce spending in general (%)

Annual Income	Labour				Conservative			
	Should	Doesn't matter	Should not	N	Should	Doesn't matter	Should not	N
All	19.2	7.4	73.4	2796	60.6	8.9	30.5	2217
Under £10,000	26.8	9.7	63.5	917	63.1	10.8	26.1	564
£10,000 - £20,000	18.3	7.0	74.7	945	58.4	9.4	32.2	733
£20,000 - £30,000	13.4	6.7	79.9	536	59.8	8.2	32.0	415
£30,000 - £40,000	12.5	3.0	84.5	264	61.3	6.8	31.9	222
Above £40,000	10.4	5.2	84.4	134	61.8	6.7	31.5	283

Table 6.17

*Table 6.17   A future Labour/Conservative government should/should not
introduce stricter laws to regulate the trade unions (%)*

Annual Income	Labour				Conservative			
	Should	Doesn't matter	Should not	N	Should	Doesn't matter	Should not	N
All	10.1	14.6	75.3	2806	65.7	12.2	22.1	2239
Under £10,000	15.3	14.1	70.6	930	79.0	6.7	14.3	581
£10,000 - £20,000	7.3	13.6	79.1	944	62.6	13.6	23.8	733
£20,000 - £30,000	8.0	14.4	77.6	536	63.2	11.7	25.1	419
£30,000 - £40,000	8.7	15.6	75.7	263	61.2	16.5	22.3	224
Above £40,000	5.3	25.6	69.1	133	53.9	17.0	29.1	282

*Table 6.18   A future Labour/Conservative government should/should not give
workers more say in the places where they work (%)*

Annual Income	Labour				Conservative			
	Should	Doesn't matter	Should not	N	Should	Doesn't matter	Should not	N
All	91.2	5.6	3.2	2829	63.5	13.5	23.0	2242
Under £10,000	91.0	6.1	2.9	938	67.8	12.7	19.5	581
£10,000 - £20,000	91.4	5.4	3.2	950	64.6	14.2	21.2	734
£20,000 - £30,000	92.1	4.4	3.5	543	61.8	13.8	24.4	421
£30,000 - £40,000	91.7	5.3	3.0	264	62.3	13.0	24.7	223
Above £40,000	85.8	9.7	4.5	134	55.1	13.1	31.8	283

Table 6.19   *A future Labour/Conservative government should/should not spend less on defence (%)*

Annual Income	Labour				Conservative			
	Should	Doesn't matter	Should not	N	Should	Doesn't matter	Should not	N
All	82.8	4.7	12.5	2834	44.8	4.8	50.4	2235
Under £10,000	76.3	5.3	18.4	938	40.0	5.4	54.6	575
£10,000 - £20,000	83.8	4.2	12.0	953	44.4	4.5	51.1	735
£20,000 - £30,000	86.2	5.1	8.7	544	48.1	4.3	47.6	422
£30,000 - £40,000	89.0	4.2	6.8	264	45.9	4.5	49.6	222
Above £40,000	94.1	2.2	3.7	135	49.8	5.3	44.9	281

Table 6.20   Should a future Labour/Conservative government :
(A) Reduce taxes & spend less on health, education & social benefits ?
(B) Keep taxes & spending on these services at the same levels as now ?
(C) Increase taxes & spend more on health, education & social benefits ?

Annual Income	Labour				Conservative			
	A	B	C	N	A	B	C	N
All	2.7	6.4	90.9	2833	6.9	66.8	26.3	2232
Under £10,000	3.8	8.6	87.6	944	5.3	63.4	31.3	582
£10,000 - £20,000	2.8	5.6	91.6	949	5.5	68.9	25.6	726
£20,000 - £30,000	1.5	4.1	94.4	537	7.9	67.1	25.0	420
£30,000 - £40,000	1.9	6.4	91.7	267	8.2	66.8	25.0	220
Above £40,000	0.7	5.9	93.4	136	10.9	67.6	21.5	284

Table 6.21   *On joining the Labour/Conservative party did the member approach*
                the party (MA) or did the party approach the member (PA) ? (%)

Annual Income	Labour				Conservative			
	MA	Don't Know	PA	N	MA	Don't Know	PA	N
All	77.5	19.9	2.6	2864	34.9	50.6	14.5	2260
Under £10,000	73.1	23.3	3.6	959	36.5	46.5	17.0	591
£10,000 - £20,000	79.5	19.1	1.4	958	36.4	48.8	14.8	740
£20,000 - £30,000	78.0	19.1	2.9	545	34.4	54.0	11.6	422
£30,000 - £40,000	79.6	18.1	2.3	265	35.7	50.2	14.1	221
Above £40,000	88.3	8.8	2.9	137	28.0	58.7	13.3	286

Table 6.22   *How often has the member attended a party meeting in the last*
                12 months ? (%)

Annual Income	Labour				Conservative			
	Not at all	Occas- ionally	Frequ- ently	N	Not at all	Occas- ionally	Frequ- ently	N
All	41.4	30.6	28.0	2874	66.2	21.6	12.2	2270
Under £10,000	37.2	29.7	33.1	963	67.6	20.3	12.1	596
£10,000 - £20,000	40.4	29.6	30.0	959	66.6	20.8	12.6	740
£20,000 - £30,000	48.4	30.9	20.7	550	66.3	21.7	12.0	424
£30,000 - £40,000	45.9	32.0	22.1	266	68.5	21.8	9.7	224
Above £40,000	41.9	39.7	18.4	136	60.5	26.9	12.6	286

Table 6.23   Is the member more or less politically active than 5 years ago ? (%)

Annual Income	Labour				Conservative			
	More active	About same	Less active	N	More active	About same	Less active	N
All	12.9	38.4	48.7	2839	9.8	62.8	27.4	1912
Under £10,000	11.5	40.1	48.4	942	7.1	56.8	36.1	505
£10,000 - £20,000	14.0	39.2	46.8	951	9.7	64.1	26.2	607
£20,000 - £30,000	15.0	34.6	50.4	547	10.3	65.8	23.9	348
£30,000 - £40,000	9.9	34.6	55.5	263	9.3	64.8	25.9	193
Above £40,000	13.2	43.4	43.4	136	14.7	65.6	19.7	259

Table 6.24   Does the member hold any office within the Labour/Conservative Party ? (%)

Annual Income	Labour			Conservative		
	Yes	No	N	Yes	No	N
All	16.1	83.9	2824	8.9	91.1	2240
Under £10,000	14.9	85.1	940	7.0	93.0	586
£10,000 - £20,000	15.9	84.1	951	8.1	91.9	726
£20,000 - £30,000	17.6	82.4	541	11.2	88.8	421
£30,000 - £40,000	21.3	78.7	258	10.3	89.7	223
Above £40,000	11.2	88.8	134	10.2	89.8	284

Table 6.25   *How much time does the member devote to party activities per month ? (%)*

Annual Income	Labour					Conservative				
	None	Up to 5 hrs	5 to 10 hrs	Over 10 hrs	N	None	Up to 5 hrs	5 to 10 hrs	Over 10 hrs	N
All	51.0	29.7	9.4	9.9	2833	75.9	15.2	4.5	4.4	2237
Under £10,000	50.7	29.4	9.5	10.4	934	76.5	14.6	4.8	4.1	583
£10,000 - £20,000	47.8	31.0	10.7	10.5	957	76.0	15.7	4.4	3.9	725
£20,000 - £30,000	53.9	29.5	8.5	8.1	542	74.1	15.8	4.5	5.6	424
£30,000 - £40,000	54.7	28.1	8.2	9.0	267	81.2	9.9	3.6	5.3	223
Above £40,000	56.4	25.6	6.0	12.0	133	72.7	18.8	5.0	3.5	282

Table 6.26   *What was the overall financial contribution made by the member in the last year ? (%)*

Annual Income	Labour				Conservative			
	0 to £10	£10 to £20	Over £20	N	0 to £10	£10 to £20	Over £20	N
All	23.9	19.6	56.5	2528	34.0	21.5	44.5	1734
Under £10,000	42.6	20.5	36.9	808	44.4	21.4	34.2	387
£10,000 - £20,000	18.0	20.6	61.4	860	35.7	25.4	38.9	575
£20,000 - £30,000	14.8	18.9	66.3	493	30.3	18.8	50.9	346
£30,000 - £40,000	10.1	17.6	72.3	238	31.3	17.3	51.4	179
Above £40,000	7.0	13.2	79.8	129	20.6	19.0	60.4	247

Table 6.27   *Is the member a local Labour/Conservative councillor ? (%)*

Annual Income	Labour			Conservative		
	Yes	No	N	Yes	No	N
All	8.0	92.0	2847	2.3	97.7	2252
Under £10,000	7.9	92.1	941	1.7	98.3	585
£10,000 - £20,000	9.1	90.9	956	2.8	97.2	737
£20,000 - £30,000	6.9	93.1	548	1.2	98.8	421
£30,000 - £40,000	7.1	92.9	267	4.5	95.5	222
Above £40,000	6.7	93.3	135	2.1	97.9	287

Table 6.28   *The Labour/Conservative leader should be elected by a system of one party member/one vote (%)*

Annual Income	Labour				Conservative			
	Agree	Neith-er	Dis-agree	N	Agree	Neith-er	Dis-agree	N
All	86.1	5.2	8.7	2846	49.5	14.6	35.9	2219
Under £10,000	89.3	4.3	6.4	951	63.6	10.9	25.5	569
£10,000 - £20,000	86.5	5.2	8.3	953	49.8	15.3	34.9	727
£20,000 - £30,000	84.2	4.9	10.9	546	42.1	19.0	38.9	420
£30,000 - £40,000	79.3	7.7	13.0	261	38.4	13.7	47.9	219
Above £40,000	81.5	8.1	10.4	135	40.1	14.1	45.8	284

Table 6.29   *People like me can have a real influence in politics if they are*
                 prepared to get involved (%)

Annual Income	Labour				Conservative			
	Agree	Neith-er	Dis-agree	N	Agree	Neith-er	Dis-agree	N
All	65.8	16.1	18.1	2838	56.8	20.2	23.0	2226
Under £10,000	71.2	13.6	15.2	944	55.9	21.7	22.4	567
£10,000 - £20,000	65.2	17.4	17.4	949	54.5	23.2	22.3	734
£20,000 - £30,000	61.1	19.2	19.7	542	57.6	15.6	26.8	422
£30,000 - £40,000	60.3	13.5	26.2	267	65.2	14.9	19.9	221
Above £40,000	61.0	18.4	20.6	136	57.1	20.2	22.7	282

Table 6.30   *Attending party meetings can be pretty tiring after a hard days*
                 work (%)

Annual Income	Labour				Conservative			
	Agree	Neith-er	Dis-agree	N	Agree	Neith-er	Dis-agree	N
All	77.3	11.4	11.3	2842	69.2	19.4	11.4	2210
Under £10,000	72.7	12.6	14.7	938	68.5	17.1	14.4	562
£10,000 - £20,000	75.8	13.3	10.9	955	67.4	21.3	11.3	727
£20,000 - £30,000	83.5	7.1	9.4	546	65.7	22.4	11.9	420
£30,000 - £40,000	84.3	8.6	7.1	267	75.0	17.3	7.7	220
Above £40,000	81.6	11.8	6.6	136	76.2	16.0	7.8	281

Table 6.31   *Someone like me could do a good job of being a local councillor (%)*

Annual Income	Labour				Conservative			
	Agree	Neith-er	Dis-agree	N	Agree	Neith-er	Dis-agree	N
All	48.7	22.0	29.3	2817	27.7	24.7	47.6	2202
Under £10,000	46.3	22.1	31.6	926	20.2	23.2	56.6	560
£10,000 - £20,000	49.3	22.8	27.9	947	25.6	25.1	49.3	722
£20,000 - £30,000	48.2	22.0	29.8	541	30.5	26.0	43.5	420
£30,000 - £40,000	53.9	21.7	24.4	267	35.6	26.5	37.9	219
Above £40,000	52.2	16.2	31.6	136	38.1	23.5	38.4	281

Table 6.32   *Being an active party member is a good way of meeting interesting people (%)*

Annual Income	Labour				Conservative			
	Agree	Neith-er	Dis-agree	N	Agree	Neith-er	Dis-agree	N
All	64.5	22.0	13.5	2838	58.7	30.5	10.8	2203
Under £10,000	79.1	13.6	7.3	941	71.9	21.3	6.8	559
£10,000 - £20,000	62.5	23.1	14.4	951	58.8	30.6	10.6	725
£20,000 - £30,000	54.2	29.3	16.5	543	55.3	33.5	11.2	418
£30,000 - £40,000	52.5	28.1	19.4	267	50.2	37.0	12.8	219
Above £40,000	41.1	30.1	28.8	136	44.3	39.4	16.3	282

Table 6.33   *The only way to be really educated about politics is to be a party activist (%)*

Annual Income	Labour				Conservative			
	Agree	Neith-er	Dis-agree	N	Agree	Neith-er	Dis-agree	N
All	41.9	11.2	46.9	2850	35.4	17.1	47.5	2209
Under £10,000	57.9	10.6	31.5	952	49.6	15.0	35.4	559
£10,000 - £20,000	38.4	12.4	49.2	951	32.6	18.8	48.6	728
£20,000 - £30,000	32.4	8.8	58.8	544	32.1	17.2	50.7	418
£30,000 - £40,000	28.1	12.7	59.2	267	30.9	15.9	53.2	220
Above £40,000	19.1	13.2	67.7	136	23.6	17.3	59.1	284

Table 6.34   *The party leadership does not pay a lot of attention to ordinary party members (%)*

Annual Income	Labour				Conservative			
	Agree	Neith-er	Dis-agree	N	Agree	Neith-er	Dis-agree	N
All	46.8	18.9	34.3	2846	42.3	23.6	34.1	2221
Under £10,000	50.1	13.8	36.1	946	47.3	20.6	32.1	567
£10,000 - £20,000	47.2	20.8	32.0	954	41.1	21.8	37.1	733
£20,000 - £30,000	44.1	22.6	33.3	544	42.2	26.5	31.3	419
£30,000 - £40,000	42.9	21.8	35.3	266	39.8	28.1	32.1	221
Above £40,000	40.4	21.3	38.3	136	37.7	26.7	35.6	281

Table 6.35   Party activity often takes time away from one's family (%)

Annual Income	Labour				Conservative			
	Agree	Neith-er	Dis-agree	N	Agree	Neith-er	Dis-agree	N
All	85.2	10.3	4.5	2839	66.9	25.5	7.6	2197
under £10,000	87.2	8.0	4.8	941	68.9	24.3	6.8	556
£10,000 - £20,000	82.9	12.3	4.8	953	66.4	25.2	8.4	726
£20,000 - £30,000	87.9	9.0	3.1	543	66.9	25.7	7.4	417
£30,000 - £40,000	83.8	10.2	6.0	266	64.5	29.1	6.4	220
Above £40,000	79.9	16.9	3.2	136	66.2	25.9	7.9	278

Table 6.36   The Labour/Conservative party would be more successful if people like me were elected to parliament (%)

Annual Income	Labour				Conservative			
	Agree	Neith-er	Dis-agree	N	Agree	Neith-er	Dis-agree	N
All	33.6	34.2	32.2	2818	21.2	32.0	46.8	2186
Under £10,000	36.6	31.8	31.6	931	23.1	31.0	45.9	554
£10,000 - £20,000	31.7	35.7	32.6	946	19.2	34.1	46.7	719
£20,000 - £30,000	31.8	35.9	32.3	541	18.8	32.4	48.8	410
£30,000 - £40,000	32.8	35.5	31.7	265	22.1	31.5	46.4	222
Above £40,000	35.6	30.4	34.0	135	25.6	28.1	46.3	281

Table 6.37   *During the last 5 years, how often has the member displayed an*
election poster in his/her window ? (%)

Annual Income	Labour				Conservative			
	Not at all	Occas-ionally	Freq-uently	N	Not at all	Occas-ionally	Freq-uently	N
All	9.5	21.6	68.9	2825	48.4	31.9	19.7	2154
Under £10,000	9.6	21.5	68.9	937	49.0	31.3	19.7	549
£10,000 - £20,000	10.1	21.0	68.9	948	47.2	34.2	18.6	705
£20,000 - £30,000	8.7	22.9	68.4	538	46.9	31.5	21.6	409
£30,000 - £40,000	7.9	21.0	71.1	267	46.7	35.2	18.1	210
Above £40,000	9.6	23.0	67.4	135	53.7	25.6	20.7	281

Table 6.38   *During the last 5 years, how often has the member donated money to*
party funds ? (%)

Annual Income	Labour				Conservative			
	Not at all	Occas-ionally	Freq-uently	N	Not at all	Occas-ionally	Freq-uently	N
All	9.4	51.0	39.6	2820	14.8	55.1	30.1	2202
Under £10,000	12.7	51.3	36.0	926	16.4	56.7	26.9	561
£10,000 - £20,000	9.1	51.8	39.1	947	15.2	58.4	26.4	722
£20,000 - £30,000	7.4	51.7	40.9	544	14.4	54.2	31.4	417
£30,000 - £40,000	5.3	50.4	44.3	266	12.3	55.5	32.2	220
Above £40,000	5.1	41.6	53.3	137	13.1	44.7	42.2	282

Table 6.39   *During the last 5 years, how often has the member delivered party leaflets ? (%)*

Annual Income	Labour				Conservative			
	Not at all	Occas-ionally	Freq-uently	N	Not at all	Occas-ionally	Freq-uently	N
All	17.5	27.2	55.3	2773	60.5	17.3	22.2	2113
Under £10,000	23.7	24.4	51.9	896	63.3	15.3	21.4	528
£10,000 - £20,000	16.5	26.9	56.6	938	61.4	18.8	19.8	695
£20,000 - £30,000	11.5	31.9	56.6	539	57.9	15.3	26.8	399
£30,000 - £40,000	10.2	28.7	61.1	265	58.8	17.5	23.7	211
Above £40,000	21.5	25.2	53.3	135	58.2	19.6	22.2	280

Table 6.40   *During the last 5 years, how often has the member attended a party meeting ? (%)*

Annual Income	Labour				Conservative			
	Not at all	Occas-ionally	Freq-uently	N	Not at all	Occas-ionally	Freq-uently	N
All	21.5	40.7	37.8	2779	50.5	32.7	16.8	2135
Under £10,000	20.8	35.8	43.4	904	51.5	29.8	18.7	534
£10,000 - £20,000	21.7	38.3	40.0	941	50.9	33.4	15.7	703
£20,000 - £30,000	23.0	46.2	30.8	539	53.3	30.6	16.1	405
£30,000 - £40,000	20.3	48.3	31.4	261	50.5	34.4	15.1	212
Above £40,000	21.6	53.0	25.4	134	43.8	38.4	17.8	281

Table 6.41   *During the last 5 years, how often has the member canvassed voters on behalf of the party ? (%)*

Annual Income	Labour				Conservative			
	Not at all	Occas-ionally	Freq-uently	N	Not at all	Occas-ionally	Freq-uently	N
All	36.8	31.4	31.8	2755	74.7	14.9	10.4	2102
Under £10,000	37.7	28.6	33.7	886	75.7	14.5	9.8	523
£10,000 - £20,000	36.6	31.1	32.3	932	76.7	13.4	9.9	688
£20,000 - £30,000	36.8	34.2	29.0	538	74.0	14.8	11.2	400
£30,000 - £40,000	33.8	33.1	33.1	263	72.2	15.6	12.2	212
Above £40,000	37.5	36.8	25.7	136	70.6	19.0	10.4	279

Table 6.42   *Where would you place yourself on a Left/Right scale within the Labour/Conservative party ? (%)*

Annual Income	Labour				Conservative			
	Left	Centre	Right	N	Left	Centre	Right	N
All	57.6	20.6	21.8	2849	13.5	25.9	60.6	2243
Under £10,000	53.0	23.4	23.6	948	9.0	22.3	68.7	579
£10,000 - £20,000	60.7	20.6	18.7	956	11.1	30.7	58.2	733
£20,000 - £30,000	61.5	17.8	20.7	545	15.6	27.3	57.1	422
£30,000 - £40,000	59.8	15.5	24.7	264	20.2	16.6	63.2	223
Above £40,000	47.8	22.1	30.1	136	20.3	26.6	53.1	286

Table 6.43   *Where would you place yourself on a Left/Right scale within British Politics ? (%)*

Annual Income	Labour				Conservative			
	Left	Centre	Right	N	Left	Centre	Right	N
All	80.2	10.3	9.5	2846	3.9	18.2	77.9	2239
Under £10,000	64.3	15.7	20.0	947	3.6	19.8	76.6	577
£10,000 - £20,000	84.1	9.9	6.0	954	3.7	21.6	74.7	730
£20,000 - £30,000	90.8	6.6	2.6	545	4.5	15.6	79.9	422
£30,000 - £40,000	93.5	4.2	2.3	264	4.9	11.2	83.9	224
Above £40,000	95.6	2.2	2.2	136	3.1	15.4	81.5	286

Table 6.44   *What thermometer rating would the Labour/Conservative member give the Conservative Party ? (%)*

Annual Income	Labour					Conservative				
	Cd	Cl	W	H	M	Cd	Cl	W	H	M
All	76.1	20.3	2.9	0.7	14.7	0.2	3.7	33.6	62.5	80.7
Under £10,000	65.2	28.2	5.1	1.5	20.1	0.0	4.2	24.7	71.1	84.0
£10,000 - £20,000	78.9	18.8	2.2	0.1	12.9	0.3	3.5	33.4	62.8	80.6
£20,000 - £30,000	84.0	14.1	1.5	0.4	11.0	0.5	4.1	36.3	59.1	79.4
£30,000 - £40,000	82.1	15.6	1.9	0.4	12.9	0.5	2.7	43.0	53.8	77.7
Above £40,000	85.2	14.1	0.7	0.0	11.0	0.0	3.1	41.3	55.6	78.5

Table 6.45   What thermometer rating would the Labour/Conservative member
             give the Labour Party ? (%)

Annual Income	Labour					Conservative				
	Cd	Cl	W	H	M	Cd	Cl	W	H	M
All	0.9	3.7	24.8	70.6	82.6	50.2	43.0	6.2	0.6	26.7
Under £10,000	1.0	3.2	18.0	77.8	85.9	48.1	43.2	7.6	1.1	28.9
£10,000 - £20,000	1.0	3.8	24.2	71.0	82.2	45.2	47.1	7.3	0.4	27.9
£20,000 - £30,000	0.7	4.1	30.2	65.0	80.5	53.1	40.9	5.7	0.3	25.5
£30,000 - £40,000	0.4	5.3	34.0	60.3	78.9	56.8	40.0	3.2	0.0	24.6
Above £40,000	1.5	2.9	37.5	58.1	78.1	58.6	37.4	4.0	0.0	23.2

Table 6.46   What thermometer rating would the Labour/Conservative member
             give the Liberal Democratic Party ? (%)

Annual Income	Labour					Conservative				
	Cd	Cl	W	H	M	Cd	Cl	W	H	M
All	33.2	44.2	20.8	1.8	36.8	32.9	50.7	15.1	1.3	36.1
Under £10,000	31.3	43.0	21.9	3.8	39.2	28.0	52.3	17.4	2.3	38.9
£10,000 - £20,000	34.3	44.7	19.7	1.3	35.4	33.6	51.4	14.1	0.9	35.6
£20,000 - £30,000	34.8	43.3	21.0	0.9	35.7	37.3	46.3	14.7	1.7	34.7
£30,000 - £40,000	32.8	45.7	21.5	0.0	36.1	31.7	51.4	16.5	0.4	35.5
Above £40,000	31.6	50.0	18.4	0.0	36.1	35.3	51.4	12.9	0.4	34.8

Table 6.47   *What thermometer rating would the Labour/Conservative member*
           give the Scottish Nationalist Party ? (%)

Annual Income	Labour					Conservative				
	Cd	Cl	W	H	M	Cd	Cl	W	H	M
All	43.9	37.2	16.1	2.8	32.1	69.0	26.5	4.2	0.3	19.1
Under £10,000	45.2	37.2	14.2	3.4	31.5	62.6	29.7	7.7	0.0	22.2
£10,000 - £20,000	44.8	35.7	16.8	2.7	31.8	68.9	27.7	2.8	0.6	18.8
£20,000 - £30,000	41.0	39.5	17.0	2.5	33.3	70.0	26.6	3.1	0.3	18.4
£30,000 - £40,000	40.8	39.9	17.2	2.1	34.0	70.3	25.6	4.1	0.0	18.1
Above £40,000	6.5	33.1	17.3	43.1	31.1	77.6	18.9	3.1	0.4	16.8

Table 6.48   *What thermometer rating would the Labour/Conservative member*
           give Plaid Cymru ? (%)

Annual Income	Labour					Conservative				
	Cd	Cl	W	H	M	Cd	Cl	W	H	M
All	47.6	37.6	13.0	1.8	29.6	82.7	15.9	1.2	0.2	12.9
Under £10,000	50.6	37.0	11.1	1.3	27.6	82.1	15.2	2.7	0.0	14.2
£10,000 - £20,000	48.0	37.1	12.7	2.2	29.5	81.7	17.1	1.0	0.2	13.4
£20,000 - £30,000	40.7	42.3	15.3	1.7	32.3	82.7	16.7	0.3	0.3	12.5
£30,000 - £40,000	45.6	36.7	14.6	3.1	32.2	85.3	14.1	0.6	0.0	11.3
Above £40,000	54.2	28.3	15.8	1.7	28.8	84.3	14.4	0.9	0.4	11.9

Table 6.49   *What thermometer rating would the Labour/Conservative member give the Green Party ? (%)*

Annual Income	Labour					Conservative				
	Cd	Cl	W	H	M	Cd	Cl	W	H	M
All	33.4	35.7	25.7	5.2	39.4	70.3	24.1	5.1	0.5	19.5
Under £10,000	39.3	35.1	21.1	4.5	35.7	68.4	24.2	5.9	1.5	20.5
£10,000 - £20,000	32.9	35.3	26.8	5.0	39.9	70.6	24.3	4.7	0.4	19.5
£20,000 - £30,000	27.1	36.6	30.4	5.9	42.7	71.9	22.8	5.0	0.3	18.8
£30,000 - £40,000	27.6	37.2	26.8	8.4	43.3	67.6	27.4	5.0	0.0	19.7
Above £40,000	34.8	35.6	26.7	2.9	38.7	72.0	22.8	5.2	0.0	18.6

Table 6.50   *What thermometer rating would the Labour/Conservative member give the BBC ? (%)*

Annual Income	Labour					Conservative				
	Cd	Cl	W	H	M	Cd	Cl	W	H	M
All	9.2	26.3	39.9	24.6	60.3	8.4	30.8	40.4	20.4	59.2
Under £10,000	13.1	32.9	34.5	19.5	56.1	10.8	29.7	35.5	24.0	59.2
£10,000 - £20,000	9.0	25.7	42.5	22.8	60.2	7.7	33.3	38.9	20.1	59.0
£20,000 - £30,000	6.1	25.6	42.1	26.2	62.4	7.5	29.8	42.9	19.8	59.5
£30,000 - £40,000	6.1	17.6	42.9	33.4	65.2	5.5	27.6	47.9	19.0	61.2
Above £40,000	4.4	6.6	42.6	46.4	71.6	9.3	30.1	44.4	16.2	57.8

Table 6.51   *What thermometer rating would the Labour/Conservative member give the European Community ? (%)*

Annual Income	Labour					Conservative				
	Cd	Cl	W	H	M	Cd	Cl	W	H	M
All	11.1	32.5	42.0	14.4	55.5	14.2	40.6	35.7	9.5	50.9
Under £10,000	14.0	32.0	36.2	17.8	54.8	17.8	41.4	30.3	10.5	48.7
£10,000 - £20,000	11.1	32.8	43.2	12.9	54.9	12.5	40.6	37.1	9.8	52.0
£20,000 - £30,000	10.5	34.7	42.4	12.4	54.8	15.3	41.8	34.5	8.4	49.9
£30,000 - £40,000	6.0	29.5	50.2	14.3	59.2	10.4	38.3	43.0	8.3	53.1
Above £40,000	6.0	29.9	50.0	14.1	58.6	14.8	39.3	35.8	10.1	51.1

Table 6.52   *What thermometer rating would the Labour/Conservative member give the Trade Union Congress ? (%)*

Annual Income	Labour					Conservative				
	Cd	Cl	W	H	M	Cd	Cl	W	H	M
All	5.7	29.1	47.8	17.4	59.9	53.7	40.0	5.5	0.8	26.3
Under £10,000	6.4	24.3	43.7	25.6	63.0	52.1	39.8	6.3	1.8	26.8
£10,000 - £20,000	4.9	28.7	50.2	16.2	60.2	50.2	41.2	7.6	1.0	28.4
£20,000 - £30,000	5.3	32.9	50.5	11.3	57.3	53.6	41.3	4.7	0.4	26.0
£30,000 - £40,000	5.1	35.8	45.5	13.6	57.5	55.8	40.1	2.9	1.2	24.4
Above £40,000	8.9	34.1	50.4	6.6	54.2	61.3	35.7	2.9	0.1	22.9

Table 6.53   *What thermometer rating would the Labour/Conservative member give the Police ? (%)*

Annual Income	Labour					Conservative				
	Cd	Cl	W	H	M	Cd	Cl	W	H	M
All	17.8	44.2	28.8	9.2	48.0	1.4	12.7	39.9	46.0	72.8
Under £10,000	14.5	34.8	34.4	16.3	54.2	1.3	8.8	29.7	60.2	77.6
£10,000 - £20,000	18.6	44.8	28.8	7.8	46.9	1.4	12.5	43.1	43.0	72.2
£20,000 - £30,000	21.9	50.6	23.2	4.3	42.7	1.2	15.0	41.8	42.0	71.7
£30,000 - £40,000	17.4	57.8	21.3	3.5	44.2	1.8	14.2	44.7	39.3	69.5
Above £40,000	18.5	51.9	28.1	1.5	43.8	1.8	15.8	44.7	37.7	69.3

Table 6.54   *What thermometer rating would the Labour/Conservative member give the House of Commons ? (%)*

Annual Income	Labour					Conservative				
	Cd	Cl	W	H	M	Cd	Cl	W	H	M
All	10.1	33.7	38.3	17.9	56.8	2.5	17.0	49.2	31.3	68.3
Under £10,000	9.7	30.8	34.7	24.8	59.9	3.1	15.1	40.9	40.9	71.3
£10,000 - £20,000	9.7	34.6	38.5	17.2	56.4	1.8	16.2	48.5	33.5	69.1
£20,000 - £30,000	12.9	34.5	40.3	12.3	53.3	3.0	18.7	50.8	27.5	66.8
£30,000 - £40,000	7.8	37.4	42.4	12.4	55.7	2.3	17.3	61.7	18.7	64.9
Above £40,000	8.8	35.3	44.1	11.8	55.1	2.5	20.0	53.6	23.9	65.4

Table 6.55 *What thermometer rating would the Labour/Conservative member give the CBI ? (%)*

Annual Income	Labour					Conservative				
	Cd	Cl	W	H	M	Cd	Cl	W	H	M
All	44.9	41.9	11.2	2.0	30.8	5.3	29.6	49.5	15.6	59.6
Under £10,000	39.7	40.3	16.1	3.9	34.8	7.1	25.0	46.0	21.9	61.8
£10,000 - £20,000	47.2	41.4	9.8	1.6	29.4	5.2	28.0	52.7	14.1	60.1
£20,000 - £30,000	49.0	41.4	8.8	0.8	28.2	4.9	33.4	44.9	16.8	59.0
£30,000 - £40,000	43.6	48.1	7.5	0.8	29.8	5.2	33.8	50.0	11.0	57.9
Above £40,000	46.2	44.7	9.1	0.0	29.2	4.6	29.5	52.1	13.8	58.6

Table 6.56 *What thermometer rating would the Labour/Conservative member give the Queen ? (%)*

Annual Income	Labour					Conservative				
	Cd	Cl	W	H	M	Cd	Cl	W	H	M
All	34.7	29.3	19.4	16.6	43.3	0.9	4.8	16.2	78.1	86.2
Under £10,000	23.9	23.6	22.0	30.5	55.4	0.2	2.9	10.7	86.2	90.4
£10,000 - £20,000	38.9	27.4	19.7	14.0	40.4	0.6	5.0	16.3	78.1	86.2
£20,000 - £30,000	41.2	36.9	14.6	7.3	34.5	1.9	3.1	18.4	76.6	84.9
£30,000 - £40,000	44.0	33.5	18.3	4.2	33.0	0.9	8.6	20.0	70.5	83.3
Above £40,000	33.3	43.0	20.0	3.7	37.2	1.8	7.4	20.8	70.0	82.2

Table 6.57   *What thermometer rating would the Labour/Conservative member give Judges ? (%)*

Annual Income	Labour					Conservative				
	Cd	Cl	W	H	M	Cd	Cl	W	H	M
All	38.1	43.5	14.9	3.5	35.0	4.4	30.8	45.6	19.2	60.6
Under £10,000	30.5	41.9	20.5	7.1	40.8	6.5	30.6	40.1	22.8	60.8
£10,000 - £20,000	42.0	42.3	13.3	2.4	32.5	3.5	29.9	48.5	18.1	61.3
£20,000 - £30,000	44.4	43.0	10.7	1.9	30.9	4.4	32.9	45.3	17.4	59.6
£30,000 - £40,000	37.5	50.2	11.6	0.7	33.1	3.4	32.9	46.4	17.3	60.0
Above £40,000	36.1	50.4	12.8	0.7	34.4	4.1	28.8	47.6	19.5	60.6

7   Employment Sector

Table 7.1   The Labour/Conservative party should try to capture the middle ground in politics (%)

Employment Sector	Labour				Conservative			
	Agree	Neith-er	Dis-agree	N	Agree	Neith-er	Dis-agree	N
All	49.9	12.1	38.0	2645	68.3	13.5	18.2	1965
Private	55.3	10.2	34.5	918	68.9	13.0	18.1	1176
Public	48.1	13.2	38.7	1296	67.8	14.2	18.0	600
Other	43.9	12.7	43.4	431	66.1	14.9	19.0	189

Table 7.2   A Labour/Conservative government should introduce a prices and incomes policy as a means of controlling inflation (%)

Employment Sector	Labour				Conservative			
	Agree	Neith-er	Dis-agree	N	Agree	Neith-er	Dis-agree	N
All	56.6	19.1	24.3	2650	39.1	12.1	48.8	1997
Private	57.6	16.2	26.2	922	38.7	11.3	50.0	1195
Public	56.4	20.2	23.4	1293	42.7	14.5	42.8	607
Other	54.9	22.1	23.0	435	30.8	9.2	60.0	195

Table 7.3   Income and wealth should be re-distributed towards ordinary working people (%)

Employment Sector	Labour				Conservative			
	Agree	Neith-er	Dis-agree	N	Agree	Neith-er	Dis-agree	N
All	86.1	9.0	4.9	2678	24.5	21.3	54.2	2000
Private	81.8	11.5	6.7	930	24.1	21.3	54.6	1193
Public	88.0	8.0	4.0	1309	26.5	21.6	51.9	611
Other	89.5	6.6	3.9	439	20.4	20.4	59.2	196

Table 7.4 *The Labour/Conservative Party should always stand by its principles even if this should lose it an election (%)*

Employment Sector	Labour				Conservative			
	Agree	Neith-er	Dis-agree	N	Agree	Neith-er	Dis-agree	N
All	67.2	12.2	20.6	2675	80.0	9.1	10.9	2028
Private	69.5	10.1	20.4	931	79.4	9.3	11.3	1207
Public	66.7	12.9	20.4	1305	81.0	8.7	10.3	621
Other	63.6	14.8	21.6	439	81.0	8.0	11.0	200

Table 7.5 *Further nuclear energy development is essential for the future prosperity of Britain (%)*

Employment Sector	Labour				Conservative			
	Agree	Neith-er	Dis-agree	N	Agree	Neith-er	Dis-agree	N
All	13.7	12.0	74.3	2668	60.1	17.5	22.4	2011
Private	15.9	13.5	70.6	922	61.4	17.2	21.4	1199
Public	12.7	11.6	75.7	1307	57.9	18.3	23.8	617
Other	12.1	10.2	77.7	439	59.0	16.4	24.6	195

Table 7.6 *A future Labour/Conservative government should not agree to a single European currency (%)*

Employment Sector	Labour				Conservative			
	Agree	Neith-er	Dis-agree	N	Agree	Neith-er	Dis-agree	N
All	24.2	19.4	56.4	2656	56.4	12.5	31.1	2015
Private	26.9	18.0	55.1	919	54.7	11.8	33.5	1199
Public	23.1	20.5	56.4	1301	58.8	14.0	27.2	617
Other	22.2	18.4	59.4	436	59.3	12.1	28.6	199

Table 7.7   *High income tax makes people less willing to work hard (%)*

Employment Sector	Labour				Conservative			
	Agree	Neith-er	Dis-agree	N	Agree	Neith-er	Dis-agree	N
All	25.2	10.7	64.1	2682	81.2	6.5	12.3	2033
Private	31.5	10.3	58.2	936	80.7	6.3	13.0	1212
Public	22.2	10.9	66.9	1308	81.4	7.5	11.1	622
Other	21.0	11.0	68.0	438	83.9	3.5	12.6	199

Table 7.8   *Britain's electoral system should be replaced by a system of proportional representation (%)*

Employment Sector	Labour				Conservative			
	Agree	Neith-er	Dis-agree	N	Agree	Neith-er	Dis-agree	N
All	57.9	13.3	28.8	2677	21.0	11.6	67.4	2019
Private	50.6	14.0	35.4	926	21.9	11.4	66.7	1202
Public	61.1	12.8	26.1	1312	21.0	11.9	67.1	620
Other	63.8	13.0	23.2	439	15.2	12.7	72.1	197

Table 7.9   *Further moves towards integration within the European Community should be resisted (%)*

Employment Sector	Labour				Conservative			
	Agree	Neith-er	Dis-agree	N	Agree	Neith-er	Dis-agree	N
All	20.8	13.0	66.2	2669	52.1	16.1	31.8	2023
Private	23.1	12.7	64.2	922	50.5	16.4	33.1	1204
Public	20.3	12.9	66.8	1311	53.1	16.0	30.9	621
Other	17.7	13.5	68.8	436	58.1	14.6	27.3	198

Table 7.10   There is no need for a Bill of Rights in this country (%)

Employment Sector	Labour				Conservative			
	Agree	Neith-er	Dis-agree	N	Agree	Neith-er	Dis-agree	N
All	10.7	9.6	79.7	2659	39.3	27.2	33.5	1967
Private	12.4	11.4	76.2	912	39.9	26.3	33.8	1168
Public	10.0	8.3	81.7	1314	37.4	29.7	32.9	604
Other	9.5	9.4	81.1	433	41.5	25.2	33.3	195

Table 7.11   A future Labour/Conservative government should introduce a directly elected Scottish Assembly with taxing powers (%)

Employment Sector	Labour				Conservative			
	Agree	Neith-er	Dis-agree	N	Agree	Neith-er	Dis-agree	N
All	61.3	22.2	16.5	2681	22.2	27.0	50.8	2006
Private	58.0	23.1	18.9	929	23.0	26.5	50.5	1197
Public	61.9	22.2	15.9	1310	20.4	30.1	49.5	614
Other	66.3	20.6	13.1	442	22.6	20.5	56.9	195

Table 7.12   Coalition governments are the best form of government for Britain (%)

Employment Sector	Labour				Conservative			
	Agree	Neith-er	Dis-agree	N	Agree	Neith-er	Dis-agree	N
All	8.3	17.1	74.6	2674	8.7	10.5	80.8	2044
Private	9.1	13.6	77.3	925	8.9	10.3	80.8	1221
Public	8.2	18.1	73.7	1314	9.0	11.5	79.5	625
Other	7.2	21.1	71.7	435	7.1	8.1	84.8	198

Table 7.13 *A future Labour/Conservative government should/should not spend money to get rid of poverty (%)*

Employment Sector	Labour				Conservative			
	Should	Doesn't Matter	Should Not	N	Should	Doesn't Matter	Should Not	N
All	98.1	0.9	1.0	2675	79.4	9.0	11.6	2009
Private	97.2	1.5	1.3	931	80.0	8.6	11.4	1200
Public	98.6	0.7	0.7	1306	78.7	9.7	11.6	610
Other	98.2	0.4	1.4	438	78.4	9.0	12.6	199

Table 7.14 *A future Labour/Conservative government should/should not encourage the growth of private medicine (%)*

Employment Sector	Labour				Conservative			
	Should	Doesn't Matter	Should Not	N	Should	Doesn't Matter	Should Not	N
All	3.7	4.6	91.7	2669	52.2	15.7	32.1	2018
Private	5.0	6.0	89.0	929	56.3	14.9	28.8	1200
Public	3.2	4.1	92.7	1302	43.9	16.8	39.3	619
Other	2.3	3.2	94.5	438	53.8	16.6	29.6	199

Table 7.15 *A future Labour/Conservative government should/should not put more money into the National Health Service (%)*

Employment Sector	Labour				Conservative			
	Should	Doesn't Matter	Should Not	N	Should	Doesn't Matter	Should Not	N
All	97.9	0.8	1.3	2678	78.6	8.0	13.4	2021
Private	98.2	0.5	1.3	931	77.9	8.4	13.7	1205
Public	97.8	1.0	1.2	1308	81.8	7.3	10.9	617
Other	97.9	0.5	1.6	439	72.9	7.5	19.6	199

Table 7.16   *A future Labour/Conservative government should/should not reduce spending in general (%)*

Employment Sector	Labour					Conservative			
	Should	Doesn't Matter	Should Not	N		Should	Doesn't Matter	Should Not	N
All	18.9	7.2	73.9	2638		59.8	8.8	31.4	2013
Private	24.0	9.2	66.8	910		60.7	9.3	30.0	1199
Public	17.2	6.2	76.6	1293		60.0	7.6	32.4	615
Other	13.3	6.2	80.5	435		53.8	9.0	37.2	199

Table 7.17   *A future Labour/Conservative government should/should not introduce stricter laws to regulate the trade unions (%)*

Employment Sector	Labour					Conservative			
	Should	Doesn't Matter	Should Not	N		Should	Doesn't Matter	Should Not	N
All	9.6	14.5	75.9	2647		64.9	12.6	22.5	2026
Private	9.9	15.5	74.6	918		64.6	13.2	22.2	1206
Public	10.2	13.6	76.2	1294		64.7	12.2	23.1	623
Other	7.1	15.4	77.5	435		67.0	11.2	21.8	197

Table 7.18   *A future Labour/Conservative government should/should not give workers more say in the places where they work (%)*

Employment Sector	Labour					Conservative			
	Should	Doesn't Matter	Should Not	N		Should	Doesn't Matter	Should Not	N
All	91.4	5.5	3.1	2672		62.1	14.0	23.9	2031
Private	89.9	6.8	3.3	930		60.0	13.6	26.4	1209
Public	92.4	4.7	2.9	1304		65.9	15.1	19.0	622
Other	91.8	5.0	3.2	438		63.0	12.5	24.5	200

Table 7.19   *A future Labour/Conservative government should/should not spend
less on defence (%)*

Employment Sector	Labour				Conservative			
	Should	Doesn't Matter	Should Not	N	Should	Doesn't Matter	Should Not	N
All	82.9	4.6	12.5	2673	45.0	4.8	50.2	2022
Private	79.5	5.7	14.8	928	45.9	4.9	49.2	1205
Public	84.2	4.2	11.6	1307	44.7	5.2	50.1	619
Other	86.3	3.4	10.3	438	39.9	3.5	56.6	198

Table 7.20   *Should a future Labour/Conservative government :*
(A) Reduce taxes & spend less on health, education & social benefits ?
(B) Keep taxes & spending on these services at the same levels as now ?
(C) Increase taxes & spend more on health, education & social benefits ?

Employment Sector	Labour				Conservative			
	A	B	C	N	A	B	C	N
All	2.4	6.1	91.5	2671	6.9	66.8	26.3	2013
Private	2.4	7.8	89.8	926	6.5	67.2	26.3	1196
Public	2.4	5.3	92.3	1307	7.1	66.1	26.8	620
Other	2.3	5.2	92.5	438	8.1	66.5	25.4	197

Table 7.21   *On joining the Labour/Conservative party did the member approach
the party (MA) or did the party approach the member (PA) ? (%)*

Employment Sector	Labour				Conservative			
	MA	Don't Know	PA	N	MA	Don't Know	PA	N
All	77.4	20.1	2.5	2695	35.4	50.4	14.2	2045
Private	74.8	22.3	2.9	930	36.0	50.7	13.3	1216
Public	78.4	19.5	2.1	1324	34.6	51.8	13.6	628
Other	79.8	18.0	2.2	441	34.3	43.8	21.9	201

Table 7.22 *How often has the member attended a party meeting in the last 12 months ? (%)*

Employment Sector	Labour				Conservative			
	Not at all	Occas-ionally	Frequ-ently	N	Not at all	Occas-ionally	Frequ-ently	N
All	42.0	30.2	27.8	2705	66.2	21.5	12.3	2056
Private	40.6	30.3	29.1	938	68.2	20.4	11.4	1224
Public	43.0	29.3	27.7	1327	63.4	22.8	13.8	632
Other	41.8	32.7	25.5	440	63.0	24.0	13.0	200

Table 7.23 *Is the member more or less politically active than 5 years ago ? (%)*

Employment Sector	Labour				Conservative			
	More active	About same	Less active	N	More active	About same	Less active	N
All	13.0	38.1	48.9	2677	10.3	63.1	26.6	1736
Private	13.2	38.1	48.7	931	10.1	64.9	25.0	1000
Public	13.3	37.9	48.8	1311	10.3	60.7	29.0	562
Other	12.0	38.6	49.4	435	11.5	60.3	28.2	174

Table 7.24 *Does the member hold any office within the Labour/Conservative Party ? (%)*

Employment Sector	Labour			Conservative		
	Yes	No	N	Yes	No	N
All	16.3	83.7	2664	8.7	91.3	2029
Private	16.1	83.9	929	8.1	91.9	1203
Public	17.4	82.6	1301	9.3	90.7	626
Other	13.4	86.6	434	11.0	89.0	200

Table 7.25   *How much time does the member devote to party activities per month ? (%)*

Employment Sector	Labour					Conservative				
	None	Up to 5 hrs	5 to 10 hrs	Over 10 hrs	N	None	Up to 5 hrs	5 to 10 hrs	Over 10 hrs	N
All	50.9	29.6	9.5	10.0	2670	75.2	16.0	4.6	4.2	2030
Private	51.4	26.8	9.8	12.0	925	76.9	14.9	4.4	3.8	1201
Public	51.3	31.7	8.8	8.2	1308	73.1	17.3	4.8	4.8	629
Other	49.0	29.5	10.3	11.2	437	72.0	18.0	5.0	5.0	200

Table 7.26   *What was the overall financial contribution made by the member in the last year ? (%)*

Employment Sector	Labour				Conservative			
	0 to £10	£10 to £20	Over £20	N	0 to £10	£10 to £20	Over £20	N
All	23.3	19.7	57.0	2391	33.6	21.1	45.3	1582
Private	27.7	22.3	50.0	822	33.8	20.8	45.4	934
Public	21.3	19.5	59.2	1170	34.9	21.8	43.3	496
Other	19.8	15.5	64.7	399	27.6	21.7	50.7	152

Table 7.27   *Is the member a local Labour/Conservative councillor ? (%)*

Employment Sector	Labour			Conservative		
	Yes	No	N	Yes	No	N
All	8.0	92.0	2687	2.2	97.8	2049
Private	10.6	89.4	930	1.9	98.1	1220
Public	6.6	93.4	1316	1.9	98.1	629
Other	6.8	93.2	441	5.5	94.5	200

Table 7.28   *The Labour/Conservative leader should be elected by a system of one party member/one vote (%)*

Employment Sector	Labour				Conservative			
	Agree	Neith-er	Dis-agree	N	Agree	Neith-er	Dis-agree	N
All	85.8	5.2	9.0	2684	49.3	14.6	36.1	2006
Private	85.9	4.9	9.2	931	50.8	14.4	34.8	1199
Public	85.8	5.8	8.4	1318	47.7	15.6	36.7	610
Other	85.3	4.6	10.1	435	44.7	12.7	42.6	197

Table 7.29   *People like me can have a real influence in politics if they are prepared to get involved (%)*

Employment Sector	Labour				Conservative			
	Agree	Neith-er	Dis-agree	N	Agree	Neith-er	Dis-agree	N
All	65.5	16.2	18.3	2675	57.3	19.6	23.1	2020
Private	65.5	16.8	17.7	927	57.5	19.6	22.9	1199
Public	65.3	17.1	17.6	1310	56.0	21.0	23.0	621
Other	66.2	12.3	21.5	438	60.0	16.0	24.0	200

Table 7.30   *Attending party meetings can be pretty tiring after a hard days work (%)*

Employment Sector	Labour				Conservative			
	Agree	Neith-er	Dis-agree	N	Agree	Neith-er	Dis-agree	N
All	77.6	11.2	11.2	2684	68.3	19.8	11.9	2007
Private	75.4	13.6	11.0	934	70.0	18.4	11.6	1195
Public	78.7	10.1	11.2	1311	67.2	21.7	11.1	613
Other	79.0	9.6	11.4	439	61.3	22.6	16.1	199

Table 7.31   *Someone like me could do a good job of being a local councillor (%)*

Employment Sector	Labour				Conservative			
	Agree	Neith-er	Dis-agree	N	Agree	Neith-er	Dis-agree	N
All	49.1	21.9	29.0	2657	29.3	24.2	46.5	2003
Private	47.7	23.7	28.6	919	29.4	25.5	45.1	1194
Public	48.9	21.1	30.0	1300	28.2	21.9	49.9	613
Other	52.5	20.8	26.7	438	32.1	23.5	44.4	196

Table 7.32   *Being an active party member is a good way of meeting interesting people (%)*

Employment Sector	Labour				Conservative			
	Agree	Neith-er	Dis-agree	N	Agree	Neith-er	Dis-agree	N
All	63.8	22.4	13.8	2678	58.1	31.1	10.8	1997
Private	67.5	20.4	12.1	932	56.5	31.0	12.5	1182
Public	63.0	23.1	13.9	1308	61.5	29.7	8.8	616
Other	58.5	24.9	16.6	438	56.8	35.7	7.5	199

Table 7.33   *The only way to be really educated about politics is to be a party activist (%)*

Employment Sector	Labour				Conservative			
	Agree	Neith-er	Dis-agree	N	Agree	Neith-er	Dis-agree	N
All	41.2	11.0	47.8	2680	33.4	17.8	48.8	2001
Private	47.9	9.9	42.2	933	32.9	18.2	48.9	1187
Public	38.0	11.4	50.6	1309	34.3	17.1	48.6	615
Other	36.5	12.4	51.1	438	33.7	17.6	48.7	199

Table 7.34   The party leadership does not pay a lot of attention to ordinary party members (%)

Employment Sector	Labour				Conservative			
	Agree	Neith-er	Dis-agree	N	Agree	Neith-er	Dis-agree	N
All	46.8	19.2	34.0	2682	41.6	24.4	34.0	2006
Private	49.9	17.1	33.0	928	43.1	25.3	31.6	1192
Public	44.2	20.6	35.2	1314	39.4	23.3	37.3	616
Other	47.7	19.6	32.7	440	39.4	22.2	38.4	198

Table 7.35   Party activity often takes time away from one's family (%)

Employment Sector	Labour				Conservative			
	Agree	Neith-er	Dis-agree	N	Agree	Neith-er	Dis-agree	N
All	85.5	10.1	4.4	2680	66.4	25.8	7.8	1987
Private	85.8	10.5	3.7	931	65.6	26.1	8.3	1179
Public	86.0	9.8	4.2	1310	68.2	24.8	7.0	614
Other	83.6	10.3	6.1	439	65.5	27.3	7.2	194

Table 7.36   The Labour/Conservative party would be more successful if people like me were elected to parliament (%)

Employment Sector	Labour				Conservative			
	Agree	Neith-er	Dis-agree	N	Agree	Neith-er	Dis-agree	N
All	33.5	34.3	32.2	2658	21.7	32.2	46.1	1987
Private	35.9	32.4	31.7	924	21.7	33.7	44.6	1179
Public	31.6	35.2	33.2	1297	19.2	31.2	49.6	613
Other	34.1	35.5	30.4	437	28.7	26.7	44.6	195

Table 7.37   *During the last 5 years, how often has the member displayed an election poster in his/her window ? (%)*

Employment Sector	Labour				Conservative			
	Not at all	Occas- ionally	Freq- uently	N	Not at all	Occas- ionally	Freq- uently	N
All	9.4	21.8	68.8	2662	48.5	32.2	19.3	1970
Private	9.2	22.0	68.8	919	48.5	31.8	19.7	1181
Public	9.6	22.7	67.7	1308	48.4	34.3	17.3	601
Other	9.2	18.6	72.2	435	48.4	28.2	23.4	188

Table 7.38   *During the last 5 years, how often has the member donated money to party funds ? (%)*

Employment Sector	Labour				Conservative			
	Not at all	Occas- ionally	Freq- uently	N	Not at all	Occas- ionally	Freq- uently	N
All	9.5	51.2	39.3	2658	14.9	55.4	29.7	2007
Private	10.7	51.2	38.1	918	15.3	55.1	29.6	1201
Public	9.0	51.3	39.7	1305	15.1	56.0	28.9	609
Other	8.7	50.8	40.5	435	12.2	54.8	33.0	197

Table 7.39   *During the last 5 years, how often has the member delivered party leaflets ? (%)*

Employment Sector	Labour				Conservative			
	Not at all	Occas- ionally	Freq- uently	N	Not at all	Occas- ionally	Freq- uently	N
All	17.2	27.2	55.6	2617	60.3	17.7	22.0	1931
Private	17.8	26.0	56.2	906	61.6	17.9	20.5	1164
Public	17.9	26.8	55.3	1280	59.0	17.6	23.4	581
Other	14.4	30.6	55.0	431	56.5	16.6	26.9	186

Table 7.40   *During the last 5 years, how often has the member attended a party meeting ? (%)*

Employment Sector	Labour				Conservative			
	Not at all	Occas-ionally	Freq-uently	N	Not at all	Occas-ionally	Freq-uently	N
All	21.3	41.0	37.7	2620	50.6	32.9	16.5	1953
Private	21.7	37.4	40.9	906	53.6	30.7	15.7	1172
Public	21.7	41.5	36.8	1283	48.6	34.3	17.1	589
Other	19.7	46.9	33.4	431	38.5	41.7	19.8	192

Table 7.41   *During the last 5 years, how often has the member canvassed voters on behalf of the party ? (%)*

Employment Sector	Labour				Conservative			
	Not at all	Occas-ionally	Freq-uently	N	Not at all	Occas-ionally	Freq-uently	N
All	36.3	31.9	31.8	2603	74.7	15.1	10.2	1933
Private	34.8	30.9	34.3	900	75.1	15.2	9.7	1163
Public	37.7	32.5	29.8	1272	75.9	14.6	9.5	581
Other	35.5	31.6	32.9	431	68.8	15.9	15.3	189

Table 7.42   *Where would you place yourself on a Left/Right scale within the Labour/Conservative party ? (%)*

Employment Sector	Labour				Conservative			
	Left	Centre	Right	N	Left	Centre	Right	N
All	58.1	20.7	21.2	2682	14.0	26.6	59.4	2033
Private	56.9	21.1	22.0	924	14.0	26.3	59.7	1213
Public	56.9	21.6	21.5	1320	14.3	27.0	58.7	622
Other	64.4	17.4	18.2	438	13.6	26.8	59.6	198

Table 7.43   *Where would you place yourself on a Left/Right scale within British Politics ? (%)*

Employment Sector	Labour				Conservative			
	Left	Centre	Right	N	Left	Centre	Right	N
All	81.3	10.1	8.6	2683	4.2	18.5	77.3	2029
Private	75.2	13.6	11.2	925	4.3	18.2	77.5	1211
Public	82.7	9.4	7.9	1319	4.3	19.5	76.2	621
Other	90.4	4.8	4.8	439	3.0	17.8	79.2	197

Table 7.44   *What thermometer rating would the Labour/Conservative member give the Conservative Party ? (%)*

Employment Sector	Labour					Conservative				
	Cd	Cl	W	H	M	Cd	Cl	W	H	M
All	76.3	20.2	2.8	0.7	14.6	0.3	3.6	34.3	61.8	80.7
Private	71.7	23.6	3.6	1.1	16.5	0.2	3.4	36.0	60.4	80.4
Public	77.9	19.2	2.3	0.6	13.9	0.3	3.9	32.1	63.7	80.9
Other	81.3	15.9	2.6	0.2	12.7	0.0	3.5	31.5	65.0	81.4

Table 7.45   *What thermometer rating would the Labour/Conservative member give the Labour Party ? (%)*

Employment Sector	Labour					Conservative				
	Cd	Cl	W	H	M	Cd	Cl	W	H	M
All	0.9	3.7	25.3	70.1	82.5	50.8	42.9	5.8	0.5	26.4
Private	1.2	3.3	22.2	73.3	83.7	53.1	40.8	5.8	0.3	25.9
Public	0.8	3.7	25.0	70.5	82.5	47.4	46.8	5.3	0.5	26.8
Other	0.5	4.8	32.7	62.0	79.6	47.6	43.8	7.6	1.0	27.8

Table 7.46   *What thermometer rating would the Labour/Conservative member give the Liberal Democratic Party ? (%)*

Employment Sector	Labour					Conservative				
	Cd	Cl	W	H	M	Cd	Cl	W	H	M
All	32.6	44.8	20.8	1.8	37.0	33.8	50.4	14.6	1.2	35.8
Private	33.0	43.7	21.1	2.2	37.0	34.8	50.3	13.7	1.2	35.5
Public	32.2	45.3	20.9	1.6	37.0	31.6	52.6	14.6	1.2	36.4
Other	33.0	45.4	19.9	1.7	36.8	34.8	44.4	20.3	0.5	36.5

Table 7.47   *What thermometer rating would the Labour/Conservative member give the Scottish Nationalist Party ? (%)*

Employment Sector	Labour					Conservative				
	Cd	Cl	W	H	M	Cd	Cl	W	H	M
All	43.8	37.5	15.8	2.9	32.2	69.8	26.2	3.7	0.3	18.8
Private	48.8	32.9	15.5	2.8	30.6	70.6	25.9	3.1	0.4	18.6
Public	41.7	40.8	14.1	3.4	32.9	68.1	27.8	3.9	0.2	18.9
Other	39.8	37.0	21.8	1.4	33.4	70.1	23.4	6.5	0.0	19.4

Table 7.48   *What thermometer rating would the Labour/Conservative member give Plaid Cymru ? (%)*

Employment Sector	Labour					Conservative				
	Cd	Cl	W	H	M	Cd	Cl	W	H	M
All	46.9	38.2	12.9	2.0	30.0	82.6	16.2	0.9	0.3	12.8
Private	51.1	35.0	11.9	2.0	28.3	84.1	14.6	1.0	0.3	12.1
Public	45.4	40.3	12.3	2.0	30.7	80.0	18.9	0.7	0.4	14.1
Other	42.2	38.8	17.0	2.0	31.9	81.5	17.1	1.4	0.0	12.9

Table 7.49   *What thermometer rating would the Labour/Conservative member give the Green Party ? (%)*

Employment Sector	Labour					Conservative				
	Cd	Cl	W	H	M	Cd	Cl	W	H	M
All	32.6	36.0	26.1	5.3	39.9	70.4	24.3	4.8	0.5	19.3
Private	34.8	36.4	23.9	4.9	38.5	72.6	22.2	4.6	0.6	18.6
Public	30.8	36.2	27.4	5.6	40.9	66.5	26.9	6.0	0.6	21.0
Other	33.1	34.8	27.0	5.1	40.0	69.6	28.0	2.4	0.0	18.5

Table 7.50   *What thermometer rating would the Labour/Conservative member give the BBC ? (%)*

Employment Sector	Labour					Conservative				
	Cd	Cl	W	H	M	Cd	Cl	W	H	M
All	8.9	25.8	40.3	25.0	60.8	8.5	30.7	40.1	20.7	59.4
Private	10.3	29.3	37.9	22.5	58.7	8.5	32.2	39.4	19.9	58.9
Public	9.0	24.0	41.1	25.9	61.2	7.4	28.1	40.7	23.8	61.2
Other	6.2	23.3	43.0	27.5	63.6	12.5	29.7	42.2	15.6	56.3

Table 7.51   *What thermometer rating would the Labour/Conservative member give the European Community ? (%)*

Employment Sector	Labour					Conservative				
	Cd	Cl	W	H	M	Cd	Cl	W	H	M
All	10.8	32.4	42.2	14.6	55.8	14.3	41.0	35.3	9.4	50.8
Private	11.9	32.4	39.5	16.2	55.6	14.0	41.1	34.6	10.3	51.3
Public	10.2	32.8	42.5	14.5	56.0	15.0	40.7	35.2	9.1	50.2
Other	10.1	31.6	46.4	11.9	55.4	14.4	40.9	35.3	9.4	49.7

Table 7.52   *What thermometer rating would the Labour/Conservative member give the Trade Union Congress ? (%)*

Employment Sector	Labour					Conservative				
	Cd	Cl	W	H	M	Cd	Cl	W	H	M
All	5.6	28.8	48.3	17.3	60.0	53.5	40.3	5.6	0.6	26.2
Private	6.4	25.9	48.1	19.6	61.2	53.4	40.9	5.1	0.6	25.9
Public	4.8	29.7	48.3	17.2	59.9	55.4	37.5	6.4	0.7	26.3
Other	5.9	32.5	48.8	12.8	57.7	48.3	44.2	6.8	0.7	28.1

Table 7.53   *What thermometer rating would the Labour/Conservative member give the Police ? (%)*

Employment Sector	Labour					Conservative				
	Cd	Cl	W	H	M	Cd	Cl	W	H	M
All	17.7	45.3	28.2	8.8	47.8	1.6	13.1	40.1	45.2	72.5
Private	17.1	40.2	31.1	11.6	50.2	2.0	14.2	39.1	44.7	72.0
Public	17.5	47.6	26.7	8.2	47.1	1.0	10.2	41.4	47.4	74.0
Other	19.3	49.3	26.3	5.1	45.0	1.1	15.7	42.4	40.8	71.4

Table 7.54   *What thermometer rating would the Labour/Conservative member give the House of Commons ? (%)*

Employment Sector	Labour					Conservative				
	Cd	Cl	W	H	M	Cd	Cl	W	H	M
All	10.2	33.6	38.4	17.8	56.8	2.4	16.6	50.6	30.4	68.2
Private	10.6	31.4	38.6	19.4	57.7	2.2	17.7	49.9	30.2	67.9
Public	9.7	34.7	38.3	17.3	56.6	2.7	14.3	51.3	31.7	68.9
Other	10.5	35.1	38.4	16.0	55.4	2.7	17.1	52.4	27.8	67.8

Table 7.55   *What thermometer rating would the Labour/Conservative member give the CBI ? (%)*

Employment Sector	Labour					Conservative				
	Cd	Cl	W	H	M	Cd	Cl	W	H	M
All	45.1	41.7	11.3	1.9	30.8	5.4	29.6	49.4	15.6	59.7
Private	42.8	41.8	12.3	3.1	32.3	5.0	30.2	48.9	15.9	59.8
Public	46.9	40.8	11.1	1.2	29.8	6.4	27.9	50.7	15.0	59.6
Other	44.8	44.0	10.2	1.0	30.4	5.4	31.0	48.1	15.5	58.9

Table 7.56   *What thermometer rating would the Labour/Conservative member give the Queen ? (%)*

Employment Sector	Labour					Conservative				
	Cd	Cl	W	H	M	Cd	Cl	W	H	M
All	34.9	30.2	19.1	15.8	42.3	1.0	5.0	16.6	77.4	85.9
Private	32.9	27.9	19.8	19.4	46.5	1.3	5.7	16.7	76.3	85.4
Public	36.4	30.3	18.5	14.8	41.3	0.5	4.6	15.9	79.0	86.7
Other	35.1	34.6	19.3	11.0	40.1	0.4	2.1	18.5	79.0	87.0

Table 7.57   *What thermometer rating would the Labour/Conservative member give Judges ? (%)*

Employment Sector	Labour					Conservative				
	Cd	Cl	W	H	M	Cd	Cl	W	H	M
All	38.2	44.0	14.5	3.3	34.8	4.3	31.7	45.5	18.5	60.2
Private	36.8	44.0	14.5	4.7	36.1	5.2	31.4	45.1	18.3	60.0
Public	38.2	44.7	14.3	2.8	34.4	3.3	29.6	47.4	19.7	61.2
Other	41.3	41.5	14.7	2.5	33.2	2.8	39.7	41.9	15.6	58.7

8   Economic Sector

Table 8.1   *The Labour/Conservative party should try to capture the middle ground in politics (%)*

Economic Sector	Labour				Conservative			
	Agree	Neith-er	Dis-agree	N	Agree	Neith-er	Dis-agree	N
All	50.7	8.6	40.7	2752	69.7	13.3	17.0	2273
Working F/T	45.8	13.3	40.9	1473	62.8	14.3	22.9	642
Working P/T	41.0	14.1	44.9	249	71.7	13.2	15.1	219
Unemployed	57.1	9.8	33.1	112	62.8	7.0	30.2	43
Retired	65.5	9.2	25.3	501	75.9	12.0	12.1	900
Looking after Home	56.7	13.3	30.0	150	67.1	15.3	17.6	346
Other	52.8	8.6	38.6	267	67.5	14.6	17.9	123

Table 8.2   *A Labour/Conservative government should introduce a prices and Incomes policy as a means of controlling inflation (%)*

Economic Sector	Labour				Conservative			
	Agree	Neith-er	Dis-agree	N	Agree	Neith-er	Dis-agree	N
All	56.9	19.2	23.9	2754	42.0	11.6	46.4	2318
Working F/T	47.1	22.3	30.6	1468	31.6	10.6	57.8	651
Working P/T	58.2	21.3	20.5	244	48.2	10.8	41.0	222
Unemployed	61.9	17.7	20.4	113	58.1	11.6	30.3	43
Retired	78.4	9.2	12.4	513	46.3	12.2	41.5	923
Looking after Home	71.1	16.1	12.8	149	45.2	9.4	45.4	352
Other	58.4	21.7	19.9	267	38.6	19.7	41.7	127

Table 8.3   *Income and wealth should be re-distributed towards ordinary working people (%)*

Economic Sector	Labour				Conservative			
	Agree	Neith-er	Dis-agree	N	Agree	Neith-er	Dis-agree	N
All	86.1	9.1	4.8	2784	25.3	20.4	54.3.	2312
Working F/T	86.1	8.8	5.1	1480	23.3	21.0	55.7	653
Working P/T	92.4	4.4	3.2	250	27.7	21.8	50.5	220
Unemployed	85.8	11.5	2.7	113	43.2	13.6	43.2	44
Retired	83.6	11.1	5.3	513	25.8	22.2	52.0	916
Looking after Home	86.3	9.8	3.9	153	23.0	14.6	62.4	355
Other	85.1	9.8	5.1	275	26.6	21.0	52.4	124

Table 8.4   *The Labour/Conservative Party should always stand by its principles even if this should lose it an election (%)*

Economic Sector	Labour				Conservative			
	Agree	Neith-er	Dis-agree	N	Agree	Neith-er	Dis-agree	N
All	67.9	11.9	20.2	2782	81.1	8.3	10.6	2370
Working F/T	61.7	13.1	25.2	1476	74.8	9.5	15.7	656
Working P/T	72.1	12.0	15.9	251	78.5	8.1	13.4	223
Unemployed	70.8	13.3	15.9	113	84.4	4.4	11.2	45
Retired	79.5	7.8	12.7	516	84.8	7.9	7.3	954
Looking after Home	72.3	12.9	14.8	155	84.9	8.0	7.1	364
Other	71.6	12.2	16.2	271	78.1	8.6	13.3	128

Table 8.5   *Further nuclear energy development is essential for the future prosperity of Britain (%)*

Economic Sector	Labour				Conservative			
	Agree	Neith-er	Dis-agree	N	Agree	Neith-er	Dis-agree	N
All	13.7	11.8	74.5	2773	60.2	17.1	22.7	2328
Working F/T	12.2	11.9	75.9	1475	59.1	15.5	25.4	658
Working P/T	10.7	9.9	79.4	253	49.3	19.3	31.4	223
Unemployed	14.2	10.6	75.2	113	73.3	8.9	17.8	45
Retired	19.8	13.4	66.8	509	63.7	17.0	19.3	922
Looking after Home	10.7	12.7	76.6	150	57.2	19.2	23.6	355
Other	14.7	9.9	75.4	273	63.2	18.4	18.4	125

Table 8.6   *A future Labour/Conservative government should not agree to a single European currency (%)*

Economic Sector	Labour				Conservative			
	Agree	Neith-er	Dis-agree	N	Agree	Neith-er	Dis-agree	N
All	24.8	19.3	55.9	2758	57.9	12.1	30.0	2348
Working F/T	18.9	18.7	62.4	1473	49.7	10.7	39.6	656
Working P/T	26.7	25.5	47.8	251	58.0	12.1	29.9	224
Unemployed	32.7	17.3	50.0	110	60.0	6.7	33.3	45
Retired	33.6	17.5	48.9	503	61.5	13.4	25.1	938
Looking after Home	36.8	20.4	42.8	152	64.7	10.1	25.2	357
Other	29.0	20.1	50.9	269	53.1	17.2	29.7	128

Table 8.7 *High·Income tax makes people less willing to work hard (%)*

Economic Sector	Labour				Conservative			
	Agree	Neith-er	Dis-agree	N	Agree	Neith-er	Dis-agree	N
All	25.9	10.8	63.3	2789	82.0	5.9	12.1	2373
Working F/T	20.9	10.7	68.4	1483	83.1	5.0	11.9	658
Working P/T	18.3	10.4	71.3	251	82.7	3.6	13.7	225
Unemployed	30.7	14.9	54.4	114	84.8	4.3	10.9	46
Retired	38.1	10.5	51.4	515	80.3	7.5	12.2	950
Looking after Home	33.6	11.8	54.6	152	83.6	4.7	11.7	365
Other	31.0	10.2	58.8	274	81.4	7.8	10.8	129

Table 8.8 *Britain's electoral system should be replaced by a system of proportional representation (%)*

Economic Sector	Labour				Conservative			
	Agree	Neith-er	Dis-agree	N	Agree	Neith-er	Dis-agree	N
All	57.7	13.4	28.9	2784	21.6	11.9	66.5	2337
Working F/T	58.8	13.4	27.8	1484	23.2	12.3	64.5	651
Working P/T	61.4	12.7	25.9	251	20.5	10.3	69.2	224
Unemployed	44.6	16.1	39.3	112	28.9	13.3	57.8	45
Retired	56.3	11.5	32.2	512	20.8	11.5	67.7	933
Looking after Home	53.9	17.5	28.6	154	20.5	11.5	68.0	356
Other	58.3	14.4	27.3	271	21.1	17.2	61.7	128

Table 8.9 *Further moves towards integration within the European Community should be resisted (%)*

Economic Sector	Labour				Conservative			
	Agree	Neith-er	Dis-agree	N	Agree	Neith-er	Dis-agree	N
All	21.3	13.3	65.4	2775	54.0	15.6	30.4	2346
Working F/T	18.3	11.4	70.3	1479	41.3	19.4	39.3	654
Working P/T	21.2	14.0	64.8	250	49.8	17.9	32.3	223
Unemployed	27.7	16.1	56.2	112	55.9	8.9	35.2	45
Retired	26.9	15.7	57.4	510	62.6	12.6	24.8	941
Looking after Home	28.5	18.5	53.0	151	56.5	16.6	26.9	356
Other	20.1	14.3	65.6	273	55.1	12.6	32.3	127

Table 8.10 *There is no need for a Bill of Rights in this country (%)*

Economic Sector	Labour				Conservative			
	Agree	Neith-er	Dis-agree	N	Agree	Neith-er	Dis-agree	N
All	11.0	9.9	79.1	2761	39.7	26.6	33.7	2263
Working F/T	9.0	8.8	82.2	1471	33.1	29.0	37.9	638
Working P/T	8.3	9.1	82.6	252	34.5	27.8	37.7	223
Unemployed	9.6	12.3	78.1	114	39.5	27.9	32.6	43
Retired	20.0	10.7	69.3	504	47.0	23.6	29.4	893
Looking after Home	11.4	14.8	73.8	149	39.5	26.1	34.4	337
Other	8.5	11.8	79.7	271	31.8	34.9	33.3	129

Table 8.11   *A future Labour/Conservative government should introduce a directly elected Scottish Assembly with taxing powers (%)*

Economic Sector	Labour				Conservative			
	Agree	Neith-er	Dis-agree	N	Agree	Neith-er	Dis-agree	N
All	61.5	21.9	16.6	2784	22.6	26.6	50.8	2307
Working F/T	62.7	22.1	15.2	1482	23.5	27.7	48.8	650
Working P/T	57.5	23.8	18.7	252	25.1	31.4	43.5	223
Unemployed	55.9	26.1	18.0	111	27.9	23.3	48.8	43
Retired	65.6	16.3	18.1	514	20.9	25.2	53.9	917
Looking after Home	54.2	24.8	21.0	153	19.8	26.6	53.6	349
Other	57.0	26.5	16.5	272	31.2	24.0	44.8	125

Table 8.12   *Coalition governments are the best form of government for Britain (%)*

Economic Sector	Labour				Conservative			
	Agree	Neith-er	Dis-agree	N	Agree	Neith-er	Dis-agree	N
All	8.6	16.9	74.5	2780	9.6	10.1	80.3	2376
Working F/T	6.4	18.4	75.2	1467	6.5	11.8	81.7	659
Working P/T	8.4	16.0	75.6	250	9.8	12.1	78.1	224
Unemployed	15.0	9.7	75.3	113	11.4	9.1	79.5	44
Retired	11.9	13.3	74.8	513	11.3	9.7	79.0	954
Looking after Home	10.5	16.3	73.2	153	9.3	7.1	83.6	364
Other	10.9	19.6	69.5	275	11.5	8.4	80.1	131

Table 8.13   *A future Labour/Conservative government should/should not spend money to get rid of poverty (%)*

Economic Sector	Labour				Conservative			
	Should	Doesn't matter	Should not	N	Should	Doesn't matter	Should not	N
All	98.0	0.9	1.1	2777	80.2	8.4	11.4	2329
Working F/T	98.1	0.8	1.1	1477	80.7	7.9	11.4	649
Working P/T	98.4	0.4	1.2	253	84.2	7.7	8.1	221
Unemployed	98.2	0.9	0.9	112	86.0	9.3	4.7	43
Retired	97.8	0.8	1.4	510	77.8	10.0	12.2	929
Looking after Home	97.4	1.3	1.3	153	83.7	5.8	10.5	361
Other	97.8	2.2	0.0	272	76.2	7.1	16.7	126

Table 8.14   *A future Labour/Conservative government should/should not encourage the growth of private medicine (%)*

Economic Sector	Labour				Conservative			
	Should	Doesn't matter	Should not	N	Should	Doesn't matter	Should not	N
All	3.6	4.7	91.7	2773	52.2	15.8	32.0	2338
Working F/T	3.2	4.5	92.3	53.3	55.6	16.0	28.4	651
Working P/T	2.4	3.6	94.0	253	51.1	10.9	38.0	221
Unemployed	4.5	5.4	90.1	111	43.5	19.6	36.9	46
Retired	4.9	4.9	90.2	507	50.3	17.5	32.2	936
Looking after Home	3.3	2.6	94.1	152	52.5	14.9	32.6	356
Other	4.8	6.6	88.6	272	52.3	12.5	35.2	128

Table 8.15   *A future Labour/Conservative government should/should not put*
more money into the National Health Service (%)

Economic Sector	Labour				Conservative			
	Should	Doesn't matter	Should not	N	Should	Doesn't matter	Should not	N
All	98.0	0.7	1.3	2784	79.3	7.6	13.1	2343
Working F/T	97.7	0.9	1.4	1479	77.5	8.7	13.8	652
Working P/T	99.6	0.4	0.0	253	85.7	5.8	8.5	223
Unemployed	98.2	0.0	1.8	112	84.8	6.5	8.7	46
Retired	98.1	1.0	0.9	513	78.7	7.6	13.7	934
Looking after Home	98.0	0.0	2.0	153	80.2	7.0	12.8	359
Other	98.2	0.4	1.4	274	77.5	6.2	16.3	129

Table 8.16   *A future Labour/Conservative government should/should not reduce*
spending in general (%)

Economic Sector	Labour				Conservative			
	Should	Doesn't matter	Should not	N	Should	Doesn't matter	Should not	N
All	19.0	7.2	73.8	2739	60.3	8.9	30.8	2323
Working F/T	15.9	6.6	77.5	1469	58.8	9.7	31.5	650
Working P/T	20.0	4.9	75.1	245	53.6	10.5	35.9	220
Unemployed	15.3	8.1	76.6	111	64.4	11.1	24.5	45
Retired	27.6	10.5	61.9	496	64.3	8.4	27.3	925
Looking after Home	20.1	4.7	75.2	149	58.0	7.3	34.7	357
Other	20.1	7.8	72.1	269	55.6	9.5	34.9	126

Table 8.17   *A future Labour/Conservative government should/should not introduce stricter laws to regulate the trade unions (%)*

Economic Sector	Labour				Conservative			
	Should	Doesn't matter	Should not	N	Should	Doesn't matter	Should not	N
All	9.8	14.8	75.4	2752	66.5	12.2	21.3	2351
Working F/T	7.6	14.8	77.6	1469	51.7	18.1	30.2	652
Working P/T	8.5	13.3	78.2	248	66.8	12.1	21.1	223
Unemployed	8.1	10.8	81.1	111	54.5	18.2	27.3	44
Retired	15.5	14.3	70.2	504	75.7	8.4	15.9	945
Looking after Home	14.1	14.8	71.1	149	71.2	10.3	18.5	358
Other	11.4	18.8	69.8	271	64.3	14.0	21.7	129

Table 8.18   *A future Labour/Conservative government should/should not give workers more say in the places where they work (%)*

Economic Sector	Labour				Conservative			
	Should	Doesn't matter	Should not	N	Should	Doesn't matter	Should not	N
All	91.3	5.5	3.2	2773	63.9	13.4	22.7	2358
Working F/T	91.5	4.9	3.6	1478	60.6	14.2	25.2	654
Working P/T	93.3	3.6	3.1	252	71.7	11.7	16.6	223
Unemployed	90.0	5.5	4.5	110	64.4	15.6	20.0	45
Retired	91.2	7.1	1.7	510	62.1	13.9	24.0	949
Looking after Home	92.1	4.5	3.4	151	70.0	12.0	18.0	357
Other	89.0	8.1	2.9	272	63.8	11.5	24.7	130

Table 8.19   *A future Labour/Conservative government should/should not spend less on defence (%)*

Economic Sector	Labour				Conservative			
	Should	Doesn't matter	Should not	N	Should	Doesn't matter	Should not	N
All	82.8	4.4	12.8	2775	44.4	4.9	50.7	2344
Working F/T	84.5	4.9	10.6	1480	49.2	4.9	45.9	652
Working P/T	87.7	2.4	9.9	252	45.5	4.0	50.5	224
Unemployed	76.6	4.5	18.9	111	35.6	4.4	60.0	45
Retired	79.0	5.1	15.9	509	42.3	5.7	52.0	941
Looking after Home	80.4	2.0	17.6	153	42.7	3.7	53.6	356
Other	80.4	3.7	15.9	270	40.5	3.2	56.3	126

Table 8.20   *Should a future Labour/Conservative government :*
(A) Reduce taxes & spend less on health, education & social benefits ?
(B) Keep taxes & spending on these services at the same levels as now ?
(C) Increase taxes & spend more on health, education & social benefits ?

Economic Sector	Labour				Conservative			
	A	B	C	N	A	B	C	N
All	2.6	6.3	91.1	2778	6.8	67.1	26.1	2344
Working F/T	2.6	6.8	90.6	1473	9.8	66.0	24.2	645
Working P/T	2.4	2.8	94.8	254	3.6	59.9	36.5	222
Unemployed	4.4	1.8	93.8	113	11.4	65.9	22.7	44
Retired	2.9	7.4	89.7	515	5.8	69.0	25.2	944
Looking after Home	1.9	5.8	92.3	154	5.8	72.0	22.2	361
Other	1.5	6.7	91.8	269	5.5	57.0	37.5	128

Table 8.21   *On joining the Labour/Conservative party did the member approach the party (MA) or did the party approach the member (PA) ? (%)*

Economic Sector	Labour				Conservative			
	MA	Don't Know	PA	N	MA	Don't Know	PA	N
All	77.4	20.0	2.6	2806	34.3	50.1	15.6	2389
Working F/T	79.5	18.8	1.7	1481	40.7	48.8	10.5	656
Working P/T	81.8	15.4	2.8	254	31.3	54.5	14.2	224
Unemployed	75.2	24.8	0.0	113	54.3	37.0	8.7	46
Retired	69.5	25.1	5.4	525	34.3	48.0	17.7	957
Looking after Home	73.2	24.2	2.6	157	22.8	57.1	20.1	373
Other	81.5	16.7	1.8	276	33.8	50.4	15.8	133

Table 8.22   *How often has the member attended a party meeting in the last 12 months ? (%)*

Economic Sector	Labour				Conservative			
	Not at all	Occas-ionally	Frequ-ently	N	Not at all	Occas-ionally	Frequ-ently	N
All	42.0	30.2	27.8	2817	65.9	22.0	12.1	2406
Working F/T	42.4	31.7	25.9	1493	68.9	20.2	10.9	660
Working P/T	45.2	31.7	23.1	252	68.1	21.2	10.7	226
Unemployed	42.1	23.7	34.2	114	61.7	29.8	8.5	47
Retired	35.4	30.5	34.1	528	62.8	24.0	13.2	967
Looking after Home	48.4	25.8	25.8	155	67.7	18.9	13.4	375
Other	45.8	25.8	28.4	275	66.4	24.4	9.2	131

Table 8.23   *Is the member more or less politically active than 5 years ago ? (%)*

Economic Sector	Labour				Conservative			
	More active	About same	Less active	N	More active	About same	Less active	N
All	12.9	38.4	48.7	2780	9.4	62.7	27.9	2024
Working F/T	13.0	36.8	50.2	1482	14.3	66.7	19.0	526
Working P/T	16.3	41.8	41.9	251	9.4	67.4	23.2	181
Unemployed	17.5	47.4	35.1	114	16.2	62.2	21.6	37
Retired	7.4	39.7	52.9	516	7.1	59.3	33.6	847
Looking after Home	14.5	43.4	42.1	152	8.0	64.8	27.2	324
Other	17.0	35.1	47.9	265	5.5	56.9	37.6	109

Table 8.24   *Does the member hold any office within the Labour/Conservative Party ? (%)*

Economic Sector	Labour			Conservative		
	Yes	No	N	Yes	No	N
All	16.0	84.0	2770	8.4	91.6	2371
Working F/T	17.2	82.8	1468	9.6	90.4	653
Working P/T	17.0	83.0	253	8.1	91.9	222
Unemployed	12.3	87.7	114	11.4	88.6	44
Retired	13.9	86.1	518	7.9	92.1	983
Looking after Home	13.9	86.1	151	8.1	91.9	369
Other	14.7	85.3	266	10.8	89.2	130

Table 8.25   How much time does the member devote to party activities per month ? (%)

Economic Sector	Labour					Conservative				
	None	Up to 5 hrs	5 to 10 hrs	Over 10 hrs	N	None	Up to 5 hrs	5 to 10 hrs	Over 10 hrs	N
All	51.2	29.5	9.4	9.9	2780	76.0	15.3	4.4	4.3	2362
Working F/T	50.7	29.1	9.1	11.1	1482	76.4	14.2	4.9	4.5	653
Working P/T	51.2	29.8	10.3	8.7	252	77.0	15.3	3.2	4.5	222
Unemployed	49.1	26.3	9.6	15.0	114	77.3	9.1	4.5	9.1	44
Retired	52.4	30.3	11.5	5.8	515	75.9	15.7	4.4	4.0	954
Looking after Home	53.4	30.4	8.8	7.4	148	75.2	16.4	4.5	3.9	359
Other	51.3	30.1	6.7	11.9	269	75.4	16.9	4.6	3.1	130

Table 8.26   What was the overall financial contribution made by the member in the last year ? (%)

Economic Sector	Labour				Conservative			
	0 to £10	£10 to £20	Over £20	N	0 to £10	£10 to £20	Over £20	N
All	23.8	19.8	56.4	2477	34.3	21.1	44.6	1788
Working F/T	14.1	20.1	65.8	1335	36.5	15.6	47.9	512
Working P/T	20.5	21.0	58.5	224	33.7	23.9	42.4	163
Unemployed	40.6	20.8	38.6	96	46.7	20.0	33.3	30
Retired	39.2	18.3	42.5	459	31.8	25.1	43.1	710
Looking after Home	37.8	20.5	41.7	127	34.3	22.1	43.6	271
Other	37.7	18.6	43.7	236	37.3	14.7	48.0	102

Table 8.27 *Is the member a local Labour/Conservative councillor ? (%)*

Economic Sector	Labour			Conservative		
	Yes	No	N	Yes	No	N
All	7.8	92.2	2793	2.3	97.7	2388
Working F/T	9.3	90.7	1489	2.6	97.4	656
Working P/T	8.3	91.7	253	2.2	97.8	227
Unemployed	9.6	90.4	114	2.2	97.8	46
Retired	4.4	95.6	517	2.4	97.6	959
Looking after Home	3.4	96.6	149	1.4	98.6	369
Other	7.4	92.6	271	3.1	96.9	131

Table 8.28 *The Labour/Conservative leader should be elected by a system of one party member/one vote (%)*

Economic Sector	Labour				Conservative			
	Agree	Neith-er	Dis-agree	N	Agree	Neith-er	Dis-agree	N
All	85.9	5.4	8.7	2788	49.9	14.5	35.6	2327
Working F/T	83.0	6.2	10.8	1476	47.5	17.4	35.1	651
Working P/T	87.7	4.4	7.9	252	48.4	14.5	37.1	221
Unemployed	83.9	4.5	11.6	112	60.5	11.6	27.9	43
Retired	90.4	5.6	4.0	522	54.0	13.7	32.3	931
Looking after Home	94.1	3.9	2.0	153	45.3	12.8	41.9	351
Other	87.2	6.6	6.2	273	43.8	10.8	45.4	130

Table 8.29   *People like me can have a real influence in politics if they are prepared to get involved (%)*

Economic Sector	Labour				Conservative			
	Agree	Neith-er	Dis-agree	N	Agree	Neith-er	Dis-agree	N
All	65.6	16.1	18.3	2780	56.5	20.1	23.4	2336
Working F/T	63.9	16.6	19.5	1479	60.6	17.0	22.4	653
Working P/T	64.0	14.4	21.6	250	57.6	18.3	24.1	224
Unemployed	71.1	10.5	18.4	114	53.5	23.3	23.2	43
Retired	69.5	16.1	14.4	509	55.7	23.0	21.3	928
Looking after Home	71.2	16.7	12.1	156	50.3	20.9	28.8	358
Other	63.6	17.3	19.1	272	57.7	14.6	27.7	130

Table 8.30   *Attending party meetings can be pretty tiring after a hard days work (%)*

Economic Sector	Labour				Conservative			
	Agree	Neith-er	Dis-agree	N	Agree	Neith-er	Dis-agree	N
All	77.2	11.3	11.5	2784	69.0	19.5	11.5	2318
Working F/T	80.5	9.7	9.8	1488	72.2	17.6	10.2	654
Working P/T	80.6	9.5	9.9	253	71.7	17.5	10.8	223
Unemployed	74.6	13.2	12.2	114	65.2	21.7	13.1	46
Retired	67.8	14.9	17.3	510	67.9	19.9	12.2	915
Looking after Home	79.1	10.5	10.4	153	65.9	21.3	12.8	352
Other	73.3	15.0	11.7	266	66.4	24.2	9.4	128

Table 8.31   *Someone like me could do a good job of being a local councillor (%)*

Economic Sector	Labour				Conservative			
	Agree	Neith-er	Dis-agree	N	Agree	Neith-er	Dis-agree	N
All	48.8	22.0	29.2	2764	27.6	24.4	48.0	2303
Working F/T	54.3	21.2	24.5	1481	39.4	27.7	32.9	649
Working P/T	43.0	21.7	35.3	249	23.0	23.0	54.0	222
Unemployed	47.3	19.6	33.1	112	31.8	29.5	38.7	44
Retired	42.8	20.8	36.4	500	23.8	24.1	52.1	913
Looking after Home	32.7	26.8	40.5	153	16.3	18.6	65.1	350
Other	45.4	26.8	27.8	269	32.8	25.6	41.6	125

Table 8.32   *Being an active party member is a good way of meeting interesting people (%)*

Economic Sector	Labour				Conservative			
	Agree	Neith-er	Dis-agree	N	Agree	Neith-er	Dis-agree	N
All	41.5	11.1	47.4	2788	59.4	30.0	10.6	2307
Working F/T	57.6	26.1	16.3	1482	49.6	36.4	14.0	645
Working P/T	61.8	24.1	14.1	249	57.0	33.9	9.1	221
Unemployed	66.7	21.1	12.2	114	63.6	25.0	11.4	44
Retired	81.1	12.3	6.6	512	66.7	25.8	7.5	911
Looking after Home	73.6	16.1	10.3	155	59.7	27.6	12.7	355
Other	65.9	19.3	14.8	270	58.8	28.2	13.0	131

Table 8.33 *The only way to be really educated about politics is to be a party activist (%)*

Economic Sector	Labour				Conservative			
	Agree	Neith-er	Dis-agree	N	Agree	Neith-er	Dis-agree	N
All	41.5	11.1	47.4	2788	35.6	17.3	47.1	2312
Working F/T	36.1	10.7	53.2	1487	27.7	19.0	53.3	649
Working P/T	37.5	13.1	49.4	251	31.5	16.9	51.6	219
Unemployed	46.4	15.2	38.4	112	28.9	17.8	53.3	45
Retired	57.8	10.1	32.1	514	41.8	17.2	41.0	917
Looking after Home	41.0	12.2	46.8	156	38.9	13.5	47.6	355
Other	42.5	10.8	46.7	268	30.7	19.7	49.6	127

Table 8.34 *The party leadership does not pay a lot of attention to ordinary party members (%)*

Economic Sector	Labour				Conservative			
	Agree	Neith-er	Dis-agree	N	Agree	Neith-er	Dis-agree	N
All	46.9	18.9	34.2	2786	42.3	24.1	33.6	2324
Working F/T	46.3	21.1	32.6	1485	38.5	27.1	34.4	649
Working P/T	44.2	20.7	35.1	251	45.7	20.1	34.2	219
Unemployed	51.8	13.2	35.0	114	47.7	22.7	29.6	44
Retired	45.2	16.1	38.7	509	43.8	22.9	33.3	924
Looking after Home	39.6	18.2	42.2	154	42.5	23.5	34.0	358
Other	57.9	13.6	28.5	273	41.5	25.4	33.1	130

Table 8.35   *Party activity often takes time away from one's family (%)*

Economic Sector	Labour				Conservative			
	Agree	Neith-er	Dis-agree	N	Agree	Neith-er	Dis-agree	N
All	84.8	10.6	4.6	2783	67.1	25.5	7.4	2292
Working F/T	84.0	11.5	4.5	1494	62.2	29.3	8.5	641
Working P/T	87.2	8.4	4.4	251	69.2	23.1	7.7	221
Unemployed	79.8	14.9	5.3	114	62.2	22.2	15.6	45
Retired	88.5	7.0	4.5	511	70.5	23.7	5.8	908
Looking after Home	87.6	8.4	4.0	154	67.4	24.0	8.6	350
Other	80.3	14.1	5.6	269	63.8	29.1	7.1	127

Table 8.36   *The Labour/Conservative party would be more successful if people like me were elected to parliament (%)*

Economic Sector	Labour				Conservative			
	Agree	Neith-er	Dis-agree	N	Agree	Neith-er	Dis-agree	N
All	33.7	34.4	31.9	2760	21.1	31.6	47.3	2281
Working F/T	33.9	35.6	30.5	1476	27.3	33.4	39.3	644
Working P/T	28.7	32.0	39.3	247	20.8	30.3	48.9	221
Unemployed	36.3	30.1	33.6	113	24.4	35.6	40.0	45
Retired	35.5	31.3	33.2	502	19.2	32.7	48.1	897
Looking after Home	25.3	38.7	36.0	150	12.6	26.3	61.1	350
Other	36.8	35.3	27.9	272	26.6	30.6	42.8	124

Table 8.37   *During the last 5 years, how often has the member displayed an election poster in his/her window ? (%)*

Economic Sector	Labour				Conservative			
	Not at all	Occas- ionally	Freq- uently	N	Not at all	Occas- ionally	Freq- uently	N
All	9.6	21.7	68.7	2767	48.9	31.8	19.3	2275
Working F/T	8.7	21.9	69.4	1472	49.1	30.3	20.6	644
Working P/T	7.1	18.8	74.1	255	45.5	34.7	19.8	213
Unemployed	11.6	15.2	73.2	112	40.9	43.2	15.9	44
Retired	13.7	23.2	63.1	504	50.7	30.5	18.8	905
Looking after Home	7.2	19.7	73.1	152	47.0	34.0	19.0	347
Other	9.9	24.3	65.8	272	49.2	34.4	16.4	122

Table 8.38   *During the last 5 years, how often has the member donated money to party funds ? (%)*

Economic Sector	Labour				Conservative			
	Not at all	Occas- ionally	Freq- uently	N	Not at all	Occas- ionally	Freq- uently	N
All	9.6	51.3	39.1	2762	14.9	55.5	29.6	2325
Working F/T	7.8	50.4	41.8	1480	17.6	53.7	28.7	654
Working P/T	8.3	59.5	32.2	252	13.8	60.6	25.6	218
Unemployed	11.7	52.3	36.0	111	23.8	57.1	19.1	42
Retired	10.7	48.8	40.5	496	14.2	54.5	31.3	932
Looking after Home	16.4	52.6	31.0	152	11.8	57.2	31.0	355
Other	13.7	51.7	34.6	271	13.7	58.9	27.4	124

Table 8.39   *During the last 5 years, how often has the member delivered party leaflets ? (%)*

Economic Sector	Labour				Conservative			
	Not at all	Occas-ionally	Freq-uently	N	Not at all	Occas-ionally	Freq-uently	N
All	17.6	27.0	55.4	2720	60.9	16.9	22.2	2222
Working F/T	13.8	28.1	58.1	1467	61.8	15.8	22.4	638
Working P/T	13.1	28.3	58.6	251	59.4	15.7	24.9	217
Unemployed	16.4	20.0	63.6	110	69.0	19.0	12.0	42
Retired	28.2	24.3	47.5	482	61.7	16.8	21.5	864
Looking after Home	23.2	29.6	47.2	142	56.9	19.4	23.7	341
Other	21.6	26.5	51.9	268	62.5	18.3	19.2	120

Table 8.40   *During the last 5 years, how often has the member attended a party meeting ? (%)*

Economic Sector	Labour				Conservative			
	Not at all	Occas-ionally	Freq-uently	N	Not at all	Occas-ionally	Freq-uently	N
All	21.7	41.1	37.2	2717	50.4	32.8	16.8	2252
Working F/T	20.1	43.6	36.3	1468	53.7	29.6	16.7	639
Working P/T	25.0	43.5	31.5	248	54.8	31.3	13.9	217
Unemployed	16.2	38.7	45.1	111	53.5	32.6	13.9	43
Retired	22.4	32.9	44.7	477	48.0	34.3	17.7	892
Looking after Home	24.7	43.2	32.1	146	49.6	34.0	16.4	341
Other	24.0	39.7	36.3	267	44.2	38.3	17.5	120

Table 8.41   *During the last 5 years, how often has the member canvassed voters on behalf of the party ? (%)*

Economic Sector	Labour				Conservative			
	Not at all	Occas- ionally	Freq- uently	N	Not at all	Occas- ionally	Freq- uently	N
All	37.0	31.1	31.9	2700	74.8	14.8	10.4	2215
Working F/T	32.5	33.0	34.5	1465	72.3	15.7	12.0	643
Working P/T	41.8	32.1	26.1	249	74.6	13.1	12.3	213
Unemployed	34.2	27.9	37.9	111	75.6	22.0	2.4	41
Retired	42.9	28.5	28.6	466	75.9	15.0	9.1	867
Looking after Home	53.1	26.6	20.3	143	76.6	12.9	10.5	334
Other	39.5	28.2	32.3	266	75.2	13.7	11.1	117

Table 8.42   *Where would you place yourself on a Left/Right scale within the Labour/Conservative party ? (%)*

Economic Sector	Labour				Conservative			
	Left	Centre	Right	N	Left	Centre	Right	N
All	57.8	20.5	21.7	2786	13.3	26.1	60.6	2360
Working F/T	59.9	18.0	22.1	1481	18.9	27.5	53.6	657
Working P/T	59.5	22.0	18.5	254	12.6	32.7	54.7	223
Unemployed	61.8	22.7	15.5	110	15.4	15.4	69.2	39
Retired	61.8	25.2	13.0	516	10.0	24.1	65.9	942
Looking after Home	50.6	22.4	27.0	152	11.4	25.7	62.9	370
Other	49.3	21.6	29.1	273	16.3	27.1	56.6	129

Table 8.43   *Where would you place yourself on a Left/Right scale within British Politics ? (%)*

Economic Sector	Labour				Conservative			
	Left	Centre	Right	N	Left	Centre	Right	N
All	80.5	10.2	9.3	2785	3.7	18.3	78.0	2353
Working F/T	87.1	7.2	5.7	1480	3.8	19.3	76.9	657
Working P/T	85.8	9.9	4.3	253	3.2	25.7	71.1	222
Unemployed	76.4	10.9	12.7	110	5.3	7.9	86.8	38
Retired	64.8	16.4	18.8	517	3.8	16.8	79.4	938
Looking after Home	71.1	13.8	15.1	152	3.0	17.4	79.6	368
Other	78.5	12.5	9.0	273	4.6	16.2	79.2	130

Table 8.44   *What thermometer rating would the Labour/Conservative member give the Conservative Party ? (%)*

Economic Sector	Labour					Conservative				
	Cd	Cl	W	H	M	Cd	Cl	W	H	M
All	76.3	20.2	2.9	0.6	14.7	0.2	3.5	33.8	62.5	80.8
Working F/T	80.4	16.7	2.4	0.5	12.6	0.6	4.0	40.0	55.4	78.1
Working P/T	82.8	15.5	1.3	0.4	11.8	0.0	4.9	38.2	56.9	79.0
Unemployed	72.0	25.2	1.9	0.9	16.8	0.0	9.1	38.6	52.3	76.8
Retired	60.8	33.1	4.9	1.2	22.1	0.1	2.8	29.9	67.2	82.8
Looking after Home	80.3	16.9	2.1	0.7	13.4	0.0	2.2	29.0	68.8	82.9
Other	75.3	19.4	4.2	1.1	15.0	0.0	6.1	34.1	59.8	78.8

Table 8.45   *What thermometer rating would the Labour/Conservative member give the Labour Party ? (%)*

Economic Sector	Labour					Conservative				
	Cd	Cl	W	H	M	Cd	Cl	W	H	M
All	0.9	3.9	25.0	70.2	82.5	50.0	43.5	6.1	0.4	26.8
Working F/T	1.2	3.9	27.9	67.0	81.0	54.2	39.1	6.4	0.3	25.3
Working P/T	1.2	3.6	28.9	66.3	81.6	52.1	43.7	3.3	0.9	25.7
Unemployed	1.8	4.5	24.1	69.6	81.9	55.0	35.0	10.0	0.0	25.9
Retired	0.2	2.3	18.1	79.4	87.0	46.4	45.6	7.6	0.4	28.6
Looking after Home	0.7	2.7	12.0	84.6	86.9	48.9	46.8	3.7	0.6	26.1
Other	0.7	6.9	26.6	65.8	80.6	51.3	45.4	3.3	0.0	25.4

Table 8.46   *What thermometer rating would the Labour/Conservative member give the Liberal Democratic Party ? (%)*

Economic Sector	Labour					Conservative				
	Cd	Cl	W	H	M	Cd	Cl	W	H	M
All	33.1	44.2	20.8	1.9	36.8	32.8	50.6	15.4	1.2	36.2
Working F/T	33.9	44.5	20.7	0.9	35.8	34.9	48.1	16.0	1.0	35.8
Working P/T	38.0	41.7	19.4	0.9	33.9	35.5	48.1	14.5	1.9	34.8
Unemployed	36.1	40.7	21.3	1.9	36.7	36.6	29.3	34.1	0.0	39.5
Retired	28.1	45.5	22.4	4.0	40.9	32.2	53.1	13.4	1.3	35.9
Looking after Home	31.5	42.7	21.0	4.8	38.0	28.4	53.4	17.4	0.8	37.8
Other	33.2	44.5	20.0	2.3	37.2	32.0	50.0	16.4	1.6	37.6

Table 8.47   What thermometer rating would the Labour/Conservative member give the Scottish Nationalist Party ? (%)

Economic Sector	Labour					Conservative				
	Cd	Cl	W	H	M	Cd	Cl	W	H	M
All	44.1	36.9	16.1	2.9	32.1	68.9	26.7	4.0	0.4	19.0
Working F/T	45.4	36.3	15.4	2.9	31.5	72.0	25.2	2.8	0.0	17.3
Working P/T	40.9	37.0	19.2	2.9	32.8	64.4	33.1	2.5	0.0	20.2
Unemployed	49.0	30.6	17.3	3.1	30.2	70.6	26.5	2.9	0.0	19.0
Retired	40.7	42.7	14.3	2.3	32.7	67.5	27.4	4.4	0.7	20.1
Looking after Home	45.5	35.7	13.4	5.4	31.5	73.2	23.0	3.3	0.5	17.3
Other	43.0	32.6	21.3	3.1	34.7	59.2	28.6	12.2	0.0	24.0

Table 8.48   What thermometer rating would the Labour/Conservative member give Plaid Cymru ? (%)

Economic Sector	Labour					Conservative				
	Cd	Cl	W	H	M	Cd	Cl	W	H	M
All	47.5	37.5	13.0	2.0	29.6	82.6	16.1	1.1	0.2	12.9
Working F/T	47.5	36.5	14.0	2.0	30.1	83.2	15.3	1.1	0.4	11.9
Working P/T	47.1	37.7	12.7	2.5	30.1	77.5	21.2	1.3	0.0	15.2
Unemployed	50.5	35.8	11.6	2.1	26.4	81.3	15.6	3.1	0.0	12.5
Retired	46.5	43.8	9.0	0.7	28.4	82.8	16.2	0.8	0.2	13.2
Looking after Home	52.7	31.3	12.5	3.5	27.3	86.0	13.1	0.9	0.0	11.8
Other	46.1	35.5	16.6	1.8	31.5	78.6	17.9	2.4	1.1	15.0

Table 8.49   *What thermometer rating would the Labour/Conservative member give the Green Party ? (%)*

Economic Sector	Labour					Conservative				
	Cd	Cl	W	H	M	Cd	Cl	W	H	M
All	33.2	36.8	25.8	4.2	39.5	70.0	24.5	5.0	0.5	19.2
Working F/T	31.5	37.4	26.3	4.8	40.2	70.6	24.2	4.7	0.5	18.9
Working P/T	27.0	33.8	31.2	8.0	44.3	60.7	31.8	7.5	0.0	22.9
Unemployed	39.4	31.2	28.4	1.0	36.7	69.4	25.0	5.6	0.0	19.6
Retired	37.7	39.0	20.2	3.1	35.3	72.9	22.4	3.8	0.9	18.5
Looking after Home	34.5	28.1	25.9	11.5	41.8	69.6	24.1	6.3	0.0	20.1
Other	37.8	29.4	26.7	6.1	38.3	65.3	27.7	6.9	0.1	21.9

Table 8.50   *What thermometer rating would the Labour/Conservative member give the BBC ? (%)*

Economic Sector	Labour					Conservative				
	Cd	Cl	W	H	M	Cd	Cl	W	H	M
All	9.5	26.1	39.6	24.8	60.3	8.4	30.6	40.5	20.5	59.3
Working F/T	8.0	24.0	41.2	26.8	61.8	8.5	31.8	40.0	19.7	59.0
Working P/T	8.5	26.2	36.3	29.0	62.3	7.0	26.0	40.9	26.1	61.8
Unemployed	15.7	27.8	38.0	18.5	54.8	11.6	34.9	37.2	16.3	54.8
Retired	10.3	31.8	35.3	22.6	58.3	8.6	32.5	38.6	20.3	58.8
Looking after Home	10.8	23.6	44.6	21.0	59.5	7.7	24.4	47.2	20.7	61.2
Other	13.4	28.0	39.9	18.7	56.9	9.8	35.0	37.4	17.8	56.9

Table 8.51   *What thermometer rating would the Labour/Conservative member give the European Community ? (%)*

Economic Sector	Labour					Conservative				
	Cd	Cl	W	H	M	Cd	Cl	W	H	M
All	11.2	32.4	41.8	14.6	55.4	14.3	20.8	35.7	29.2	50.7
Working F/T	9.9	32.3	43.7	14.1	56.1	14.6	39.1	35.8	10.5	51.6
Working P/T	13.5	33.2	38.4	14.9	53.8	11.4	43.4	36.1	9.1	51.9
Unemployed	19.6	32.0	35.1	13.3	49.7	26.3	31.6	26.3	15.8	47.1
Retired	9.7	33.7	40.9	15.7	56.8	14.1	40.6	36.5	8.8	50.7
Looking after Home	17.1	28.7	37.2	17.0	52.1	13.3	44.1	35.9	6.7	49.7
Other	12.4	32.3	41.0	14.3	54.6	16.2	41.9	32.4	9.5	48.7

Table 8.52   *What thermometer rating would the Labour/Conservative member give the Trade Union Congress ? (%)*

Economic Sector	Labour					Conservative				
	Cd	Cl	W	H	M	Cd	Cl	W	H	M
All	5.8	28.9	47.8	17.5	59.9	53.7	39.9	5.6	0.8	26.3
Working F/T	6.0	31.2	47.2	15.6	58.8	54.9	39.0	5.6	0.5	25.6
Working P/T	3.3	26.6	53.9	16.2	61.0	51.4	45.7	2.1	0.8	26.5
Unemployed	11.8	23.5	36.3	28.4	60.8	54.3	31.4	14.3	0.0	26.2
Retired	4.9	24.5	47.7	22.9	62.9	50.4	40.9	7.4	1.3	28.2
Looking after Home	5.1	29.9	46.0	19.0	60.9	58.7	37.4	2.9	1.0	24.2
Other	6.3	27.6	51.2	14.9	59.3	58.1	38.7	3.2	0.0	22.7

Table 8.53   *What thermometer rating would the Labour/Conservative member give the Police ? (%)*

Economic Sector	Labour					Conservative				
	Cd	Cl	W	H	M	Cd	Cl	W	H	M
All	17.8	44.6	28.4	9.2	47.9	1.4	12.5	39.9	46.2	73.0
Working F/T	20.0	48.5	24.8	6.7	45.2	1.4	18.4	40.3	39.9	70.1
Working P/T	20.6	48.2	25.1	6.1	45.2	2.7	10.9	40.7	45.7	72.0
Unemployed	24.3	39.3	23.4	13.0	46.4	0.0	19.0	33.3	47.7	71.9
Retired	11.7	34.0	38.3	16.0	55.9	1.0	9.7	40.1	49.2	74.6
Looking after Home	9.2	43.0	35.9	11.9	54.7	0.9	8.3	39.0	51.8	75.4
Other	16.5	42.5	31.2	9.8	48.2	3.2	15.1	39.9	41.8	70.9

Table 8.54   *What thermometer rating would the Labour/Conservative member give the House of Commons ? (%)*

Economic Sector	Labour					Conservative				
	Cd	Cl	W	H	M	Cd	Cl	W	H	M
All	10.3	33.5	38.2	18.0	56.8	2.4	17.0	49.2	31.4	68.3
Working F/T	11.0	34.5	38.5	16.0	55.3	1.8	20.6	48.5	29.1	67.2
Working P/T	9.3	37.0	36.6	17.1	56.2	3.4	15.2	56.9	24.5	66.7
Unemployed	13.3	39.0	31.4	16.3	53.3	5.3	13.2	55.3	26.2	66.7
Retired	8.4	29.8	36.8	25.0	61.4	2.3	14.2	48.2	35.3	69.9
Looking after Home	5.6	21.8	52.8	19.8	62.5	2.2	16.9	50.8	30.1	68.6
Other	12.0	35.7	35.3	17.0	55.2	5.0	23.1	39.7	32.2	65.6

Table 8.55   *What thermometer rating would the Labour/Conservative member give the CBI ? (%)*

Economic Sector	Labour					Conservative				
	Cd	Cl	W	H	M	Cd	Cl	W	H	M
All	44.6	42.2	11.3	1.9	30.8	5.5	29.8	49.0	15.7	59.5
Working F/T	47.0	42.5	9.2	1.3	29.3	5.0	34.3	47.2	13.5	57.8
Working P/T	47.8	42.5	9.2	0.5	29.0	4.3	31.6	47.9	16.2	60.0
Unemployed	49.5	38.7	10.8	1.0	28.5	10.3	37.9	44.8	7.0	53.4
Retired	36.3	42.0	17.5	4.2	36.0	5.9	28.5	49.8	15.8	60.4
Looking after Home	34.2	46.2	16.2	3.4	36.9	5.0	21.2	54.2	19.6	62.3
Other	45.4	40.6	12.2	1.8	30.4	7.1	26.2	46.4	20.3	59.7

Table 8.56   *What thermometer rating would the Labour/Conservative member give the Queen ? (%)*

Economic Sector	Labour					Conservative				
	Cd	Cl	W	H	M	Cd	Cl	W	H	M
All	34.8	29.6	19.3	16.3	43.0	1.0	4.7	15.8	78.5	86.4
Working F/T	40.9	31.5	17.7	9.9	37.6	2.3	7.8	20.1	69.8	81.8
Working P/T	37.3	32.8	18.4	11.5	39.0	0.5	6.3	19.8	73.4	84.9
Unemployed	33.6	24.3	16.8	25.3	46.9	2.4	9.5	16.7	71.4	81.8
Retired	21.2	24.5	23.3	31.0	56.1	0.2	3.3	12.7	83.8	89.1
Looking after Home	21.1	31.7	21.8	25.4	52.2	0.0	1.1	13.1	85.8	89.8
Other	32.5	27.2	21.3	19.0	45.5	2.3	3.9	17.2	76.6	84.8

Table 8.57   *What thermometer rating would the Labour/Conservative member*
               give Judges ? (%)

Economic Sector	Labour					Conservative				
	Cd	Cl	W	H	M	Cd	Cl	W	H	M
All	38.3	43.4	14.7	3.6	34.8	4.4	31.0	45.7	18.9	60.5
Working F/T	41.7	43.6	12.4	2.3	32.3	5.3	36.7	43.4	14.6	57.5
Working P/T	41.4	45.6	10.0	3.0	32.9	4.0	36.3	44.3	15.4	59.1
Unemployed	39.8	42.7	12.6	4.9	33.4	7.7	25.6	43.6	23.1	61.5
Retired	28.7	42.8	23.0	5.5	41.7	3.2	26.9	49.3	20.6	62.6
Looking after Home	28.7	49.3	16.2	5.8	39.4	4.8	24.8	47.6	22.8	62.6
Other	37.8	38.6	17.5	6.1	36.6	6.0	36.8	33.3	23.9	60.0

9   Trade Union Membership

Table 9.1   *The Labour/Conservative party should try to capture the middle ground in politics (%)*

TU Membership	Labour				Conservative			
	Agree	Neith-er	Dis-agree	N	Agree	Neith-er	Dis-agree	N
All	50.6	12.1	37.3	2771	70.1	13.2	16.7	2191
TU Member	46.6	12.6	40.8	1770	61.9	16.4	21.7	226
Non-TU Member	57.8	11.2	31.0	1001	71.0	12.9	16.1	1965

Table 9.2   *A Labour/Conservative government should introduce a prices and incomes policy as a means of controlling inflation (%)*

TU Membership	Labour				Conservative			
	Agree	Neith-er	Dis-agree	N	Agree	Neith-er	Dis-agree	N
All	57.0	19.1	23.9	2770	42.5	11.7	45.8	2236
TU Member	52.7	20.2	27.1	1765	39.8	13.0	47.2	231
Non-TU Member	64.5	17.1	18.4	1005	42.8	11.5	45.7	2005

Table 9.3   *Income and wealth should be re-distributed towards ordinary working people (%)*

TU Membership	Labour				Conservative			
	Agree	Neith-er	Dis-agree	N	Agree	Neith-er	Dis-agree	N
All	85.9	9.1	5.0	2804	25.5	20.2	54.3	2234
TU Member	87.4	8.1	4.5	1787	29.7	24.1	46.2	236
Non-TU Member	83.3	10.9	5.8	1017	25.0	19.8	55.2	1998

Table 9.4   *The Labour/Conservative Party should always stand by its principles even if this should lose it an election (%)*

TU Membership	Labour				Conservative			
	Agree	Neith-er	Dis-agree	N	Agree	Neith-er	Dis-agree	N
All	67.5	12.0	20.5	2799	81.5	8.4	10.1	2288
TU Member	64.8	13.0	22.2	1779	70.1	14.5	15.4	234
Non-TU Member	72.0	10.5	17.5	1020	82.8	7.7	9.5	2054

Table 9.5   *Further nuclear energy development is essential for the future prosperity of Britain (%)*

TU Membership	Labour				Conservative			
	Agree	Neith-er	Dis-agree	N	Agree	Neith-er	Dis-agree	N
All	13.9	11.8	74.3	2789	59.8	16.9	23.3	2249
TU Member	13.0	11.6	75.4	1782	56.4	16.2	27.4	234
Non-TU Member	15.4	12.3	72.3	1007	60.1	17.1	22.8	2015

Table 9.6   *A future Labour/Conservative government should not agree to a single European currency (%)*

TU Membership	Labour				Conservative			
	Agree	Neith-er	Dis-agree	N	Agree	Neith-er	Dis-agree	N
All	24.9	19.2	55.9	2777	57.8	12.3	29.9	2269
TU Member	21.9	19.8	58.3	1773	51.9	11.5	36.6	235
Non-TU Member	30.2	18.0	51.8	1004	58.5	12.4	29.1	2034

Table 9.7   *High income tax makes people less willing to work hard (%)*

TU Membership	Labour				Conservative			
	Agree	Neith-er	Dis-agree	N	Agree	Neith-er	Dis-agree	N
All	25.9	10.8	63.3	2804	81.6	6.2	12.2	2290
TU Member	22.0	11.0	67.0	1790	76.7	11.9	11.4	236
Non-TU Member	32.7	10.6	56.7	1014	82.1	5.6	12.3	2054

Table 9.8   *Britain's electoral system should be replaced by a system of proportional representation (%)*

TU Membership	Labour				Conservative			
	Agree	Neith-er	Dis-agree	N	Agree	Neith-er	Dis-agree	N
All	58.1	13.0	28.9	2806	21.5	11.9	66.6	2256
TU Member	56.6	13.6	29.8	1786	24.0	14.6	61.4	233
Non-TU Member	60.7	12.0	27.3	1020	21.2	11.6	67.2	2023

Table 9.9   *Further moves towards integration within the European Community should be resisted (%)*

TU Membership	Labour				Conservative			
	Agree	Neith-er	Dis-agree	N	Agree	Neith-er	Dis-agree	N
All	21.6	13.1	65.3	2797	54.2	15.5	30.3	2267
TU Member	19.4	12.3	68.3	1785	39.5	20.2	40.3	233
Non-TU Member	25.4	14.7	59.9	1012	55.9	14.9	29.2	2034

Table 9.10   There is no need for a Bill of Rights in this country (%)

TU Membership	Labour					Conservative			
	Agree	Neith-er	Dis-agree	N		Agree	Neith-er	Dis-agree	N
All	11.1	10.0	78.9	2783		40.0	26.5	33.5	2184
TU Member	9.6	8.7	81.7	1777		29.5	30.0	40.5	227
Non-TU Member	14.0	12.0	74.0	1006		41.2	26.1	32.7	1957

Table 9.11   A future Labour/Conservative government should introduce a directly elected Scottish Assembly with taxing powers (%)

TU Membership	Labour					Conservative			
	Agree	Neith-er	Dis-agree	N		Agree	Neith-er	Dis-agree	N
All	61.1	22.3	16.6	2800		22.9	26.3	50.8	2231
TU Member	63.0	21.9	15.1	1785		25.8	31.4	42.8	229
Non-TU Member	57.9	23.0	19.1	1015		22.6	25.7	51.7	2002

Table 9.12   Coalition governments are the best form of government for Britain (%)

TU Membership	Labour					Conservative			
	Agree	Neith-er	Dis-agree	N		Agree	Neith-er	Dis-agree	N
All	8.6	16.7	74.7	2801		9.5	10.0	80.5	2292
TU Member	6.7	17.3	76.0	1791		8.9	10.5	80.6	235
Non-TU Member	11.9	15.7	72.4	1010		9.6	9.9	80.5	2057

Table 9.13 *A future Labour/Conservative government should/should not spend money to get rid of poverty (%)*

TU Membership	Labour				Conservative			
	Should	Doesn't matter	Should not	N	Should	Doesn't matter	Should not	N
All	98.0	1.0	1.0	2795	80.2	8.4	11.4	2248
TU Member	98.3	1.0	0.7	1781	79.0	12.2	8.8	229
Non-TU Member	97.6	0.9	1.5	1014	80.3	8.0	11.7	2019

Table 9.14 *A future Labour/Conservative government should/should not encourage the growth of private medicine (%)*

TU Membership	Labour				Conservative			
	Should	Doesn't matter	Should not	N	Should	Doesn't matter	Should not	N
All	3.6	4.7	91.7	2790	51.9	16.0	32.1	2255
TU Member	3.3	4.2	92.5	1781	43.6	17.1	39.3	234
Non-TU Member	4.1	5.5	90.4	1009	52.8	15.9	31.3	2021

Table 9.15 *A future Labour/Conservative government should/should not put more money into the National Health Service (%)*

TU Membership	Labour				Conservative			
	Should	Doesn't matter	Should not	N	Should	Doesn't matter	Should not	N
All	98.0	0.7	1.3	2801	79.5	7.6	12.9	2263
TU Member	98.1	0.8	1.1	1784	78.7	8.1	13.2	235
Non-TU Member	97.8	0.5	1.7	1017	79.5	7.5	13.0	2028

Table 9.16   *A future Labour/Conservative government should/should not reduce spending in general (%)*

TU Membership	Labour				Conservative			
	Should	Doesn't matter	Should not	N	Should	Doesn't matter	Should not	N
All	19.2	7.2	73.6	2758	60.6	8.9	30.5	2244
TU Member	17.3	6.9	75.8	1768	54.7	12.1	33.2	232
Non-TU Member	22.6	7.9	69.5	990	61.2	8.6	30.2	2012

Table 9.17   *A future Labour/Conservative government should/should not introduce stricter laws to regulate the trade unions (%)*

TU Membership	Labour				Conservative			
	Should	Doesn't matter	Should not	N	Should	Doesn't matter	Should not	N
All	9.8	14.7	75.5	2768	66.5	12.2	21.3	2268
TU Member	7.1	13.4	79.5	1769	47.6	15.1	37.3	233
Non-TU Member	14.6	17.0	68.4	999	68.7	11.8	19.5	2035

Table 9.18   *A future Labour/Conservative government should/should not give workers more say in the places where they work (%)*

TU Membership	Labour				Conservative			
	Should	Doesn't matter	Should not	N	Should	Doesn't matter	Should not	N
All	91.1	5.7	3.2	2792	63.7	13.4	22.9	2276
TU Member	91.4	5.1	3.5	1782	65.5	13.6	20.9	235
Non-TU Member	90.5	6.7	2.8	1010	63.4	13.4	23.2	2041

Table 9.19   *A future Labour/Conservative government should/should not spend less on defence (%)*

TU Membership	Labour				Conservative			
	Should	Doesn't matter	Should not	N	Should	Doesn't matter	Should not	N
All	82.9	4.8	12.3	2795	44.0	5.0	51.0	2263
TU Member	83.1	4.9	12.0	1783	44.4	6.3	49.1	234
Non-TU Member	82.5	4.6	12.9	1012	43.9	4.9	51.2	2029

Table 9.20   *Should a future Labour/Conservative government :*
(A) Reduce taxes & spend less on health, education & social benefits ?
(B) Keep taxes & spending on these services at the same levels as now ?
(C) Increase taxes & spend more on health, education & social benefits ?

TU Membership	Labour				Conservative			
	A	B	C	N	A	B	C	N
All	2.7	6.3	91.0	2793	6.5	67.1	26.4	2260
TU Member	3.1	5.4	91.5	1778	3.1	65.9	31.0	232
Non-TU Member	2.0	7.9	90.1	1015	6.9	67.2	25.9	2028

Table 9.21   *On joining the Labour/Conservative party did the member approach the party (MA) or did the party approach the member (PA) ? (%)*

TU Membership	Labour				Conservative			
	MA	Don't Know	PA	N	MA	Don't Know	PA	N
All	77.6	19.8	2.6	2823	34.6	50.3	15.1	2303
TU Member	80.0	17.9	2.1	1795	36.9	51.1	12.0	233
Non-TU Member	73.5	23.2	3.3	1028	34.3	50.2	15.5	2070

224

Table 9.22   *How often has the member attended a party meeting in the last 12 months ? (%)*

TU Membership	Labour				Conservative			
	Not at all	Occas-ionally	Frequ-ently	N	Not at all	Occas-ionally	Frequ-ently	N
All	41.7	30.5	27.8	2837	66.0	21.9	12.1	2320
TU Member	37.7	32.1	30.2	1802	70.5	20.9	8.6	234
Non-TU Member	48.7	27.6	23.7	1035	65.5	22.1	12.4	2086

Table 9.23   *Is the member more or less politically active than 5 years ago ? (%)*

TU Membership	Labour				Conservative			
	More active	About same	Less active	N	More active	About same	Less active	N
All	13.0	38.6	48.4	2801	9.6	62.6	27.8	1943
TU Member	13.9	38.3	47.8	1783	7.5	71.0	21.5	186
Non-TU Member	11.2	39.3	49.5	1018	9.7	61.8	28.5	1757

Table 9.24   *Does the member hold any office within the Labour/Conservative Party ? (%)*

TU Membership	Labour			Conservative		
	Yes	No	N	Yes	No	N
All	16.0	84.0	2789	8.2	91.8	2291
TU Member	18.9	81.1	1774	9.1	90.9	232
Non-TU Member	11.0	89.0	1015	8.2	91.8	2059

Table 9.25 *How much time does the member devote to party activities per month ? (%)*

TU Membership	Labour					Conservative				
	None	Up to 5 hrs	5 to 10 hrs	Over 10 hrs	N	None	Up to 5 hrs	5 to 10 hrs	Over 10 hrs	N
All	51.3	29.6	9.3	9.8	2796	76.0	15.5	4.4	4.1	2278
TU Member	47.1	31.2	9.9	11.8	1783	77.6	15.5	2.6	4.3	232
Non-TU Member	58.6	26.8	8.3	6.3	1013	75.9	15.4	4.6	4.1	2046

Table 9.26 *What was the overall financial contribution made by the member in the last year ? (%)*

TU Membership	Labour				Conservative			
	0 to £10	£10 to £20	Over £20	N	0 to £10	£10 to £20	Over £20	N
All	24.0	19.6	56.4	2492	33.8	21.7	44.5	1712
TU Member	18.5	19.6	61.9	1618	38.5	20.7	40.8	179
Non-TU Member	34.1	19.7	46.2	874	33.3	21.8	44.9	1533

Table 9.27 *Is the member a local Labour/Conservative councillor ? (%)*

TU Membership	Labour			Conservative		
	Yes	No	N	Yes	No	N
All	7.9	92.1	2813	2.2	97.8	2306
TU Member	9.4	90.6	1789	2.6	97.4	235
Non-TU Member	5.3	94.7	1024	2.1	97.9	2071

Table 9.28   *The Labour/Conservative leader should be elected by a system of one*
party member/one vote (%)

TU Membership	Labour				Conservative			
	Agree	Neith-er	Dis-agree	N	Agree	Neith-er	Dis-agree	N
All	85.9	5.4	8.7	2811	50.0	14.3	35.7	2248
TU Member	84.8	5.5	9.7	1788	47.2	19.8	33.0	233
Non-TU Member	87.9	5.3	6.8	1023	50.3	13.7	36.0	2015

Table 9.29   *People like me can have a real influence in politics if they are*
prepared to get involved (%)

TU Membership	Labour				Conservative			
	Agree	Neith-er	Dis-agree	N	Agree	Neith-er	Dis-agree	N
All	65.6	16.1	18.3	2804	56.1	20.4	23.5	2252
TU Member	66.0	15.5	18.5	1785	58.9	19.5	21.6	231
Non-TU Member	65.0	17.0	18.0	1019	55.8	20.4	23.8	2021

Table 9.30   *Attending party meetings can be pretty tiring after a hard days*
work (%)

TU Membership	Labour				Conservative			
	Agree	Neith-er	Dis-agree	N	Agree	Neith-er	Dis-agree	N
All	77.2	11.4	11.4	2807	69.0	19.6	11.4	2237
TU Member	80.4	9.4	10.2	1789	70.3	18.9	10.8	232
Non-TU Member	71.5	14.9	13.6	1018	68.9	19.7	11.4	2005

Table 9.31   Someone like me could do a good job of being a local councillor (%)

TU Membership	Labour				Conservative			
	Agree	Neith-er	Dis-agree	N	Agree	Neith-er	Dis-agree	N
All	48.5	22.1	29.4	2783	27.1	24.4	48.5	2223
TU Member	52.4	22.1	25.5	1776	33.0	24.8	42.2	230
Non-TU Member	41.7	22.0	36.3	1007	26.4	24.4	49.2	1993

Table 9.32   Being an active party member is a good way of meeting interesting people (%)

TU Membership	Labour				Conservative			
	Agree	Neith-er	Dis-agree	N	Agree	Neith-er	Dis-agree	N
All	64.2	22.2	13.6	2801	59.8	29.7	10.5	2227
TU Member	62.5	23.2	14.3	1786	50.9	34.3	14.8	230
Non-TU Member	67.3	20.3	12.4	1015	60.8	29.1	10.1	1997

Table 9.33   The only way to be really educated about politics is to be a party activist (%)

TU Membership	Labour				Conservative			
	Agree	Neith-er	Dis-agree	N	Agree	Neith-er	Dis-agree	N
All	41.5	11.2	47.3	2809	35.9	17.3	46.8	2231
TU Member	41.4	11.1	47.5	1794	29.4	18.2	52.4	231
Non-TU Member	41.7	11.3	47.0	1015	36.7	17.2	46.1	2000

Table 9.34   *The party leadership does not pay a lot of attention to ordinary party members (%)*

TU Membership	Labour				Conservative			
	Agree	Neith-er	Dis-agree	N	Agree	Neith-er	Dis-agree	N
All	46.9	19.1	34.0	2809	42.4	24.1	33.5	2241
TU Member	47.9	19.1	33.0	1793	40.6	28.0	31.4	229
Non-TU Member	45.1	19.0	35.9	1016	42.6	23.7	33.7	2012

Table 9.35   *Party activity often takes time away from one's family (%)*

TU Membership	Labour				Conservative			
	Agree	Neith-er	Dis-agree	N	Agree	Neith-er	Dis-agree	N
All	85.0	10.6	4.4	2805	67.4	25.3	7.3	2212
TU Member	86.2	9.7	4.1	1787	67.8	25.7	6.5	230
Non-TU Member	82.7	12.3	5.0	1018	67.3	25.3	7.4	1982

Table 9.36   *The Labour/Conservative party would be more successful if people like me were elected to parliament (%)*

TU Membership	Labour				Conservative			
	Agree	Neith-er	Dis-agree	N	Agree	Neith-er	Dis-agree	N
All	33.7	34.0	32.3	2783	20.9	31.7	47.4	2202
TU Member	33.7	35.7	30.6	1772	23.2	36.5	40.3	233
Non-TU Member	33.6	31.1	35.3	1011	20.7	31.1	48.2	1969

Table 9.37   *During the last 5 years, how often has the member displayed an election poster in his/her window ? (%)*

TU Membership	Labour				Conservative			
	Not at all	Occas-ionally	Freq-uently	N	Not at all	Occas-ionally	Freq-uently	N
All	9.6	21.7	68.7	2782	49.0	31.8	19.2	2208
TU Member	8.5	20.0	71.5	1783	49.6	31.0	19.4	226
Non-TU Member	11.5	24.7	63.8	999	49.0	31.9	19.1	1982

Table 9.38   *During the last 5 years, how often has the member donated money to party funds ? (%)*

TU Membership	Labour				Conservative			
	Not at all	Occas-ionally	Freq-uently	N	Not at all	Occas-ionally	Freq-uently	N
All	9.6	50.9	39.5	2778	14.9	55.2	29.9	2252
TU Member	7.7	49.9	42.4	1784	14.2	50.9	34.9	232
Non-TU Member	13.2	52.7	34.1	994	14.9	55.7	29.4	2020

Table 9.39   *During the last 5 years, how often has the member delivered party leaflets ? (%)*

TU Membership	Labour				Conservative			
	Not at all	Occas-ionally	Freq-uently	N	Not at all	Occas-ionally	Freq-uently	N
All	17.3	27.2	55.5	2735	61.4	16.7	21.9	2157
TU Member	13.5	26.8	59.7	1766	63.6	16.8	19.6	225
Non-TU Member	24.3	27.9	47.8	969	49.0	31.9	19.1	1932

Table 9.40   *During the last 5 years, how often has the member attended a party meeting ? (%)*

TU Membership	Labour				Conservative			
	Not at all	Occas-ionally	Freq-uently	N	Not at all	Occas-ionally	Freq-uently	N
All	21.5	41.1	37.4	2741	50.8	32.5	16.7	2189
TU Member	18.3	41.1	40.6	1764	55.8	28.3	15.9	226
Non-TU Member	27.3	41.0	31.7	977	50.3	33.0	16.7	1963

Table 9.41   *During the last 5 years, how often has the member canvassed voters on behalf of the party ? (%)*

TU Membership	Labour				Conservative			
	Not at all	Occas-ionally	Freq-uently	N	Not at all	Occas-ionally	Freq-uently	N
All	37.1	31.1	31.8	2717	75.1	14.7	10.2	2154
TU Member	31.7	32.4	35.9	1757	76.1	13.3	10.6	226
Non-TU Member	47.0	28.9	24.1	960	75.0	14.9	10.1	1928

Table 9.42   *Where would you place yourself on a Left/Right scale within the Labour/Conservative party ? (%)*

TU Membership	Labour				Conservative			
	Left	Centre	Right	N	Left	Centre	Right	N
All	57.6	20.6	21.8	2810	13.2	25.9	60.9	2276
TU Member	60.9	19.0	20.1	1791	5.2	22.1	72.7	229
Non-TU Member	51.8	23.4	24.8	1019	12.5	25.3	62.2	2047

Table 9.43   *Where would you place yourself on a Left/Right scale within British Politics ? (%)*

TU Membership	Labour				Conservative			
	Left	Centre	Right	N	Left	Centre	Right	N
All	80.1	10.4	9.5	2807	3.8	18.2	78.0	2269
TU Member	83.7	8.7	7.6	1791	5.2	22.1	72.7	231
Non-TU Member	73.7	13.4	12.9	1016	3.6	17.8	78.6	2038

Table 9.44   *What thermometer rating would the Labour/Conservative member give the Conservative Party ? (%)*

TU Membership	Labour					Conservative				
	Cd	Cl	W	H	M	Cd	Cl	W	H	M
All	76.1	20.3	3.0	0.6	14.7	0.2	3.6	33.5	62.7	80.9
TU Member	78.7	18.1	2.7	0.5	13.4	0.9	5.5	38.7	54.9	77.4
Non-TU Member	71.3	24.4	3.5	0.8	17.1	0.1	3.4	32.9	63.6	81.3

Table 9.45   *What thermometer rating would the Labour/Conservative member give the Labour Party ? (%)*

TU Membership	Labour					Conservative				
	Cd	Cl	W	H	M	Cd	Cl	W	H	M
All	1.0	3.8	24.9	70.3	82.6	50.0	43.5	6.0	0.5	26.8
TU Member	1.0	3.7	25.8	69.5	82.3	43.7	45.0	10.0	1.3	29.6
Non-TU Member	1.0	4.0	23.4	71.6	83.0	50.8	43.3	5.5	0.4	26.5

Table 9.46   *What thermometer rating would the Labour/Conservative member give the Liberal Democratic Party ? (%)*

TU Membership	Labour					Conservative				
	Cd	Cl	W	H	M	Cd	Cl	W	H	M
All	32.9	44.5	20.8	1.8	36.9	32.6	50.8	15.4	1.2	36.4
TU Member	35.8	43.7	19.2	1.3	35.2	28.7	53.9	15.2	2.2	38.3
Non-TU Member	27.7	46.1	23.6	2.6	39.9	33.0	50.4	15.4	1.2	36.1

Table 9.47   *What thermometer rating would the Labour/Conservative member give the Scottish Nationalist Party ? (%)*

TU Membership	Labour					Conservative				
	Cd	Cl	W	H	M	Cd	Cl	W	H	M
All	44.0	37.1	16.0	2.9	32.2	68.7	27.1	4.0	0.2	19.2
TU Member	45.0	36.2	16.3	2.5	31.7	68.8	27.3	3.9	0.0	18.7
Non-TU Member	42.0	38.9	15.5	3.6	33.1	68.7	27.1	4.0	0.2	19.3

Table 9.48   *What thermometer rating would the Labour/Conservative member give Plaid Cymru ? (%)*

TU Membership	Labour					Conservative				
	Cd	Cl	W	H	M	Cd	Cl	W	H	M
All	47.5	37.6	13.0	1.9	29.7	82.3	16.3	1.1	0.3	13.1
TU Member	47.9	36.7	13.8	1.6	29.8	79.8	16.6	3.1	0.5	14.5
Non-TU Member	46.8	39.3	11.5	2.4	29.6	82.6	16.3	0.9	0.2	12.9

Table 9.49   *What thermometer rating would the Labour/Conservative member give the Green Party ? (%)*

TU Membership	Labour					Conservative				
	Cd	Cl	W	H	M	Cd	Cl	W	H	M
All	33.1	35.9	25.9	5.1	39.6	69.9	24.4	5.2	0.5	19.7
TU Member	33.1	36.7	25.5	4.7	39.5	67.2	27.1	5.2	0.5	19.6
Non-TU Member	33.1	34.3	26.6	6.0	39.7	70.2	24.1	5.2	0.5	19.7

Table 9.50   *What thermometer rating would the Labour/Conservative member give the BBC ? (%)*

TU Membership	Labour					Conservative				
	Cd	Cl	W	H	M	Cd	Cl	W	H	M
All	9.2	26.3	39.8	24.7	60.5	8.3	30.6	40.2	20.9	59.5
TU Member	8.7	27.2	40.2	23.9	60.3	7.9	31.7	37.9	22.5	59.2
Non-TU Member	10.1	24.6	39.1	26.2	60.7	8.4	30.4	40.5	20.7	59.5

Table 9.51   *What thermometer rating would the Labour/Conservative member give the European Community ? (%)*

TU Membership	Labour					Conservative				
	Cd	Cl	W	H	M	Cd	Cl	W	H	M
All	11.1	32.6	41.7	14.6	55.5	14.2	40.4	35.8	9.6	50.9
TU Member	10.4	32.5	42.9	14.2	55.8	16.8	34.2	32.7	16.3	52.0
Non-TU Member	12.3	32.8	39.5	15.5	55.1	13.8	41.3	36.3	8.6	50.8

Table 9.52   *What thermometer rating would the Labour/Conservative member give the Trade Union Congress ? (%)*

TU Membership	Labour					Conservative				
	Cd	Cl	W	H	M	Cd	Cl	W	H	M
All	5.7	29.0	47.5	17.8	60.0	53.4	39.9	5.8	0.9	26.4
TU Member	5.2	27.4	48.9	18.5	60.1	46.5	40.6	10.7	2.2	31.1
Non-TU Member	6.5	32.1	45.0	16.4	58.7	54.4	39.8	5.1	0.7	25.8

Table 9.53   *What thermometer rating would the Labour/Conservative member give the Police ? (%)*

TU Membership	Labour					Conservative				
	Cd	Cl	W	H	M	Cd	Cl	W	H	M
All	17.9	44.4	28.4	9.3	48.0	1.4	12.7	39.6	46.3	72.9
TU Member	20.0	46.1	26.3	7.6	46.0	1.8	14.3	42.6	41.3	71.6
Non-TU Member	14.1	41.3	32.3	12.3	51.5	1.4	12.5	39.3	46.8	73.1

Table 9.54   *What thermometer rating would the Labour/Conservative member give the House of Commons ? (%)*

TU Membership	Labour					Conservative				
	Cd	Cl	W	H	M	Cd	Cl	W	H	M
All	10.1	33.8	38.1	18.0	56.7	2.4	16.9	49.1	31.6	68.4
TU Member	11.3	34.5	37.6	16.6	55.6	3.1	17.5	50.7	28.7	67.0
Non-TU Member	8.0	32.6	38.9	20.5	58.8	2.4	16.8	48.9	31.9	68.6

Table 9.55   **What thermometer rating would the Labour/Conservative member give the CBI ? (%)**

TU Membership	Labour					Conservative				
	Cd	Cl	W	H	M	Cd	Cl	W	H	M
All	45.0	41.7	11.2	2.1	30.9	5.4	29.3	49.2	16.1	59.8
TU Member	47.6	40.3	10.7	1.4	29.4	5.8	41.3	42.6	10.3	55.5
Non-TU Member	40.0	44.4	12.1	3.5	33.8	5.6	27.6	50.0	16.8	60.4

Table 9.56   **What thermometer rating would the Labour/Conservative member give the Queen ? (%)**

TU Membership	Labour					Conservative				
	Cd	Cl	W	H	M	Cd	Cl	W	H	M
All	34.8	29.3	19.4	16.5	43.3	0.9	4.6	15.9	78.6	86.5
TU Member	38.0	30.9	18.0	13.1	39.7	1.8	6.0	18.0	74.2	83.6
Non-TU Member	29.0	26.6	21.9	22.5	49.6	0.8	4.4	15.7	79.1	86.8

Table 9.57   **What thermometer rating would the Labour/Conservative member give Judges ? (%)**

TU Membership	Labour					Conservative				
	Cd	Cl	W	H	M	Cd	Cl	W	H	M
All	38.1	43.6	14.8	3.5	34.9	4.7	31.1	45.3	18.9	60.5
TU Member	41.8	42.1	13.6	2.5	32.8	4.6	37.4	41.6	16.4	58.4
Non-TU Member	31.4	46.4	17.1	5.1	38.7	4.6	30.3	45.8	19.3	60.8

10 Gender

Table 10.1   *The Labour/Conservative party should try to capture the middle ground in politics (%)*

Gender	Labour				Conservative			
	Agree	Neith-er	Dis-agree	N	Agree	Neith-er	Dis-agree	N
All	51.0	12.0	37.0	2831	69.5	13.4	17.1	2261
Female	44.6	12.7	42.7	1148	69.0	14.0	17.0	1163
Male	55.3	11.6	33.1	1683	70.0	12.9	17.1	1098

Table 10.2   *A Labour/Conservative government should introduce a prices and incomes policy as a means of controlling inflation (%)*

Gender	Labour				Conservative			
	Agree	Neith-er	Dis-agree	N	Agree	Neith-er	Dis-agree	N
All	57.6	18.8	23.6	2833	41.7	11.7	46.6	2300
Female	59.4	22.5	18.1	1142	47.8	12.8	39.4	1183
Male	56.4	16.3	27.3	1691	35.3	10.4	54.3	1117

Table 10.3   *Income and wealth should be re-distributed towards ordinary working people (%)*

Gender	Labour				Conservative			
	Agree	Neith-er	Dis-agree	N	Agree	Neith-er	Dis-agree	N
All	86.0	9.1	4.9	2867	25.1	20.3	54.6	2295
Female	85.9	8.9	5.2	1166	25.4	17.9	56.7	1180
Male	86.0	9.2	4.8	1701	24.7	22.9	52.4	1115

239

Table 10.4   *The Labour/Conservative Party should always stand by its principles even if this should lose it an election (%)*

Gender	Labour				Conservative			
	Agree	Neith-er	Dis-agree	N	Agree	Neith-er	Dis-agree	N
All	67.9	11.9	20.2	2862	81.3	8.2	10.5	2352
Female	71.0	11.8	17.2	1165	84.0	7.7	8.3	1217
Male	65.7	12.0	22.3	1697	78.4	8.8	12.8	1135

Table 10.5   *Further nuclear energy development is essential for the future prosperity of Britain (%)*

Gender	Labour				Conservative			
	Agree	Neith-er	Dis-agree	N	Agree	Neith-er	Dis-agree	N
All	14.0	11.8	74.2	2852	60.5	16.9	22.6	2310
Female	9.4	12.0	78.6	1162	54.7	19.5	25.8	1180
Male	17.1	11.7	71.2	1690	66.5	14.1	19.4	1130

Table 10.6   *A future Labour/Conservative government should not agree to a single European currency (%)*

Gender	Labour				Conservative			
	Agree	Neith-er	Dis-agree	N	Agree	Neith-er	Dis-agree	N
All	25.3	19.0	55.7	2839	57.8	12.1	30.1	2332
Female	28.0	23.6	48.4	1151	63.2	12.8	24.0	1202
Male	23.4	15.9	60.7	1688	52.1	11.4	36.5	1130

Table 10.7   *High income tax makes people less willing to work hard (%)*

Gender	Labour				Conservative			
	Agree	Neith-er	Dis-agree	N	Agree	Neith-er	Dis-agree	N
All	26.2	10.9	62.9	2868	82.1	6.0	11.9	2354
Female	23.0	11.3	65.7	1172	82.0	5.3	12.7	1220
Male	28.4	10.6	61.0	1696	82.1	6.9	11.0	1134

Table 10.8   *Britain's electoral system should be replaced by a system of proportional representation (%)*

Gender	Labour				Conservative			
	Agree	Neith-er	Dis-agree	N	Agree	Neith-er	Dis-agree	N
All	58.0	13.2	28.8	2864	21.7	11.8	66.5	2323
Female	60.4	15.1	24.5	1168	20.5	13.4	66.1	1196
Male	56.3	11.9	31.8	1696	23.0	10.1	66.9	1127

Table 10.9   *Further moves towards integration within the European Community should be resisted (%)*

Gender	Labour				Conservative			
	Agree	Neith-er	Dis-agree	N	Agree	Neith-er	Dis-agree	N
All	21.6	13.3	65.1	2856	53.8	15.6	30.6	2332
Female	22.9	15.1	62.0	1158	57.7	16.0	26.3	1202
Male	20.8	11.9	67.3	1698	49.6	15.2	35.2	1130

Table 10.10   There is no need for a Bill of Rights in this country (%)

Gender	Labour				Conservative			
	Agree	Neith-er	Dis-agree	N	Agree	Neith-er	Dis-agree	N
All	11.2	10.0	78.8	2838	40.0	26.6	33.4	2250
Female	9.2	11.0	79.8	1158	37.5	29.6	32.9	1146
Male	12.6	9.3	78.1	1680	42.6	23.4	34.0	1104

Table 10.11   A future Labour/Conservative government should introduce a directly elected Scottish Assembly with taxing powers (%)

Gender	Labour				Conservative			
	Agree	Neith-er	Dis-agree	N	Agree	Neith-er	Dis-agree	N
All	61.3	22.2	16.5	2861	22.6	26.6	50.8	2295
Female	58.9	24.4	16.7	1164	21.1	30.3	48.6	1175
Male	62.9	20.6	16.5	1697	24.1	22.8	53.1	1120

Table 10.12   Coalition governments are the best form of government for Britain (%)

Gender	Labour				Conservative			
	Agree	Neith-er	Dis-agree	N	Agree	Neith-er	Dis-agree	N
All	8.7	16.6	74.7	2860	9.3	10.1	80.6	2356
Female	9.0	17.5	73.5	1165	9.7	10.0	80.3	1217
Male	8.5	16.0	75.5	1695	8.9	10.1	81.0	1139

Table 10.13   *A future Labour/Conservative government should/should not spend money to get rid of poverty (%)*

Gender	Labour				Conservative			
	Should	Doesn't matter	Should not	N	Should	Doesn't matter	Should not	N
All	98.0	1.0	1.0	2895	80.1	8.4	11.5	2310
Female	98.3	0.5	1.2	1174	82.6	7.2	10.2	1189
Male	97.9	1.2	0.9	1685	77.4	9.8	12.8	1121

Table 10.14   *A future Labour/Conservative government should/should not encourage the growth of private medicine (%)*

Gender	Labour				Conservative			
	Should	Doesn't matter	Should not	N	Should	Doesn't matter	Should not	N
All	3.7	4.7	91.6	2852	52.0	15.9	32.1	2319
Female	3.0	3.2	93.8	1166	49.3	16.1	34.6	1194
Male	4.2	5.7	90.1	1686	54.8	15.7	29.5	1125

Table 10.15   *A future Labour/Conservative government should/should not put more money into the National Health Service (%)*

Gender	Labour				Conservative			
	Should	Doesn't matter	Should not	N	Should	Doesn't matter	Should not	N
All	98.0	0.7	1.3	2865	79.1	7.6	13.3	2326
Female	98.8	0.3	0.9	1175	81.8	6.4	11.8	1199
Male	97.5	1.0	1.5	1690	76.1	9.0	14.9	1127

Table 10.16   *A future Labour/Conservative government should/should not reduce*
spending in general (%)

Gender	Labour				Conservative			
	Should	Doesn't matter	Should not	N	Should	Doesn't matter	Should not	N
All	19.5	7.2	73.3	2817	60.7	8.7	30.6	2307
Female	20.2	6.2	73.6	1148	57.8	7.9	34.3	1182
Male	19.0	8.0	73.0	1669	63.7	9.6	26.7	1125

Table 10.17   *A future Labour/Conservative government should/should not*
introduce stricter laws to regulate the trade unions (%)

Gender	Labour				Conservative			
	Should	Doesn't matter	Should not	N	Should	Doesn't matter	Should not	N
All	10.1	14.7	75.2	2827	66.2	12.2	21.6	2333
Female	12.2	13.8	74.0	1150	71.0	10.5	18.5	1204
Male	8.7	15.3	76.0	1677	61.3	13.9	24.8	1129

Table 10.18   *A future Labour/Conservative government should/should not give*
workers more say in the places where they work (%)

Gender	Labour				Conservative			
	Should	Doesn't matter	Should not	N	Should	Doesn't matter	Should not	N
All	91.2	5.6	3.2	2854	63.6	13.5	22.9	2340
Female	92.4	4.5	3.1	1168	68.8	13.2	18.0	1207
Male	90.4	6.5	3.1	1686	58.2	13.6	28.2	1133

Table 10.19   A future Labour/Conservative government should/should not spend
               less on defence (%)

Gender	Labour				Conservative			
	Should	Doesn't matter	Should not	N	Should	Doesn't matter	Should not	N
All	82.7	4.7	12.6	2856	44.0	5.0	51.0	2326
Female	85.8	2.9	11.3	1170	40.7	4.8	54.5	1194
Male	80.6	5.9	13.5	1686	47.5	5.2	47.3	1132

Table 10.20   Should a future Labour/Conservative government :
(A) Reduce taxes & spend less on health, education & social benefits ?
(B) Keep taxes & spending on these services at the same levels as now ?
(C) Increase taxes & spend more on health, education & social benefits ?

Gender	Labour				Conservative			
	A	B	C	N	A	B	C	N
All	2.7	6.4	90.9	2858	6.8	67.2	26.0	2327
Female	2.8	4.9	92.3	1173	5.6	68.9	25.5	1205
Male	2.6	7.4	90.0	1685	8.1	65.3	26.6	1122

Table 10.21   On joining the Labour/Conservative party did the member approach
               the party (MA) or did the party approach the member (PA) ? (%)

Gender	Labour				Conservative			
	MA	Don't Know	PA	N	MA	Don't Know	PA	N
All	77.5	20.0	2.5	2889	34.1	50.5	15.4	2370
Female	75.3	21.7	3.0	1186	30.4	51.3	18.3	1233
Male	79.0	18.8	2.2	1703	38.2	49.6	12.2	1137

Table 10.22   *How often has the member attended a party meeting in the last 12 months ? (%)*

Gender	Labour				Conservative			
	Not at all	Occas-ionally	Frequ-ently	N	Not at all	Occas-ionally	Frequ-ently	N
All	41.6	30.6	27.8	2901	65.9	22.0	12.1	2388
Female	48.2	28.3	23.5	1186	63.0	23.7	13.3	1243
Male	37.0	32.2	30.8	1715	69.0	20.3	10.7	1145

Table 10.23   *Is the member more or less politically active than 5 years ago ? (%)*

Gender	Labour				Conservative			
	More active	About same	Less active	N	More active	About same	Less active	N
All	13.0	38.4	48.6	2862	9.4	62.8	27,8	2008
Female	13.2	39.5	47.3	1175	8.8	60.4	30.8	1068
Male	12.8	37.6	49.6	1687	10.0	65.6	24.4	940

Table 10.24   *Does the member hold any office within the Labour/Conservative Party ? (%)*

Gender	Labour			Conservative		
	Yes	No	N	Yes	No	N
All	16.0	84.0	2849	8.5	91.5	2354
Female	15.0	85.0	1165	8.0	92.0	1227
Male	16.6	83.4	1684	9.1	90.9	1127

Table 10.25   *How much time does the member devote to party activities per month ? (%)*

Gender	Labour					Conservative				
	None	Up to 5 hrs	5 to 10 hrs	Over 10 hrs	N	None	Up to 5 hrs	5 to 10 hrs	Over 10 hrs	N
All	51.2	29.5	9.4	9.9	2859	75.9	15.4	4.5	4.2	2343
Female	55.8	28.5	9.2	6.5	1165	74.2	17.0	4.6	4.2	1215
Male	48.1	30.2	9.5	12.2	1694	77.7	13.7	4.3	4.3	1128

Table 10.26   *What was the overall financial contribution made by the member in the last year ? (%)*

Gender	Labour				Conservative			
	0 to £10	£10 to £20	Over £20	N	0 to £10	£10 to £20	Over £20	N
All	24.4	19.7	55.9	2545	34.0	21.2	44.8	1776
Female	25.4	20.8	53.8	1003	32.1	23.5	44.4	876
Male	23.7	19.0	57.3	1542	35.8	19.1	45.1	900

Table 10.27   *Is the member a local Labour/Conservative councillor ? (%)*

Gender	Labour			Conservative		
	Yes	No	N	Yes	No	N
All	7.9	92.1	2874	2.4	97.6	2371
Female	5.2	94.7	1174	1.6	98.4	1233
Male	9.7	90.3	1700	3.2	96.8	1138

*Table 10.28   The Labour/Conservative leader should be elected by a system of one
party member/one vote (%)*

Gender	Labour				Conservative			
	Agree	Neith-er	Dis-agree	N	Agree	Neith-er	Dis-agree	N
All	86.0	5.3	8.7	2871	49.7	14.4	35.9	2311
Female	86.8	5.3	7.9	1170	51.3	13.2	35.5	1183
Male	85.5	5.3	9.2	1701	48.0	15.7	36.3	1128

*Table 10.29   People like me can have a real influence in politics if they are
prepared to get involved (%)*

Gender	Labour				Conservative			
	Agree	Neith-er	Dis-agree	N	Agree	Neith-er	Dis-agree	N
All	66.0	16.0	18.0	2860	56.5	20.2	23.3	2320
Female	64.1	16.4	19.5	1159	54.6	20.5	24.9	1195
Male	67.3	15.8	16.9	1701	58.4	20.1	21.5	1125

*Table 10.30   Attending party meetings can be pretty tiring after a hard days
work (%)*

Gender	Labour				Conservative			
	Agree	Neith-er	Dis-agree	N	Agree	Neith-er	Dis-agree	N
All	77.1	11.4	11.5	2864	69.1	19.6	11.3	2301
Female	79.2	9.9	10.9	1163	70.4	17.4	12.2	1181
Male	75.7	12.4	11.9	1701	67.9	22.0	10.1	1120

Table 10.31   Someone like me could do a good job of being a local councillor (%)

Gender	Labour				Conservative			
	Agree	Neith-er	Dis-agree	N	Agree	Neith-er	Dis-agree	N
All	48.6	22.0	29.4	2838	27.6	24.6	47.8	2287
Female	41.7	22.4	35.9	1149	20.5	22.4	57.1	1173
Male	53.3	21.7	25.0	1689	35.0	26.8	38.2	1114

Table 10.32   Being an active party member is a good way of meeting interesting people (%)

Gender	Labour				Conservative			
	Agree	Neith-er	Dis-agree	N	Agree	Neith-er	Dis-agree	N
All	64.6	21.9	13.5	2861	59.4	30.0	10.6	2293
Female	62.0	22.9	15.1	1160	64.1	26.9	9.0	1185
Male	66.3	21.2	12.5	1701	54.3	33.4	12.3	1108

Table 10.33   The only way to be really educated about politics is to be a party activist (%)

Gender	Labour				Conservative			
	Agree	Neith-er	Dis-agree	N	Agree	Neith-er	Dis-agree	N
All	41.8	11.2	47.0	2869	35.6	17.1	47.3	2298
Female	38.5	11.4	50.1	1165	38.2	14.5	47.3	1185
Male	44.1	11.1	44.8	1704	32.7	19.9	47.4	1113

Table 10.34   *The party leadership does not pay a lot of attention to ordinary party members (%)*

Gender	Labour				Conservative			
	Agree	Neith-er	Dis-agree	N	Agree	Neith-er	Dis-agree	N
All	46.9	19.0	34.1	2867	42.0	24.2	33.8	2307
Female	44.5	19.6	35.9	1163	41.8	24.3	33.9	1188
Male	48.6	18.6	32.8	1704	42.2	24.1	33.7	1119

Table 10.35   *Party activity often takes time away from one's family (%)*

Gender	Labour				Conservative			
	Agree	Neith-er	Dis-agree	N	Agree	Neith-er	Dis-agree	N
All	85.0	10.4	4.6	2862	67.0	25.7	7.3	2278
Female	85.0	10.0	5.0	1165	68.4	23.7	7.9	1171
Male	85.0	10.7	4.3	1697	65.6	27.8	6.6	1107

Table 10.36   *The Labour/Conservative party would be more successful if people like me were elected to parliament (%)*

Gender	Labour				Conservative			
	Agree	Neith-er	Dis-agree	N	Agree	Neith-er	Dis-agree	N
All	33.8	34.0	32.2	2838	21.3	31.6	47.1	2266
Female	28.7	32.7	38.8	1145	17.1	29.9	53.0	1164
Male	37.3	34.9	27.8	1693	25.7	33.4	40.9	1102

Table 10.37 *During the last 5 years, how often has the member displayed an election poster in his/her window ? (%)*

Gender	Labour				Conservative			
	Not at all	Occas-ionally	Freq-uently	N	Not at all	Occas-ionally	Freq-uently	N
All	9.6	21.6	68.8	2845	48.9	31.7	19.4	2268
Female	8.0	20.9	71.1	1166	47.5	32.6	19.9	1163
Male	10.8	22.0	67.2	1679	50.4	30.9	18.7	1105

Table 10.38 *During the last 5 years, how often has the member donated money to party funds ? (%)*

Gender	Labour				Conservative			
	Not at all	Occas-ionally	Freq-uently	N	Not at all	Occas-ionally	Freq-uently	N
All	9.6	51.0	39.4	2840	14.8	55.6	29.6	2314
Female	11.0	53.5	35.5	1159	13.6	56.3	30.1	1191
Male	8.6	49.3	42.1	1681	16.1	54.8	29.1	1123

Table 10.39 *During the last 5 years, how often has the member delivered party leaflets ? (%)*

Gender	Labour				Conservative			
	Not at all	Occas-ionally	Freq-uently	N	Not at all	Occas-ionally	Freq-uently	N
All	17.6	27.0	55.4	2792	60.9	16.9	22.2	2216
Female	18.3	29.1	52.6	1136	58.2	17.3	24.5	1133
Male	17.2	25.6	57.2	1656	63.7	16.5	19.8	1083

Table 10.40   *During the last 5 years, how often has the member attended a party meeting ? (%)*

Gender	Labour				Conservative			
	Not at all	Occas- ionally	Freq- uently	N	Not at all	Occas- ionally	Freq- uently	N
All	21.5	40.7	37.8	2797	50.5	32.8	16.7	2246
Female	24.2	43.5	32.3	1142	47.7	34.4	17.9	1160
Male	19.6	38.9	41.5	1655	53.5	31.0	15.5	1086

Table 10.41   *During the last 5 years, how often has the member canvassed voters on behalf of the party ? (%)*

Gender	Labour				Conservative			
	Not at all	Occas- ionally	Freq- uently	N	Not at all	Occas- ionally	Freq- uently	N
All	37.0	31.1	31.9	2772	74.6	14.9	10.5	2209
Female	43.3	31.6	25.1	1125	75.7	14.1	10.2	1124
Male	32.7	30.9	36.4	1647	73.4	15.7	10.9	1085

Table 10.42   *Where would you place yourself on a Left/Right scale within the Labour/Conservative party ? (%)*

Gender	Labour				Conservative			
	Left	Centre	Right	N	Left	Centre	Right	N
All	57.5	20.6	21.9	2869	13.4	25.9	60.7	2341
Female	57.7	22.1	20.2	1174	12.3	27.5	60.2	1213
Male	57.5	19.4	23.1	1695	14.3	24.4	61.3	1128

Table 10.43   *Where would you place yourself on a Left/Right scale within British Politics ? (%)*

Gender	Labour				Conservative			
	Left	Centre	Right	N	Left	Centre	Right	N
All	79.9	10.3	9.8	2868	3.6	18.1	78.3	2334
Female	81.7	9.6	8.7	1173	3.9	19.3	76.8	1205
Male	78.7	10.8	10.5	1695	3.9	19.3	76.8	1129

Table 10.44   *What thermometer rating would the Labour/Conservative member give the Conservative Party ? (%)*

Gender	Labour					Conservative				
	Cd	Cl	W	H	M	Cd	Cl	W	H	M
All	76.0	20.4	3.0	0.6	14.8	0.2	3.5	33.8	62.5	80.9
Female	80.4	17.3	2.0	0.3	12.2	0.2	2.7	30.2	66.9	82.5
Male	73.0	22.5	3.7	0.8	16.5	0.3	4.4	37.5	57.8	79.1

Table 10.45   *What thermometer rating would the Labour/Conservative member give the Labour Party ? (%)*

Gender	Labour					Conservative				
	Cd	Cl	W	H	M	Cd	Cl	W	H	M
All	1.0	3.8	24.7	70.5	82.7	50.3	43.2	6.1	0.4	26.7
Female	1.1	3.7	25.5	69.7	82.4	52.1	42.4	5.1	0.4	25.7
Male	0.9	3.8	24.2	71.1	82.9	48.5	44.0	7.1	0.4	27.6

Table 10.46   *What thermometer rating would the Labour/Conservative member give the Liberal Democratic Party ? (%)*

Gender	Labour					Conservative				
	Cd	Cl	W	H	M	Cd	Cl	W	H	M
All	32.9	44.3	20.9	1.9	36.9	32.7	51.0	15.2	1.1	36.2
Female	32.5	45.5	19.9	2.1	36.6	31.1	51.8	15.7	1.4	37.0
Male	33.2	43.5	21.6	1.7	37.2	34.2	50.1	14.6	1.1	35.6

Table 10.47   *What thermometer rating would the Labour/Conservative member give the Scottish Nationalist Party ? (%)*

Gender	Labour					Conservative				
	Cd	Cl	W	H	M	Cd	Cl	W	H	M
All	43.8	37.3	16.0	2.9	32.2	69.2	26.5	4.0	0.3	18.9
Female	38.0	41.3	17.7	3.0	34.7	69.4	26.4	4.0	0.2	18.6
Male	47.5	34.7	14.9	2.9	30.7	69.1	26.6	4.0	0.3	19.2

Table 10.48   *What thermometer rating would the Labour/Conservative member give Plaid Cymru ? (%)*

Gender	Labour					Conservative				
	Cd	Cl	W	H	M	Cd	Cl	W	H	M
All	47.4	37.8	12.9	1.9	29.7	82.8	15.9	1.1	0.2	12.8
Female	42.0	43.2	12.8	2.0	31.6	81.8	17.5	0.7	0.0	13.4
Male	50.7	34.4	13.0	1.9	28.6	83.6	14.5	1.5	0.4	12.4

Table 10.49   *What thermometer rating would the Labour/Conservative member give the Green Party ? (%)*

Gender	Labour					Conservative				
	Cd	Cl	W	H	M	Cd	Cl	W	H	M
All	33.2	36.0	25.7	5.1	39.5	70.3	24.2	4.9	0.6	19.4
Female	27.5	35.6	29.9	7.0	43.2	65.6	28.0	5.7	0.7	21.2
Male	37.2	36.2	22.8	3.8	37.0	74.7	20.8	4.1	0.4	17.7

Table 10.50   *What thermometer rating would the Labour/Conservative member give the BBC ? (%)*

Gender	Labour					Conservative				
	Cd	Cl	W	H	M	Cd	Cl	W	H	M
All	9.4	26.3	39.7	24.6	60.3	8.5	30.9	40.4	20.2	59.1
Female	8.5	27.1	40.1	24.3	60.8	7.8	27.1	42.7	22.4	60.8
Male	10.0	25.9	39.4	24.7	60.0	9.2	34.8	38.0	18.0	57.4

Table 10.51   *What thermometer rating would the Labour/Conservative member give the European Community ? (%)*

Gender	Labour					Conservative				
	Cd	Cl	W	H	M	Cd	Cl	W	H	M
All	11.2	32.4	41.8	14.6	55.5	14.4	40.7	35.7	9.2	50.7
Female	11.6	34.1	40.6	13.7	54.7	13.2	42.5	37.0	7.3	50.3
Male	10.9	31.4	42.6	15.1	56.1	15.4	39.2	34.6	10.8	51.1

Table 10.52   *What thermometer rating would the Labour/Conservative member give the Trade Union Congress ? (%)*

Gender	Labour					Conservative				
	Cd	Cl	W	H	M	Cd	Cl	W	H	M
All	5.6	29.0	47.6	17.8	60.1	54.0	39.6	5.6	0.8	26.2
Female	4.3	29.7	49.4	16.6	60.3	58.2	37.1	3.9	0.8	24.1
Male	6.5	28.4	46.5	18.6	60.0	50.9	41.4	6.8	0.9	27.7

Table 10.53   *What thermometer rating would the Labour/Conservative member give the Police ? (%)*

Gender	Labour					Conservative				
	Cd	Cl	W	H	M	Cd	Cl	W	H	M
All	17.7	44.3	28.5	9.5	48.2	1.5	12.6	39.8	46.1	72.9
Female	19.5	46.3	26.6	7.6	46.5	0.9	9.7	37.1	52.3	75.1
Male	16.5	43.0	29.8	10.7	49.3	1.9	15.7	42.7	39.7	70.7

Table 10.54   *What thermometer rating would the Labour/Conservative member give the House of Commons ? (%)*

Gender	Labour					Conservative				
	Cd	Cl	W	H	M	Cd	Cl	W	H	M
All	10.2	33.6	38.2	18.0	56.8	2.4	17.1	49.3	31.2	68.3
Female	9.3	36.2	39.8	14.7	56.1	1.8	16.1	49.8	32.3	69.3
Male	10.8	31.9	37.1	20.2	57.3	2.9	18.2	48.8	30.1	67.3

Table 10.55   *What thermometer rating would the Labour/Conservative member give the CBI ? (%)*

Gender	Labour					Conservative				
	Cd	Cl	W	H	M	Cd	Cl	W	H	M
All	44.9	41.7	11.2	2.2	31.0	5.6	29.5	49.2	15.7	59.7
Female	44.2	43.3	10.8	1.7	31.1	5.9	26.3	50.5	17.3	60.4
Male	45.4	40.7	11.5	2.4	30.8	5.2	31.7	48.4	14.7	59.2

Table 10.56   *What thermometer rating would the Labour/Conservative member give the Queen ? (%)*

Gender	Labour					Conservative				
	Cd	Cl	W	H	M	Cd	Cl	W	H	M
All	34.6	29.3	19.3	16.8	43.5	0.9	4.7	16.0	78.4	86.4
Female	33.9	31.0	18.0	17.1	43.9	0.5	2.6	13.8	83.1	88.7
Male	35.1	28.1	20.2	16.6	43.2	1.5	6.9	18.3	73.3	83.9

Table 10.57   *What thermometer rating would the Labour/Conservative member give Judges ? (%)*

Gender	Labour					Conservative				
	Cd	Cl	W	H	M	Cd	Cl	W	H	M
All	37.9	43.5	15.0	3.6	35.0	4.5	30.8	45.9	18.8	60.5
Female	38.7	45.7	12.4	3.2	34.3	4.1	29.4	47.9	18.6	60.9
Male	37.4	42.1	16.8	3.7	35.6	4.9	32.2	44.0	18.9	60.1

11 Age

Table 11.1   *The Labour/Conservative party should try to capture the middle ground in politics (%)*

Age	Labour				Conservative			
	Agree	Neith-er	Dis-agree	N	Agree	Neith-er	Dis-agree	N
All	50.9	12.1	37.0	2820	69.6	13.3	17.1	2271
25 and under	37.4	9.9	52.7	91	47.8	4.3	47.9	23
26 to 45	40.9	14.2	44.9	1214	56.2	17.8	26.0	331
46 to 65	55.7	11.3	33.0	1016	66.9	13.8	19.3	939
66 and over	68.1	8.8	23.1	499	77.2	11.6	11.2	978

Table 11.2   *A Labour/Conservative government should introduce a prices and incomes policy as a means of controlling inflation (%)*

Age	Labour				Conservative			
	Agree	Neith-er	Dis-agree	N	Agree	Neith-er	Dis-agree	N
All	57.5	18.9	23.6	2821	42.1	11.4	46.5	2311
25 and under	29.2	39.3	31.5	89	21.7	17.4	60.9	23
26 to 45	44.4	25.4	30.2	1202	34.1	13.5	52.4	334
46 to 65	63.9	14.9	21.2	1024	39.1	9.5	51.4	947
66 and over	80.8	7.9	11.3	506	48.2	12.4	39.4	1007

Table 11.3   *Income and wealth should be re-distributed towards ordinary working people (%)*

Age	Labour				Conservative			
	Agree	Neith-er	Dis-agree	N	Agree	Neith-er	Dis-agree	N
All	86.0	9.0	5.0	2855	25.4	20.3	54.3	2306
25 and under	80.4	12.0	7.6	92	22.7	9.1	68.2	22
26 to 45	89.2	7.3	3.5	1220	25.9	18.8	55.3	336
46 to 65	83.9	10.2	5.9	1032	24.7	19.3	56.0	944
66 and over	83.6	10.4	6.0	511	26.0	21.9	52.1	1004

Table 11.4 The Labour/Conservative Party should always stand by its principles even if this should lose it an election (%)

Age	Labour				Conservative			
	Agree	Neith-er	Dis-agree	N	Agree	Neith-er	Dis-agree	N
All	67.8	11.9	20.3	2850	81.2	8.2	10.6	2366
25 and under	68.9	11.1	20.0	90	56.5	13.0	30.5	23
26 to 45	63.1	13.7	23.2	1215	71.8	12.6	15.6	340
46 to 65	65.9	12.1	22.0	1029	79.6	7.6	12.8	955
66 and over	82.2	7.6	10.2	516	86.4	7.1	6.5	1048

Table 11.5 Further nuclear energy development is essential for the future prosperity of Britain (%)

Age	Labour				Conservative			
	Agree	Neith-er	Dis-agree	N	Agree	Neith-er	Dis-agree	N
All	13.9	11.8	74.3	2840	60.2	16.8	23.0	2323
25 and under	8.7	12.0	79.3	92	54.5	27.3	18.2	22
26 to 45	9.4	10.6	80.0	1217	49.1	22.2	28.7	338
46 to 65	16.3	12.4	71.3	1031	60.5	14.2	25.3	954
66 and over	21.0	13.4	65.6	500	63.8	17.3	18.9	1009

Table 11.6 A future Labour/Conservative government should not agree to a single European currency (%)

Age	Labour				Conservative			
	Agree	Neith-er	Dis-agree	N	Agree	Neith-er	Dis-agree	N
All	25.2	19.0	55.8	2828	57.9	12.0	30.1	2343
25 and under	27.5	24.2	48.3	91	60.9	8.7	30.4	23
26 to 45	20.7	21.5	57.8	1207	56.2	11.8	32.0	338
46 to 65	25.3	16.5	58.2	1029	54.0	11.1	34.9	950
66 and over	35.5	17.4	47.1	501	61.9	12.9	25.2	1032

Table 11.7   *High income tax makes people less willing to work hard (%)*

Age	Labour				Conservative			
	Agree	Neith-er	Dis-agree	N	Agree	Neith-er	Dis-agree	N
All	26.1	10.9	63.0	2856	82.2	5.9	11.9	2367
25 and under	24.2	7.7	68.1	91	78.3	0.0	21.7	23
26 to 45	17.0	11.3	71.7	1216	80.5	6.8	12.7	339
46 to 65	29.9	10.4	59.7	1039	84.8	4.3	10.9	959
66 and over	40.0	11.6	48.4	510	80.4	7.2	12.4	1046

Table 11.8   *Britain's electoral system should be replaced by a system of proportional representation (%)*

Age	Labour				Conservative			
	Agree	Neith-er	Dis-agree	N	Agree	Neith-er	Dis-agree	N
All	58.0	13.2	28.8	2853	21.8	11.8	66.4	2333
25 and under	64.1	17.4	18.5	92	21.7	17.4	60.9	23
26 to 45	60.1	14.5	25.4	1217	23.1	17.2	59.7	337
46 to 65	56.2	11.7	32.1	1035	21.9	10.8	67.3	948
66 and over	55.2	12.6	32.2	509	21.2	10.9	67.9	1025

Table 11.9   *Further moves towards integration within the European Community should be resisted (%)*

Age	Labour				Conservative			
	Agree	Neith-er	Dis-agree	N	Agree	Neith-er	Dis-agree	N
All	21.5	13.3	65.2	2845	54.2	15.4	30.4	2345
25 and under	15.2	19.6	65.2	92	52.2	17.4	30.4	23
26 to 45	18.3	14.3	67.4	1214	38.2	21.8	40.0	340
46 to 65	23.4	10.0	66.6	1031	48.9	15.3	35.8	948
66 and over	26.8	16.5	56.7	508	64.4	13.2	22.4	1034

Table 11.10 *There is no need for a Bill of Rights in this country (%)*

Age	Labour				Conservative			
	Agree	Neith-er	Dis-agree	N	Agree	Neith-er	Dis-agree	N
All	11.2	9.9	78.9	2827	39.9	26.4	33.7	2260
25 and under	5.4	19.6	75.0	92	30.4	34.8	34.8	23
26 to 45	8.0	9.2	82.8	1211	31.6	31.6	36.8	335
46 to 65	11.1	8.2	80.7	1029	36.5	26.1	37.4	926
66 and over	20.4	13.5	66.1	495	46.1	24.7	29.2	976

Table 11.11 *A future Labour/Conservative government should introduce a directly elected Scottish Assembly with taxing powers (%)*

Age	Labour				Conservative			
	Agree	Neith-er	Dis-agree	N	Agree	Neith-er	Dis-agree	N
All	61.3	22.1	16.6	2851	22.8	26.3	50.9	2305
25 and under	58.7	29.3	12.0	92	21.7	26.1	52.2	23
26 to 45	62.4	23.9	13.7	1214	22.7	35.4	41.9	339
46 to 65	59.0	21.3	19.7	1033	25.6	23.7	50.7	944
66 and over	63.7	18.4	17.9	512	20.2	25.6	54.2	999

Table 11.12 *Coalition governments are the best form of government for Britain (%)*

Age	Labour				Conservative			
	Agree	Neith-er	Dis-agree	N	Agree	Neith-er	Dis-agree	N
All	8.7	16.6	74.7	2848	9.6	10.0	80.4	2373
25 and under	10.9	27.2	61.9	92	4.3	17.4	78.3	23
26 to 45	7.2	18.2	74.6	1214	5.0	13.5	81.5	341
46 to 65	8.7	15.4	75.9	1035	8.0	9.6	82.4	962
66 and over	11.6	13.6	74.8	507	12.7	9.1	78.2	1047

Table 11.13   *A future Labour/Conservative government should/should not spend money to get rid of poverty (%)*

Age	Labour				Conservative			
	Should	Doesn't matter	Should not	N	Should	Doesn't matter	Should not	N
All	98.1	0.9	1.0	2847	80.3	8.4	11.3	2325
25 and under	98.9	0.0	1.1	91	60.9	13.0	26.1	23
26 to 45	98.5	0.7	0.8	1215	80.5	8.0	11.5	338
46 to 65	97.3	1.3	1.4	1029	82.6	7.2	10.2	940
66 and over	98.4	1.0	0.6	512	78.5	9.6	11.9	1024

Table 11.14   *A future Labour/Conservative government should/should not encourage the growth of private medicine (%)*

Age	Labour				Conservative			
	Should	Doesn't matter	Should not	N	Should	Doesn't matter	Should not	N
All	3.7	4.7	91.6	2840	52.0	15.8	32.2	2335
25 and under	4.3	3.3	92.4	92	73.9	26.1	0.0	23
26 to 45	2.1	4.5	93.4	1214	53.0	18.6	28.4	338
46 to 65	4.7	4.6	90.7	1030	51.4	13.4	35.2	946
66 and over	5.4	5.4	89.2	504	51.8	16.9	31.3	1028

Table 11.15   *A future Labour/Conservative government should/should not put more money into the National Health Service (%)*

Age	Labour				Conservative			
	Should	Doesn't matter	Should not	N	Should	Doesn't matter	Should not	N
All	98.0	0.7	1.3	2853	79.2	7.5	13.3	2343
25 and under	97.8	1.1	1.1	92	73.9	17.4	8.7	23
26 to 45	98.0	0.7	1.3	1215	82.3	6.5	11.2	339
46 to 65	98.0	0.5	1.5	1032	79.5	7.3	13.2	948
66 and over	98.1	1.0	0.9	514	78.0	7.7	14.3	1033

Table 11.16   A future Labour/Conservative government should/should not reduce spending in general (%)

Age	Labour				Conservative			
	Should	Doesn't matter	Should not	N	Should	Doesn't matter	Should not	N
All	19.4	7.3	73.3	2805	60.7	8.6	30.7	2323
25 and under	6.5	8.7	84.8	92	43.5	17.4	39.1	23
26 to 45	13.3	6.5	80.2	1206	54.4	10.9	34.7	338
46 to 65	23.3	6.3	70.4	1018	60.0	8.7	31.3	941
66 and over	28.8	11.0	60.2	489	63.9	7.5	28.6	1021

Table 11.17   A future Labour/Conservative government should/should not introduce stricter laws to regulate the trade unions (%)

Age	Labour				Conservative			
	Should	Doesn't matter	Should not	N	Should	Doesn't matter	Should not	N
All	10.0	14.7	75.3	2815	66.4	12.2	21.4	2350
25 and under	13.0	14.1	72.9	92	60.9	17.4	21.7	23
26 to 45	5.5	14.9	79.6	1212	52.7	20.2	27.1	336
46 to 65	11.9	14.9	73.2	1015	58.3	13.7	28.0	947
66 and over	16.5	14.1	69.4	496	78.3	8.0	13.7	1044

Table 11.18   A future Labour/Conservative government should/should not give workers more say in the places where they work (%)

Age	Labour				Conservative			
	Should	Doesn't matter	Should not	N	Should	Doesn't matter	Should not	N
All	91.2	5.6	3.2	2842	63.9	13.4	22.7	2357
25 and under	87.9	11.0	1.1	91	47.8	13.0	39.2	23
26 to 45	92.8	4.0	3.2	1215	62.4	14.2	23.4	338
46 to 65	89.7	6.4	3.9	1027	64.2	13.6	22.2	951
66 and over	91.0	6.9	2.1	509	64.5	13.1	22.4	1045

Table 11.19   *A future Labour/Conservative government should/should not spend*
                less on defence (%)

Age	Labour				Conservative			
	Should	Doesn't matter	Should not	N	Should	Doesn't matter	Should not	N
All	82.8	4.7	12.5	2844	44.3	4.9	50.8	2343
25 and under	81.5	8.7	9.8	92	26.1	8.7	65.2	23
26 to 45	86.2	4.0	9.8	1215	46.6	7.1	46.3	337
46 to 65	80.3	4.8	14.9	1029	48.5	3.8	47.7	947
66 and over	79.9	5.5	14.6	508	40.1	5.0	54.9	1036

Table 11.20   *Should a future Labour/Conservative government :*
(A) Reduce taxes & spend less on health, education & social benefits ?
(B) Keep taxes & spending on these services at the same levels as now ?
(C) Increase taxes & spend more on health, education & social benefits ?

Age	Labour				Conservative			
	A	B	C	N	A	B	C	N
All	2.7	6.3	91.0	2846	6.7	67.3	26.0	2341
25 and under	7.6	7.6	84.8	92	9.1	72.7	18.2	22
26 to 45	1.6	6.0	92.4	1207	8.1	63.9	28.0	335
46 to 65	3.4	5.8	90.8	1034	7.1	66.6	26.3	944
66 and over	2.9	7.6	89.5	513	6.0	68.8	25.2	1040

Table 11.21   *On joining the Labour/Conservative party did the member approach*
the party (MA) or did the party approach the member (PA) ? (%)

Age	Labour				Conservative			
	MA	Don't Know	PA	N	MA	Don't Know	PA	N
All	77.5	20.0	2.5	2879	34.4	50.3	15.3	2386
25 and under	87.0	12.0	1.0	92	39.1	60.9	0.0	23
26 to 45	82.2	16.5	1.3	1216	48.8	40.4	10.8	342
46 to 65	74.4	23.1	2.5	1044	32.4	55.2	12.4	958
66 and over	71.0	23.3	5.7	527	31.5	48.7	19.8	1063

Table 11.22   *How often has the member attended a party meeting in the last*
12 months ? (%)

Age	Labour				Conservative			
	Not at all	Occas-ionally	Frequ-ently	N	Not at all	Occas-ionally	Frequ-ently	N
All	41.6	30.7	27.7	2890	66.2	21.9	11.9	2403
25 and under	55.4	28.3	16.3	92	60.9	17.4	21.7	23
26 to 45	47.5	29.2	23.3	1221	69.9	18.7	11.4	342
46 to 65	35.6	32.3	32.1	1048	66.5	21.0	12.5	967
66 and over	37.4	31.4	31.2	529	64.8	23.9	11.3	1071

Table 11.23   *Is the member more or less politically active than 5 years ago ? (%)*

Age	Labour				Conservative			
	More active	About same	Less active	N	More active	About same	Less active	N
All	13.0	38.3	48.7	2853	9.2	62.8	28.0	2020
25 and under	11.2	29.2	59.6	89	33.3	41.7	25.0	12
26 to 45	15.4	34.7	49.9	1213	18.0	59.2	22.8	255
46 to 65	13.8	43.0	43.2	1036	10.6	70.2	19.2	819
66 and over	5.8	39.2	55.0	515	5.1	57.6	37.3	934

Table 11.24   Does the member hold any office within the Labour/Conservative Party ? (%)

Age	Labour			Conservative		
	Yes	No	N	Yes	No	N
All	16.0	84.0	2839	8.5	91.5	2365
25 and under	5.5	94.5	91	21.7	78.3	23
26 to 45	16.5	83.5	1203	9.5	90.5	338
46 to 65	17.6	82.4	1028	9.7	90.3	952
66 and over	13.2	86.8	517	6.9	93.1	1052

Table 11.25   How much time does the member devote to party activities per month ? (%)

Age	Labour					Conservative				
	None	Up to 5 hrs	5 to 10 hrs	Over 10 hrs	N	None	Up to 5 hrs	5 to 10 hrs	Over 10 hrs	N
All	51.2	29.6	9.4	9.8	2848	76.1	15.2	4.5	4.2	2353
25 and under	58.7	30.4	3.3	7.6	92	69.6	8.7	8.7	13.0	23
26 to 45	52.8	27.8	8.7	10.7	1214	74.6	15.5	5.7	4.2	335
46 to 65	47.1	31.1	10.6	11.2	1032	74.8	16.6	4.1	4.5	948
66 and over	54.5	30.4	9.6	5.5	510	77.8	14.0	4.3	3.9	1047

Table 11.26   What was the overall financial contribution made by the member in the last year ? (%)

Age	Labour				Conservative			
	0 to £10	£10 to £20	Over £20	N	0 to £10	£10 to £20	Over £20	N
All	24.4	19.6	56.0	2537	34.1	21.3	44.6	1781
25 and under	42.9	23.4	33.7	77	27.8	11.1	61.1	18
26 to 45	19.1	19.3	61.6	1062	39.4	15.7	44.9	249
46 to 65	21.5	19.8	58.7	932	34.5	18.9	46.6	751
66 and over	39.5	18.9	41.6	466	32.1	25.8	42.1	763

Table 11.27 Is the member a local Labour/Conservative councillor ? (%)

Age	Labour			Conservative		
	Yes	No	N	Yes	No	N
All	7.8	92.2	2863	2.4	97.6	2382
25 and under	2.2	97.8	92	0.0	100.0	23
26 to 45	8.7	91.3	1221	2.1	97.9	341
46 to 65	9.5	90.5	1032	3.2	96.8	964
66 and over	3.5	96.5	518	1.7	98.3	1054

Table 11.28 The Labour/Conservative leader should be elected by a system of one party member/one vote (%)

Age	Labour				Conservative			
	Agree	Neith-er	Dis-agree	N	Agree	Neith-er	Dis-agree	N
All	86.0	5.3	8.7	2859	49.9	14.3	35.8	2323
25 and under	81.3	8.8	9.9	91	47.8	13.0	39.2	23
26 to 45	82.1	6.3	11.6	1211	49.7	17.6	32.7	340
46 to 65	88.2	4.6	7.2	1040	46.3	14.1	39.6	943
66 and over	91.7	3.9	4.4	517	53.4	13.5	33.1	1017

Table 11.29 People like me can have a real influence in politics if they are prepared to get involved (%)

Age	Labour				Conservative			
	Agree	Neith-er	Dis-agree	N	Agree	Neith-er	Dis-agree	N
All	66.0	16.0	18.0	2848	56.5	20.1	23.4	2335
25 and under	60.9	21.7	17.4	92	68.2	9.1	22.7	22
26 to 45	64.0	15.7	20.3	1216	61.4	16.2	22.4	339
46 to 65	66.6	15.8	17.6	1036	55.8	17.3	26.9	949
66 and over	70.6	16.3	13.1	504	55.2	24.3	20.5	1025

269

Table 11.30   *Attending party meetings can be pretty tiring after a hard days work (%)*

Age	Labour				Conservative			
	Agree	Neith-er	Dis-agree	N	Agree	Neith-er	Dis-agree	N
All	77.2	11.4	11.4	2852	69.2	19.5	11.3	2314
25 and under	75.3	16.9	7.8	89	73.9	26.1	0.0	23
26 to 45	81.7	9.7	8.6	1221	68.3	22.2	9.5	338
46 to 65	75.4	11.5	13.1	1035	72.5	17.3	10.2	947
66 and over	70.4	14.4	15.2	507	66.2	20.6	13.2	1006

Table 11.31   *Someone like me could do a good job of being a local councillor (%)*

Age	Labour				Conservative			
	Agree	Neith-er	Dis-agree	N	Agree	Neith-er	Dis-agree	N
All	48.6	22.0	29.4	2826	27.5	24.4	48.1	2301
25 and under	50.5	20.9	28.6	91	40.9	27.3	31.8	22
26 to 45	52.8	22.0	25.2	1212	37.8	28.9	33.3	336
46 to 65	48.8	22.0	29.2	1035	29.5	23.6	46.9	942
66 and over	37.5	22.1	40.4	488	21.9	23.6	54.5	1001

Table 11.32   *Being an active party member is a good way of meeting interesting people (%)*

Age	Labour				Conservative			
	Agree	Neith-er	Dis-agree	N	Agree	Neith-er	Dis-agree	N
All	64.5	21.9	13.6	2849	59.5	29.9	10.6	2306
25 and under	48.9	27.8	23.3	90	50.0	50.0	0.0	22
26 to 45	55.5	26.4	18.1	1214	43.5	41.7	14.8	336
46 to 65	67.0	21.3	11.7	1037	55.2	32.0	12.8	945
66 and over	83.7	11.6	4.7	508	69.0	23.6	7.4	1003

Table 11.33   *The only way to be really educated about politics is to be a party activist (%)*

Age	Labour				Conservative			
	Agree	Neith-er	Dis-agree	N	Agree	Neith-er	Dis-agree	N
All	41.7	11.3	47.0	2858	35.8	17.0	47.2	2309
25 and under	24.2	12.1	63.7	91	33.3	9.5	57.2	21
26 to 45	31.6	11.3	57.1	1218	22.8	18.1	59.1	337
46 to 65	45.6	12.4	42.0	1035	29.9	17.4	52.7	944
66 and over	61.1	8.8	30.1	514	45.7	16.4	37.9	1007

Table 11.34   *The party leadership does not pay a lot of attention to ordinary party members (%)*

Age	Labour				Conservative			
	Agree	Neith-er	Dis-agree	N	Agree	Neith-er	Dis-agree	N
All	46.9	19.0	34.1	2855	42.3	24.1	33.6	2320
25 and under	58.7	14.1	27.2	92	36.4	50.0	13.6	22
26 to 45	47.1	21.0	31.9	1218	34.9	26.9	38.2	338
46 to 65	45.9	18.0	36.1	1037	43.2	23.4	33.4	946
66 and over	46.5	17.1	36.4	508	44.0	23.2	32.8	1014

Table 11.35   *Party activity often takes time away from one's family (%)*

Age	Labour				Conservative			
	Agree	Neith-er	Dis-agree	N	Agree	Neith-er	Dis-agree	N
All	85.0	10.4	4.6	2850	67.2	25.5	7.3	2289
25 and under	63.6	30.7	5.7	88	45.5	45.5	9.0	22
26 to 45	84.3	11.0	4.7	1216	59.6	31.5	8.9	337
46 to 65	85.6	10.0	4.4	1041	67.9	24.5	7.6	934
66 and over	89.1	6.3	4.6	505	69.7	23.9	6.4	996

Table 11.36 *The Labour/Conservative party would be more successful if people like me were elected to parliament (%)*

Age	Labour				Conservative			
	Agree	Neith-er	Dis-agree	N	Agree	Neith-er	Dis-agree	N
All	33.7	34.1	32.2	2827	21.3	31.5	47.2	2276
25 and under	39.1	32.6	28.3	92	34.8	26.1	39.1	23
26 to 45	33.3	35.8	30.9	1209	26.7	35.0	38.3	337
46 to 65	33.4	32.9	33.7	1031	20.4	30.9	48.7	932
66 and over	34.5	32.7	32.8	495	19.9	31.0	49.1	984

Table 11.37 *During the last 5 years, how often has the member displayed an election poster in his/her window ? (%)*

Age	Labour				Conservative			
	Not at all	Occas-ionally	Freq-uently	N	Not at all	Occas-ionally	Freq-uently	N
All	9.5	21.6	68.9	2833	48.9	31.7	19.4	2273
25 and under	7.9	28.1	64.0	89	52.2	17.4	30.4	23
26 to 45	7.0	19.6	73.4	1216	47.0	32.7	20.3	336
46 to 65	11.0	22.8	66.2	1028	49.7	31.3	19.0	932
66 and over	13.0	23.2	63.8	500	48.7	32.1	19.2	982

Table 11.38 *During the last 5 years, how often has the member donated money to party funds ? (%)*

Age	Labour				Conservative			
	Not at all	Occas-ionally	Freq-uently	N	Not at all	Occas-ionally	Freq-uently	N
All	9.6	51.0	39.4	2828	14.8	55.1	30.1	2321
25 and under	17.8	56.7	25.5	90	26.1	43.5	30.4	23
26 to 45	10.0	53.3	36.7	1215	23.1	54.9	22.0	337
46 to 65	8.2	48.3	43.5	1028	14.8	54.8	30.4	947
66 and over	10.3	49.7	40.0	495	11.8	55.8	32.4	1014

Table 11.39   *During the last 5 years, how often has the member delivered party leaflets ? (%)*

Age	Labour				Conservative			
	Not at all	Occas-ionally	Freq-uently	N	Not at all	Occas-ionally	Freq-uently	N
All	17.5	27.1	55.4	2781	61.0	16.9	22.1	2221
25 and under	15.7	31.5	52.8	89	60.9	0.0	39.1	23
26 to 45	13.0	28.5	58.5	1215	59.3	16.9	23.8	337
46 to 65	16.9	25.1	58.0	1009	59.2	18.2	22.6	933
66 and over	30.8	27.1	42.1	468	63.4	16.1	20.5	928

Table 11.40   *During the last 5 years, how often has the member attended a party meeting ? (%)*

Age	Labour				Conservative			
	Not at all	Occas-ionally	Freq-uently	N	Not at all	Occas-ionally	Freq-uently	N
All	21.4	40.9	37.7	2786	50.6	32.6	16.8	2247
25 and under	25.6	46.7	27.7	90	39.1	34.8	26.1	23
26 to 45	21.2	45.0	33.8	1210	55.7	27.1	17.2	336
46 to 65	20.0	38.6	41.4	1017	51.9	31.7	16.4	935
66 and over	24.3	34.1	41.6	469	48.0	35.4	16.6	953

Table 11.41   *During the last 5 years, how often has the member canvassed voters on behalf of the party ? (%)*

Age	Labour				Conservative			
	Not at all	Occas-ionally	Freq-uently	N	Not at all	Occas-ionally	Freq-uently	N
All	37.0	31.1	31.9	2761	74.6	14.9	10.5	2212
25 and under	37.8	34.4	27.8	90	73.9	4.3	21.8	23
26 to 45	34.2	33.0	32.8	1210	71.3	18.5	10.2	335
46 to 65	36.7	29.9	33.4	1004	74.8	13.4	11.8	927
66 and over	45.1	28.4	26.5	457	75.7	15.3	9.0	927

Table 11.42   *Where would you place yourself on a Left/Right scale within the Labour/Conservative party ? (%)*

Age	Labour				Conservative			
	Left	Centre	Right	N	Left	Centre	Right	N
All	57.5	20.5	22.0	2858	13.4	25.9	60.7	2357
25 and under	61.8	13.5	24.7	89	18.2	4.5	77.3	22
26 to 45	61.3	18.4	20.3	1215	19.8	29.9	50.3	338
46 to 65	55.6	21.9	22.5	1035	17.6	27.7	54.7	956
66 and over	51.6	23.5	24.9	519	7.4	23.3	69.3	1041

Table 11.43   *Where would you place yourself on a Left/Right scale within British Politics ? (%)*

Age	Labour				Conservative			
	Left	Centre	Right	N	Left	Centre	Right	N
All	79.9	10.3	9.8	2857	3.7	18.0	78.3	2351
25 and under	83.1	11.2	5.7	89	0.0	8.7	91.3	23
26 to 45	89.9	6.6	3.5	1215	4.1	22.2	73.7	338
46 to 65	75.9	12.0	12.1	1034	4.2	19.9	75.9	954
66 and over	63.7	15.4	20.9	519	3.2	15.2	81.6	1036

Table 11.44   *What thermometer rating would the Labour/Conservative member give the Conservative Party ? (%)*

Age	Labour					Conservative				
	Cd	Cl	W	H	M	Cd	Cl	W	H	M
All	76.0	20.4	3.0	0.6	14.7	0.2	3.5	33.7	62.6	80.8
25 and under	85.7	13.2	1.1	0.0	11.1	0.0	4.3	26.1	69.6	80.8
26 to 45	83.8	14.2	1.5	0.5	10.8	0.6	6.5	38.5	54.4	77.8
46 to 65	72.2	23.1	4.0	0.7	16.5	0.2	3.8	39.2	56.8	79.0
66 and over	62.2	31.8	5.2	0.8	21.5	0.1	2.3	27.1	70.5	83.6

Table 11.45   *What thermometer rating would the Labour/Conservative member give the Labour Party ? (%)*

Age	Labour					Conservative				
	Cd	Cl	W	H	M	Cd	Cl	W	H	M
All	0.9	3.7	24.8	70.6	82.6	50.1	43.4	6.1	0.4	26.7
25 and under	2.2	9.8	27.2	60.8	76.2	73.9	26.1	0.0	0.0	15.8
26 to 45	0.9	4.6	31.0	63.5	79.9	56.8	38.4	4.2	0.6	23.2
46 to 65	1.2	2.9	21.3	74.6	84.3	52.3	41.6	5.7	0.4	26.1
66 and over	0.4	2.3	17.0	80.3	86.7	44.9	47.3	7.3	0.5	28.8

Table 11.46   *What thermometer rating would the Labour/Conservative member give the Liberal Democratic Party ? (%)*

Age	Labour					Conservative				
	Cd	Cl	W	H	M	Cd	Cl	W	H	M
All	32.8	44.4	21.0	1.8	36.9	32.7	50.7	15.2	1.4	36.2
25 and under	39.6	36.3	24.1	0.0	34.4	56.5	30.4	13.0	0.1	28.4
26 to 45	33.4	45.5	19.6	1.5	35.7	33.3	48.3	17.1	1.3	36.2
46 to 65	34.2	43.2	20.8	1.8	36.6	32.1	50.2	16.4	1.3	36.7
66 and over	27.2	45.0	24.2	3.6	41.3	32.5	52.6	13.4	1.5	35.9

Table 11.47   *What thermometer rating would the Labour/Conservative member give the Scottish Nationalist Party ? (%)*

Age	Labour					Conservative				
	Cd	Cl	W	H	M	Cd	Cl	W	H	M
All	43.8	37.3	16.0	2.9	32.2	68.7	27.0	4.0	0.3	19.1
25 and under	42.3	36.3	21.3	0.1	31.6	78.9	21.1	0.0	0.0	12.4
26 to 45	42.5	38.0	16.8	2.7	32.9	69.5	28.9	1.5	0.1	17.8
46 to 65	47.4	34.2	14.9	3.5	30.9	69.3	25.8	4.5	0.4	19.1
66 and over	40.0	42.3	15.1	2.6	33.0	67.5	27.6	4.6	0.3	19.9

Table 11.48 What thermometer rating would the Labour/Conservative member give Plaid Cymru ? (%)

Age	Labour					Conservative				
	Cd	Cl	W	H	M	Cd	Cl	W	H	M
All	47.4	37.8	12.9	1.9	29.7	82.4	16.2	1.1	0.3	13.0
25 and under	49.3	33.8	16.9	0.0	29.6	94.1	5.9	0.0	0.0	6.5
26 to 45	44.9	38.5	14.3	2.3	31.1	81.1	18.5	0.4	0.0	12.2
46 to 65	51.3	34.5	12.2	2.0	28.5	82.6	15.5	1.5	0.4	13.0
66 and over	45.2	43.9	10.1	0.8	28.4	82.5	16.2	1.1	0.2	13.4

Table 11.49 What thermometer rating would the Labour/Conservative member give the Green Party ? (%)

Age	Labour					Conservative				
	Cd	Cl	W	H	M	Cd	Cl	W	H	M
All	33.2	36.0	25.7	5.1	39.5	70.0	24.5	5.0	0.5	19.5
25 and under	20.5	28.4	44.3	6.8	48.1	52.4	42.9	4.6	0.1	21.6
26 to 45	27.6	35.9	30.4	6.1	42.8	62.8	29.5	7.0	0.7	22.1
46 to 65	39.2	36.6	20.1	4.1	36.1	69.3	25.4	5.0	0.3	19.6
66 and over	37.7	36.5	21.5	4.3	36.1	74.3	20.9	4.1	0.7	18.4

Table 11.50 What thermometer rating would the Labour/Conservative member give the BBC ? (%)

Age	Labour					Conservative				
	Cd	Cl	W	H	M	Cd	Cl	W	H	M
All	9.3	26.3	39.8	24.6	60.3	8.6	30.4	40.5	20.5	59.3
25 and under	12.2	34.4	36.7	16.7	54.9	9.1	50.0	18.2	22.7	57.5
26 to 45	8.7	26.0	41.4	23.9	60.3	8.5	32.2	41.0	18.3	57.7
46 to 65	9.5	23.3	39.6	27.6	61.9	7.5	29.0	41.4	22.1	60.5
66 and over	10.0	31.7	36.9	21.4	57.9	9.6	30.6	40.0	19.8	58.6

Table 11.51   *What thermometer rating would the Labour/Conservative member*
give the European Community ? (%)

Age	Labour					Conservative				
	Cd	Cl	W	H	M	Cd	Cl	W	H	M
All	11.1	32.5	41.8	14.6	55.5	14.3	40.7	35.6	9.4	50.8
25 and under	18.2	29.5	44.3	8.0	50.6	35.0	30.0	30.0	5.0	42.0
26 to 45	11.1	35.0	42.4	11.5	54.2	14.4	39.0	36.3	10.3	51.6
46 to 65	11.5	29.4	41.5	17.6	56.6	14.2	41.5	34.7	9.6	50.6
66 and over	8.5	33.7	40.4	17.4	57.7	13.7	40.9	36.4	9.0	51.0

Table 11.52   *What thermometer rating would the Labour/Conservative member*
give the Trade Union Congress ? (%)

Age	Labour					Conservative				
	Cd	Cl	W	H	M	Cd	Cl	W	H	M
All	5.6	29.0	47.7	17.7	60.1	53.3	40.1	5.7	0.9	26.4
25 and under	12.9	18.8	48.2	20.1	57.7	55.6	38.9	5.4	0.1	22.1
26 to 45	5.6	32.4	48.8	13.2	58.0	55.0	41.3	3.3	0.4	24.4
46 to 65	5.6	27.6	46.3	20.5	61.2	54.2	39.2	5.3	1.3	26.5
66 and over	3.8	24.8	47.6	23.8	63.4	51.4	40.6	7.0	1.0	27.2

Table 11.53   *What thermometer rating would the Labour/Conservative member*
give the Police ? (%)

Age	Labour					Conservative				
	Cd	Cl	W	H	M	Cd	Cl	W	H	M
All	17.7	44.4	28.6	9.3	48.1	1.4	12.6	39.9	46.1	72.9
25 and under	20.5	51.1	22.7	5.7	43.7	0.0	8.7	52.2	39.1	76.5
26 to 45	22.0	50.4	22.6	5.0	43.0	1.2	17.1	38.1	43.6	71.1
46 to 65	15.7	41.3	31.5	11.5	50.7	2.3	16.3	41.3	40.1	69.9
66 and over	10.6	34.4	38.4	16.6	56.0	0.6	7.6	38.9	52.9	76.2

Table 11.54   **What thermometer rating would the Labour/Conservative member give the House of Commons ? (%)**

Age	Labour					Conservative				
	Cd	Cl	W	H	M	Cd	Cl	W	H	M
All	10.2	33.7	38.2	17.9	56.7	2.3	17.3	49.0	31.4	68.3
25 and under	16.9	48.3	27.0	7.8	46.7	4.8	23.8	47.6	23.8	63.3
26 to 45	11.5	38.2	37.9	12.4	53.4	3.8	23.0	47.3	25.9	64.7
46 to 65	8.6	29.6	38.8	23.0	59.7	1.7	18.8	50.5	29.0	67.8
66 and over	8.8	28.2	39.7	23.3	61.0	2.2	13.7	48.2	35.9	70.3

Table 11.55   **What thermometer rating would the Labour/Conservative member give the CBI ? (%)**

Age	Labour					Conservative				
	Cd	Cl	W	H	M	Cd	Cl	W	H	M
All	44.9	41.7	11.2	2.2	30.9	5.4	29.8	49.0	15.8	59.7
25 and under	43.2	44.6	12.2	0.0	29.6	0.0	35.7	57.1	7.2	60.0
26 to 45	48.7	43.0	7.8	0.5	27.8	8.8	35.1	45.6	10.5	55.1
46 to 65	44.1	40.5	12.2	3.2	32.2	5.0	30.4	49.5	15.1	59.0
66 and over	36.4	40.5	18.5	4.6	36.7	4.4	26.8	49.7	19.1	62.5

Table 11.56   **What thermometer rating would the Labour/Conservative member give the Queen ? (%)**

Age	Labour					Conservative				
	Cd	Cl	W	H	M	Cd	Cl	W	H	M
All	34.5	29.3	19.3	16.9	43.4	1.0	4.6	16.0	78.4	86.3
25 and under	44.9	23.6	22.5	9.0	34.4	8.7	0.0	39.1	52.2	76.0
26 to 45	43.9	33.4	15.5	7.2	34.1	1.5	8.6	22.0	67.9	81.4
46 to 65	29.3	27.6	20.4	22.7	49.1	1.5	5.6	17.4	75.5	84.4
66 and over	20.3	23.6	26.1	30.0	56.6	0.1	2.5	12.1	85.3	90.0

Table 11.57   *What thermometer rating would the Labour/Conservative member*
                 give Judges ? (%)

Age	Labour					Conservative				
	Cd	Cl	W	H	M	Cd	Cl	W	H	M
All	37.9	43.5	15.0	3.6	35.0	4.6	31.1	45.5	18.8	60.4
25 and under	38.6	51.1	9.1	1.2	30.3	0.0	42.9	52.4	4.7	58.3
26 to 45	44.8	44.4	8.7	2.1	30.5	4.4	42.1	42.1	11.4	55.9
46 to 65	34.8	41.7	18.9	4.6	37.2	5.6	30.7	46.8	16.9	59.4
66 and over	26.2	43.7	24.2	5.9	43.0	3.6	26.9	45.1	24.4	63.2

12 Religion

Table 12.1   *The Labour/Conservative party should try to capture the middle*
                 ground in politics (%)

Religion	Labour				Conservative			
	Agree	Neith-er	Dis-agree	N	Agree	Neith-er	Dis-agree	N
All	51.0	12.1	36.9	2814	69.7	13.4	16.9	2283
Non-Religious	38.5	14.3	47.2	1282	57.6	17.6	24.8	245
Catholic	54.6	8.5	36.9	295	73.4	13.0	13.6	154
Anglican	66.7	10.3	23.0	798	71.3	12.7	16.0	1742
Non-Conformist	56.5	11.6	31.9	439	67.6	14.8	17.6	142

Table 12.2   *A Labour/Conservative government should introduce a prices and*
                 Incomes policy as a means of controlling inflation (%)

Religion	Labour				Conservative			
	Agree	Neith-er	Dis-agree	N	Agree	Neith-er	Dis-agree	N
All	57.4	18.9	23.7	2816	42.2	11.6	46.2	2325
Non-Religious	48.5	22.7	28.8	1270	31.4	11.8	56.8	245
Catholic	58.3	18.0	23.7	295	52.2	14.9	32.9	161
Anglican	69.0	13.7	17.3	810	42.9	11.5	45.6	1778
Non-Conformist	60.8	18.1	21.1	441	40.4	4.5	55.1	141

Table 12.3   *Income and wealth should be re-distributed towards ordinary working*
                 people (%)

Religion	Labour				Conservative			
	Agree	Neith-er	Dis-agree	N	Agree	Neith-er	Dis-agree	N
All	86.1	9.0	4.9	2850	25.3	20.1	54.6	2321
Non-Religious	90.5	6.4	3.1	1297	21.5	22.4	56.1	246
Catholic	79.5	13.1	7.4	297	34.0	18.2	47.8	159
Anglican	81.9	11.2	6.9	812	24.8	20.2	55.0	1777
Non-Conformist	85.1	9.7	5.2	444	29.5	17.3	53.2	139

Table 12.4   *The Labour/Conservative Party should always stand by its principles*
even if this should lose it an election (%)

Religion	Labour				Conservative			
	Agree	Neith-er	Dis-agree	N	Agree	Neith-er	Dis-agree	N
All	67.7	11.9	20.4	2846	81.2	8.3	10.5	2378
Non-Religious	67.2	13.7	19.1	1284	74.9	9.6	15.5	251
Catholic	66.6	11.5	21.9	296	79.1	8.6	12.3	163
Anglican	68.3	8.7	23.0	819	82.5	8.2	9.3	1821
Non-Conformist	68.9	13.0	18.1	447	77.6	7.0	15.4	143

Table 12.5   *Further nuclear energy development is essential for the future*
prosperity of Britain (%)

Religion	Labour				Conservative			
	Agree	Neith-er	Dis-agree	N	Agree	Neith-er	Dis-agree	N
All	13.9	11.9	74.2	2833	60.4	16.7	22.9	2338
Non-Religious	10.3	10.8	78.9	1293	63.8	14.6	21.6	246
Catholic	18.3	11.9	69.8	295	54.0	19.6	26.4	163
Anglican	18.0	13.3	68.7	807	60.5	17.2	22.3	1786
Non-Conformist	14.2	12.3	73.5	438	60.8	10.5	28.7	143

Table 12.6   *A future Labour/Conservative government should not agree to a*
single European currency (%)

Religion	Labour				Conservative			
	Agree	Neith-er	Dis-agree	N	Agree	Neith-er	Dis-agree	N
All	25.2	19.0	55.8	2823	57.8	11.9	30.3	2357
Non-Religious	17.2	20.7	62.1	1284	53.4	13.0	33.6	247
Catholic	26.6	15.0	58.4	293	55.6	9.9	34.5	162
Anglican	36.9	17.0	46.1	814	58.8	11.9	29.3	1807
Non-Conformist	25.9	20.6	53.5	432	56.0	12.1	31.9	141

Table 12.7   High Income tax makes people less willing to work hard (%)

Religion	Labour				Conservative			
	Agree	Neith-er	Dis-agree	N	Agree	Neith-er	Dis-agree	N
All	26.1	11.0	62.9	2852	81.8	6.0	12.2	2383
Non-Religious	15.3	9.8	74.9	1298	80.9	6.8	12.3	251
Catholic	35.5	9.8	54.7	296	86.1	4.2	9.7	165
Anglican	38.3	11.1	50.6	817	81.2	6.3	12.5	1823
Non-Conformist	28.8	15.2	56.0	441	86.1	2.8	11.1	144

Table 12.8   Britain's electoral system should be replaced by a system of proportional representation (%)

Religion	Labour				Conservative			
	Agree	Neith-er	Dis-agree	N	Agree	Neith-er	Dis-agree	N
All	58.0	13.2	28.8	2845	21.7	11.8	66.5	2350
Non-Religious	60.0	14.7	25.3	1295	22.1	11.1	66.8	244
Catholic	56.0	12.1	31.9	298	22.7	11.7	65.6	163
Anglican	57.6	11.0	31.4	809	20.9	11.8	67.3	1803
Non-Conformist	54.0	13.5	32.5	443	30.7	13.6	55.7	140

Table 12.9   Further moves towards integration within the European Community should be resisted (%)

Religion	Labour				Conservative			
	Agree	Neith-er	Dis-agree	N	Agree	Neith-er	Dis-agree	N
All	21.5	13.2	65.3	2839	54.0	15.4	30.6	2359
Non-Religious	17.0	14.2	68.8	1299	54.8	17.3	27.9	248
Catholic	19.9	12.1	68.0	297	46.6	11.8	41.6	161
Anglican	29.8	10.6	59.6	803	55.5	15.6	28.9	1805
Non-Conformist	20.5	15.5	64.0	440	43.4	13.8	42.8	145

Table 12.10   *There is no need for a Bill of Rights in this country (%)*

Religion	Labour				Conservative			
	Agree	Neith-er	Dis-agree	N	Agree	Neith-er	Dis-agree	N
All	11.3	9.9	78.8	2818	39.7	26.4	33.9	2272
Non-Religious	8.1	7.5	84.4	1284	37.6	27.3	35.1	242
Catholic	12.6	9.2	78.2	294	41.3	25.2	33.5	155
Anglican	15.8	12.3	71.9	804	39.9	26.9	33.2	1733
Non-Conformist	11.6	12.8	75.6	439	40.1	19.7	40.2	142

Table 12.11   *A future Labour/Conservative government should introduce a directly elected Scottish Assembly with taxing powers (%)*

Religion	Labour				Conservative			
	Agree	Neith-er	Dis-agree	N	Agree	Neith-er	Dis-agree	N
All	61.3	22.1	16.6	2845	22.8	26.3	50.9	2321
Non-Religious	65.2	22.2	12.6	1295	25.1	27.2	47.7	243
Catholic	65.2	17.1	17.7	299	23.8	28.1	48.1	160
Anglican	56.8	20.5	22.7	811	21.4	26.2	52.4	1773
Non-Conformist	55.2	28.2	16.6	440	34.5	24.8	40.7	145

Table 12.12   *Coalition governments are the best form of government for Britain (%)*

Religion	Labour				Conservative			
	Agree	Neith-er	Dis-agree	N	Agree	Neith-er	Dis-agree	N
All	8.7	16.8	74.5	2846	9.5	10.1	80.4	2388
Non-Religious	7.0	18.9	74.1	1293	6.9	12.6	80.5	246
Catholic	9.5	15.9	74.6	296	10.4	9.1	80.5	164
Anglican	10.9	14.2	74.9	819	9.7	9.5	80.8	1831
Non-Conformist	9.1	16.2	74.7	438	11.6	14.3	74.1	147

Table 12.13   A future Labour/Conservative government should/should not spend money to get rid of poverty (%)

Religion	Labour				Conservative			
	Should	Doesn't matter	Should not	N	Should	Doesn't matter	Should not	N
All	98.0	0.9	1.1	2845	80.4	8.3	11.3	2342
Non-Religious	98.2	1.1	0.7	1290	68.7	10.2	21.1	246
Catholic	97.3	0.3	2.4	297	79.0	10.5	10.5	162
Anglican	97.8	0.9	1.3	820	81.5	8.2	10.3	1788
Non-Conformist	98.4	0.9	0.7	438	87.0	4.1	8.9	146

Table 12.14   A future Labour/Conservative government should/should not encourage the growth of private medicine (%)

Religion	Labour				Conservative			
	Should	Doesn't matter	Should not	N	Should	Doesn't matter	Should not	N
All	3.7	4.5	91.8	2837	52.0	15.8	32.2	2352
Non-Religious	2.2	2.7	95.1	1289	50.0	18.3	31.7	246
Catholic	6.4	6.4	87.2	297	55.6	12.3	32.1	162
Anglican	5.3	6.9	87.8	813	51.8	15.8	32.4	1798
Non-Conformist	3.7	4.3	92.0	438	54.8	15.1	30.1	146

Table 12.15   A future Labour/Conservative government should/should not put more money into the National Health Service (%)

Religion	Labour				Conservative			
	Should	Doesn't matter	Should not	N	Should	Doesn't matter	Should not	N
All	98.0	0.7	1.3	2850	79.3	7.5	13.2	2358
Non-Religious	98.3	0.8	0.9	1293	68.4	11.7	19.9	247
Catholic	97.0	1.7	1.3	297	82.2	6.7	11.1	163
Anglican	97.8	0.4	1.8	819	80.9	6.9	12.2	1803
Non-Conformist	98.2	0.5	1.3	441	75.9	8.3	15.8	145

Table 12.16   A future Labour/Conservative government should/should not reduce spending in general (%)

Religion	Labour				Conservative			
	Should	Doesn't matter	Should not	N	Should	Doesn't matter	Should not	N
All	19.5	7.3	73.2	2803	60.5	8.8	30.7	2337
Non-Religious	11.4	5.0	83.6	1274	65.9	9.2	24.9	249
Catholic	27.6	10.9	61.5	294	62.5	6.9	30.6	160
Anglican	27.1	8.6	64.3	801	60.1	8.9	31.0	1785
Non-Conformist	23.7	9.0	67.3	434	55.2	8.4	36.4	143

Table 12.17   A future Labour/Conservative government should/should not introduce stricter laws to regulate the trade unions (%)

Religion	Labour				Conservative			
	Should	Doesn't matter	Should not	N	Should	Doesn't matter	Should not	N
All	10.2	14.7	75.1	2815	66.5	12.1	21.4	2365
Non-Religious	6.3	13.0	80.7	1280	63.1	14.9	22.0	249
Catholic	10.8	17.6	71.6	295	64.0	12.8	23.2	164
Anglican	15.8	15.5	68.7	804	67.5	11.7	20.8	1805
Non-Conformist	10.8	15.8	73.4	436	62.6	11.6	25.8	147

Table 12.18   A future Labour/Conservative government should/should not give workers more say in the places where they work (%)

Religion	Labour				Conservative			
	Should	Doesn't matter	Should not	N	Should	Doesn't matter	Should not	N
All	91.2	5.6	3.2	2839	63.7	13.4	22.9	2372
Non-Religious	92.8	4.1	3.1	1291	61.4	12.9	25.7	249
Catholic	89.2	8.4	2.4	296	65.0	12.9	22.1	163
Anglican	89.1	7.2	3.7	816	63.5	13.7	22.8	1814
Non-Conformist	91.7	5.3	3.0	436	69.2	11.0	19.8	146

Table 12.19   A future Labour/Conservative government should/should not spend
less on defence (%)

Religion	Labour				Conservative			
	Should	Doesn't matter	Should not	N	Should	Doesn't matter	Should not	N
All	82.7	4.6	12.7	2841	44.3	5.0	50.7	2360
Non-Religious	88.4	3.2	8.4	1292	53.4	5.2	41.4	249
Catholic	83.5	4.0	12.5	297	52.5	6.2	41.3	162
Anglican	74.2	6.3	19.5	811	41.9	4.7	53.4	1803
Non-Conformist	81.2	6.1	12.7	441	49.3	6.2	44.5	146

Table 12.20   Should a future Labour/Conservative government :
(A) Reduce taxes & spend less on health, education & social benefits ?
(B) Keep taxes & spending on these services at the same levels as now ?
(C) Increase taxes & spend more on health, education & social benefits ?

Religion	Labour				Conservative			
	A	B	C	N	A	B	C	N
All	2.6	6.3	91.1	2842	6.7	67.1	26.2	2358
Non-Religious	2.0	5.2	92.8	1288	9.0	67.2	23.8	244
Catholic	1.7	6.8	91.5	292	4.9	68.3	26.8	164
Anglican	3.6	8.3	88.1	822	6.3	67.2	26.5	1804
Non-Conformist	2.7	5.7	91.6	440	9.6	64.4	26.0	146

Table 12.21   On joining the Labour/Conservative party did the member approach the party (MA) or did the party approach the member (PA) ? (%)

Religion	Labour				Conservative			
	MA	Don't Know	PA	N	MA	Don't Know	PA	N
All	77.4	20.0	2.6	2874	34.5	50.1	15.4	2396
Non-Religious	80.4	17.4	2.2	1299	37.7	49.8	12.5	247
Catholic	79.7	18.3	2.0	300	35.4	47.0	17.6	164
Anglican	72.3	24.6	3.1	829	33.9	50.2	15.9	1837
Non-Conformist	76.9	20.0	3.1	446	36.5	52.7	10.8	148

Table 12.22   How often has the member attended a party meeting in the last 12 months ? (%)

Religion	Labour				Conservative			
	Not at all	Occas-ionally	Frequ-ently	N	Not at all	Occas-ionally	Frequ-ently	N
All	41.5	30.6	27.9	2885	66.2	22.0	11.8	2414
Non-Religious	44.7	29.6	25.7	1303	70.8	17.2	12.0	250
Catholic	38.2	34.2	27.6	301	68.9	20.7	10.4	164
Anglican	39.8	32.0	28.2	834	65.0	22.7	12.3	1853
Non-Conformist	37.4	28.4	34.2	447	69.4	21.8	8.8	147

Table 12.23   Is the member more or less politically active than 5 years ago ? (%)

Religion	Labour				Conservative			
	More active	About same	Less active	N	More active	About same	Less active	N
All	13.0	38.4	48.6	2850	9.3	62.8	27.9	2032
Non-Religious	13.7	35.3	51.0	1292	9.9	63.4	26.7	191
Catholic	14.7	35.1	50.2	299	3.7	66.4	29.9	134
Anglican	10.8	44.2	45.0	817	9.4	62.1	28.5	1587
Non-Conformist	14.0	39.1	46.9	442	13.3	67.5	19.2	120

Table 12.24   *Does the member hold any office within the Labour/Conservative Party ? (%)*

Religion	Labour			Conservative		
	Yes	No	N	Yes	No	N
All	16.0	84.0	2837	8.4	91.6	2379
Non-Religious	15.2	84.8	1285	8.1	91.9	248
Catholic	14.7	85.3	293	11.8	88.2	161
Anglican	15.1	84.9	821	8.4	91.6	1823
Non-Conformist	21.0	79.0	438	4.8	95.2	147

Table 12.25   *How much time does the member devote to party activities per month ? (%)*

Religion	Labour					Conservative				
	None	Up to 5 hrs	5 to 10 hrs	Over 10 hrs	N	None	Up to 5 hrs	5 to 10 hrs	Over 10 hrs	N
All	51.0	29.7	9.5	9.8	2846	76.2	15.2	4.4	4.2	2368
Non-Religious	51.5	29.1	9.2	10.2	1298	76.8	14.2	4.1	4.9	246
Catholic	52.9	27.9	8.8	10.4	297	77.6	13.7	4.3	4.4	161
Anglican	50.3	31.6	9.3	8.8	813	75.7	15.5	4.6	4.2	1816
Non-Conformist	49.5	29.0	11.0	10.5	438	80.7	13.8	2.8	2.7	145

Table 12.26   *What was the overall financial contribution made by the member in the last year ? (%)*

Religion	Labour				Conservative			
	0 to £10	£10 to £20	Over £20	N	0 to £10	£10 to £20	Over £20	N
All	24.3	19.8	55.9	2535	34.2	21.3	44.5	1796
Non-Religious	17.8	19.0	63.2	1158	37.6	17.5	44.9	189
Catholic	32.4	21.1	46.5	256	35.6	19.5	44.9	118
Anglican	30.5	20.7	48.8	714	33.0	21.8	45.2	1375
Non-Conformist	26.5	19.7	53.8	407	41.2	22.8	36.0	114

Table 12.27   Is the member a local Labour/Conservative councillor ? (%)

Religion	Labour			Conservative		
	Yes	No	N	Yes	No	N
All	7.9	92.1	2861	2.3	97.7	2393
Non-Religious	6.7	93.3	1301	1.6	98.4	248
Catholic	10.5	89.5	295	1.8	98.2	165
Anglican	7.7	92.3	822	2.3	97.7	1834
Non-Conformist	10.2	89.8	443	2.7	97.3	146

Table 12.28   The Labour/Conservative leader should be elected by a system of one party member/one vote (%)

Religion	Labour				Conservative			
	Agree	Neith-er	Dis-agree	N	Agree	Neith-er	Dis-agree	N
All	86.1	5.2	8.7	2854	50.0	14.3	35.7	2338
Non-Religious	82.2	6.5	11.3	1290	49.6	18.0	32.4	244
Catholic	85.6	6.4	8.0	299	45.6	21.9	32.5	160
Anglican	91.8	2.8	5.4	818	50.4	13.2	36.4	1789
Non-Conformist	87.2	4.7	8.1	447	51.0	13.1	35.9	145

Table 12.29   People like me can have a real influence in politics if they are prepared to get involved (%)

Religion	Labour				Conservative			
	Agree	Neith-er	Dis-agree	N	Agree	Neith-er	Dis-agree	N
All	65.9	16.1	18.0	2843	56.4	20.3	23.3	2348
Non-Religious	60.8	17.8	21.4	1293	56.4	16.9	26.7	243
Catholic	68.2	14.0	17.8	299	51.2	24.7	24.1	162
Anglican	70.3	14.8	14.9	811	56.5	20.4	23.1	1797
Non-Conformist	71.1	15.0	13.9	440	60.3	19.9	19.8	146

Table 12.30   Attending party meetings can be pretty tiring after a hard days work (%)

Religion	Labour				Conservative			
	Agree	Neith-er	Dis-agree	N	Agree	Neith-er	Dis-agree	N
All	77.2	11.5	11.3	2846	69.1	19.5	11.4	2326
Non-Religious	77.9	11.4	10.7	1295	64.5	26.4	9.1	242
Catholic	78.5	9.1	12.4	297	72.0	17.4	10.6	161
Anglican	77.7	12.2	10.1	811	69.6	18.8	11.6	1779
Non-Conformist	73.1	12.0	14.9	443	68.1	18.8	13.1	144

Table 12.31   Someone like me could do a good job of being a local councillor (%)

Religion	Labour				Conservative			
	Agree	Neith-er	Dis-agree	N	Agree	Neith-er	Dis-agree	N
All	48.7	21.9	29.4	2821	27.5	24.5	48.0	2314
Non-Religious	49.4	21.7	28.9	1288	31.5	23.7	44.8	241
Catholic	50.7	19.4	29.9	294	27.5	24.4	48.1	160
Anglican	44.7	24.2	31.1	805	26.2	24.2	49.6	1770
Non-Conformist	52.5	20.0	27.5	434	36.4	29.4	34.2	143

Table 12.32   Being an active party member is a good way of meeting interesting people (%)

Religion	Labour				Conservative			
	Agree	Neith-er	Dis-agree	N	Agree	Neith-er	Dis-agree	N
All	64.5	22.0	13.5	2844	59.2	30.0	10.8	2317
Non-Religious	56.5	26.9	16.6	1294	50.2	38.1	11.7	239
Catholic	70.1	16.0	13.9	294	60.2	31.7	8.1	161
Anglican	72.5	16.4	11.1	815	60.6	28.5	10.9	1776
Non-Conformist	69.4	22.0	8.6	441	56.0	33.3	10.7	141

Table 12.33   *The only way to be really educated about politics is to be a party activist (%)*

Religion	Labour				Conservative			
	Agree	Neith-er	Dis-agree	N	Agree	Neith-er	Dis-agree	N
All	41.9	11.1	47.0	2854	35.8	17.1	47.1	2321
Non-Religious	36.0	11.5	52.5	1294	28.2	17.0	54.8	241
Catholic	48.7	11.1	40.2	298	44.9	12.7	42.4	153
Anglican	46.8	10.3	42.9	817	36.2	17.9	45.9	1780
Non-Conformist	45.4	11.5	43.1	445	32.4	13.4	54.2	142

Table 12.34   *The party leadership does not pay a lot of attention to ordinary party members (%)*

Religion	Labour				Conservative			
	Agree	Neith-er	Dis-agree	N	Agree	Neith-er	Dis-agree	N
All	47.1	18.8	34.1	2852	42.3	24.0	33.7	2333
Non-Religious	50.5	20.9	28.6	1296	40.9	25.6	33.5	242
Catholic	54.1	13.5	32.4	296	41.5	30.8	27.7	159
Anglican	41.6	17.4	41.0	815	42.7	22.8	34.5	1790
Non-Conformist	42.2	18.4	39.4	445	40.1	27.5	32.4	142

Table 12.35   *Party activity often takes time away from one's family (%)*

Religion	Labour				Conservative			
	Agree	Neith-er	Dis-agree	N	Agree	Neith-er	Dis-agree	N
All	85.1	10.4	4.5	2843	67.0	25.5	7.5	2302
Non-Religious	83.9	11.7	4.4	1292	59.8	32.0	8.2	241
Catholic	84.2	11.1	4.7	297	70.2	22.4	7.4	161
Anglican	86.1	9.1	4.8	814	67.6	25.3	7.1	1760
Non-Conformist	87.3	8.6	4.1	440	68.6	21.4	10.0	140

Table 12.36   *The Labour/Conservative party would be more successful if people like me were elected to parliament (%)*

Religion	Labour				Conservative			
	Agree	Neith-er	Dis-agree	N	Agree	Neith-er	Dis-agree	N
All	33.9	33.9	32.2	2822	21.2	31.6	47.2	2292
Non-Religious	33.8	35.2	31.0	1288	21.1	37.2	41.7	242
Catholic	34.1	33.1	32.8	293	24.0	31.8	44.2	154
Anglican	31.8	32.9	35.3	806	20.4	31.4	48.2	1754
Non-Conformist	38.2	32.4	29.4	435	29.6	25.4	45.0	142

Table 12.37   *During the last 5 years, how often has the member displayed an election poster in his/her window ? (%)*

Religion	Labour				Conservative			
	Not at all	Occas-ionally	Freq-uently	N	Not at all	Occas-ionally	Freq-uently	N
All	9.5	21.7	68.8	2831	49.0	31.7	19.3	2282
Non-Religious	9.0	20.1	70.9	1290	49.0	28.6	22.4	241
Catholic	8.9	21.2	69.9	293	41.2	34.6	24.2	153
Anglican	9.3	25.7	65.0	809	49.3	32.1	18.6	1749
Non-Conformist	11.8	19.6	68.6	439	54.7	28.8	16.5	139

Table 12.38   *During the last 5 years, how often has the member donated money to party funds ? (%)*

Religion	Labour				Conservative			
	Not at all	Occas-ionally	Freq-uently	N	Not at all	Occas-ionally	Freq-uently	N
All	9.5	51.1	39.4	2824	15.0	55.3	29.7	2333
Non-Religious	9.3	51.5	39.2	1293	16.3	55.6	28.1	239
Catholic	8.9	50.3	40.8	292	17.8	51.6	30.6	157
Anglican	9.3	25.7	65.0	809	14.4	55.0	30.6	1793
Non-Conformist	11.8	19.6	68.6	439	16.7	62.5	20.8	144

Table 12.39   *During the last 5 years, how often has the member delivered party leaflets ? (%)*

Religion	Labour				Conservative			
	Not at all	Occas-ionally	Freq-uently	N	Not at all	Occas-ionally	Freq-uently	N
All	17.6	27.0	55.4	2778	61.0	17.1	21.9	2228
Non-Religious	14.4	28.0	57.6	1281	63.8	14.0	22.2	235
Catholic	17.0	24.7	58.3	288	55.7	22.8	21.5	149
Anglican	22.2	26.3	51.5	776	60.4	17.0	22.6	1711
Non-Conformist	18.9	26.6	54.5	433	69.2	16.5	14.3	133

Table 12.40   *During the last 5 years, how often has the member attended a party meeting ? (%)*

Religion	Labour				Conservative			
	Not at all	Occas-ionally	Freq-uently	N	Not at all	Occas-ionally	Freq-uently	N
All	21.3	40.8	37.9	2782	50.8	32.7	16.5	2258
Non-Religious	21.4	42.1	36.5	1278	55.0	27.7	17.3	238
Catholic	17.8	40.2	42.0	286	53.0	32.5	14.5	151
Anglican	22.1	42.0	35.9	784	49.9	33.3	16.8	1729
Non-Conformist	21.9	33.3	44.8	434	52.9	33.6	13.5	140

Table 12.41   *During the last 5 years, how often has the member canvassed voters on behalf of the party ? (%)*

Religion	Labour				Conservative			
	Not at all	Occas-ionally	Freq-uently	N	Not at all	Occas-ionally	Freq-uently	N
All	36.8	31.2	32.0	2758	74.9	14.8	10.3	2219
Non-Religious	35.6	31.9	32.5	1274	78.4	12.1	9.5	232
Catholic	36.1	27.4	36.5	288	71.0	16.6	12.4	145
Anglican	39.8	31.4	28.8	767	74.7	14.9	10.4	1704
Non-Conformist	35.7	31.5	32.8	429	76.1	16.7	7.2	138

Table 12.42 *Where would you place yourself on a Left/Right scale within the Labour/Conservative party ? (%)*

Religion	Labour				Conservative			
	Left	Centre	Right	N	Left	Centre	Right	N
All	57.6	20.5	21.9	2857	13.2	25.9	60.9	2371
Non-Religious	58.1	16.8	25.1	1294	17.6	21.6	60.8	245
Catholic	55.9	20.2	23.9	297	12.7	28.5	58.8	165
Anglican	44.2	25.9	29.9	820	12.1	25.7	62.2	1814
Non-Conformist	52.2	22.0	25.8	446	21.1	32.7	46.2	147

Table 12.43 *Where would you place yourself on a Left/Right scale within British Politics ? (%)*

Religion	Labour				Conservative			
	Left	Centre	Right	N	Left	Centre	Right	N
All	80.2	10.2	9.6	2854	3.6	18.2	78.2	2365
Non-Religious	91.4	4.6	4.0	1293	3.3	13.4	83.3	246
Catholic	73.7	12.5	13.8	297	3.0	26.7	70.3	165
Anglican	63.3	17.6	19.1	819	3.7	18.0	78.3	1807
Non-Conformist	76.9	11.2	11.9	445	4.1	19.0	76.9	147

Table 12.44 *What thermometer rating would the Labour/Conservative member give the Conservative Party ? (%)*

Religion	Labour					Conservative				
	Cd	Cl	W	H	M	Cd	Cl	W	H	M
All	76.0	20.5	2.8	0.7	14.6	0.2	3.6	33.6	62.6	80.9
Non-Religious	85.5	12.8	1.1	0.6	10.4	0.0	5.7	39.6	54.7	78.1
Catholic	68.0	26.4	4.6	1.0	17.9	0.0	6.1	31.9	62.0	80.7
Anglican	69.3	26.5	3.5	0.7	18.2	0.2	2.9	32.5	64.4	81.5
Non-Conformist	65.5	28.7	5.3	0.5	18.7	0.7	5.5	39.0	54.8	77.6

Table 12.45   *What thermometer rating would the Labour/Conservative member*
give the Labour Party ? (%)

Religion	Labour					Conservative				
	Cd	Cl	W	H	M	Cd	Cl	W	H	M
All	0.9	3.8	24.6	70.7	82.7	50.2	43.2	6.1	0.5	26.7
Non-Religious	1.1	5.2	31.2	62.5	79.8	55.3	42.2	2.5	0.0	24.2
Catholic	1.0	4.0	20.1	74.9	83.5	44.1	50.0	5.9	0.0	27.3
Anglican	0.6	2.2	18.2	79.0	85.8	50.5	42.5	6.4	0.6	26.8
Non-Conformist	0.9	2.5	20.0	76.6	84.8	44.9	46.4	8.7	0.0	29.2

Table 12.46   *What thermometer rating would the Labour/Conservative member*
give the Liberal Democratic Party ? (%)

Religion	Labour					Conservative				
	Cd	Cl	W	H	M	Cd	Cl	W	H	M
All	32.9	44.3	20.9	1.9	36.9	32.6	50.8	15.3	1.3	36.3
Non-Religious	37.1	44.5	17.5	0.9	34.2	37.8	47.2	14.2	0.8	33.8
Catholic	33.7	40.7	23.2	2.4	37.4	34.7	50.7	14.6	0.0	35.3
Anglican	28.2	46.3	22.1	3.4	39.4	31.8	51.4	15.4	1.4	36.6
Non-Conformist	28.3	42.7	27.1	1.9	40.2	32.1	49.6	16.1	2.2	36.9

Table 12.47   *What thermometer rating would the Labour/Conservative member*
give the Scottish Nationalist Party ? (%)

Religion	Labour					Conservative				
	Cd	Cl	W	H	M	Cd	Cl	W	H	M
All	43.8	37.3	16.0	2.9	32.2	69.0	26.7	3.9	0.4	19.0
Non-Religious	43.0	37.0	17.2	2.8	32.5	67.9	27.9	3.7	0.5	18.9
Catholic	41.8	35.7	18.3	4.2	33.8	66.7	30.3	2.0	1.0	18.8
Anglican	47.5	36.9	12.5	3.1	30.5	69.3	26.3	4.2	0.2	19.0
Non-Conformist	40.8	39.9	17.0	2.3	33.2	70.0	27.0	3.0	0.0	20.4

Table 12.48 *What thermometer rating would the Labour/Conservative member give Plaid Cymru ? (%)*

Religion	Labour					Conservative				
	Cd	Cl	W	H	M	Cd	Cl	W	H	M
All	47.5	37.7	12.9	1.9	29.7	82.7	16.0	1.1	0.2	12.9
Non-Religious	45.1	38.4	14.6	1.9	30.7	80.1	18.8	1.1	0.0	12.4
Catholic	45.8	37.8	13.1	3.3	30.2	77.4	21.5	1.1	0.0	14.7
Anglican	53.2	36.5	8.9	1.4	27.1	83.3	15.3	1.1	0.3	12.8
Non-Conformist	45.3	37.8	14.8	2.1	30.8	85.6	13.4	1.0	0.0	13.0

Table 12.49 *What thermometer rating would the Labour/Conservative member give the Green Party ? (%)*

Religion	Labour					Conservative				
	Cd	Cl	W	H	M	Cd	Cl	W	H	M
All	33.3	35.8	25.7	5.2	39.4	70.2	24.4	4.9	0.5	19.5
Non-Religious	29.2	34.8	30.2	5.8	42.0	68.8	25.0	5.8	0.4	19.7
Catholic	34.2	38.1	23.1	4.6	37.8	60.2	32.7	6.2	0.9	21.6
Anglican	40.2	35.5	19.8	4.5	35.7	71.6	23.5	4.4	0.5	19.1
Non-Conformist	32.5	38.0	24.3	5.2	39.3	65.5	26.4	7.3	0.8	21.7

Table 12.50 *What thermometer rating would the Labour/Conservative member give the BBC ? (%)*

Religion	Labour					Conservative				
	Cd	Cl	W	H	M	Cd	Cl	W	H	M
All	9.2	26.3	39.8	24.7	60.4	8.4	30.5	40.5	20.6	59.3
Non-Religious	7.7	24.1	42.7	25.5	61.8	12.1	39.3	33.9	14.7	54.3
Catholic	14.2	26.6	38.4	20.8	56.3	6.9	31.3	39.4	22.4	60.1
Anglican	11.0	29.4	35.2	24.4	58.9	8.0	28.6	42.2	21.2	60.1
Non-Conformist	7.1	27.1	40.6	25.2	61.5	9.3	37.9	32.1	20.7	57.3

Table 12.51   *What thermometer rating would the Labour/Conservative member give the European Community ? (%)*

Religion	Labour					Conservative				
	Cd	Cl	W	H	M	Cd	Cl	W	H	M
All	11.0	32.6	41.8	14.6	55.5	14.2	40.7	35.8	9.3	50.8
Non-Religious	10.8	34.3	42.0	12.9	55.1	22.4	42.9	27.0	7.7	45.5
Catholic	8.6	29.2	44.6	17.6	58.1	10.3	34.2	41.9	13.6	55.9
Anglican	12.5	34.8	37.5	15.2	54.0	13.2	41.2	36.7	8.9	51.1
Non-Conformist	10.7	25.6	46.7	17.0	58.0	15.5	37.9	34.5	12.1	51.7

Table 12.52   *What thermometer rating would the Labour/Conservative member give the Trade Union Congress ? (%)*

Religion	Labour					Conservative				
	Cd	Cl	W	H	M	Cd	Cl	W	H	M
All	5.6	28.9	47.8	17.7	60.0	53.6	39.9	5.6	0.9	26.3
Non-Religious	5.6	31.0	49.1	14.3	58.7	60.6	35.2	4.1	0.1	24.0
Catholic	4.6	29.3	42.4	23.7	62.0	51.1	40.0	7.8	1.1	25.7
Anglican	5.9	27.7	46.1	20.3	60.8	53.5	40.0	5.4	1.1	26.5
Non-Conformist	6.1	24.6	50.6	18.7	61.4	43.6	47.5	8.9	0.0	29.6

Table 12.53   *What thermometer rating would the Labour/Conservative member give the Police ? (%)*

Religion	Labour					Conservative				
	Cd	Cl	W	H	M	Cd	Cl	W	H	M
All	17.8	44.3	28.5	9.4	48.1	1.4	12.6	39.7	46.3	72.9
Non-Religious	22.6	51.7	21.7	4.0	42.2	1.3	20.4	40.8	37.5	68.5
Catholic	16.1	41.3	29.7	12.9	49.9	2.6	11.9	36.4	49.1	72.6
Anglican	11.9	37.9	34.5	15.7	54.9	1.3	11.0	40.2	47.5	73.8
Non-Conformist	15.1	36.6	37.0	11.3	51.9	2.1	20.3	35.0	42.6	70.6

Table 12.54 **What thermometer rating would the Labour/Conservative member give the House of Commons ? (%)**

Religion	Labour					Conservative				
	Cd	Cl	W	H	M	Cd	Cl	W	H	M
All	10.1	33.7	38.3	17.9	56.8	2.4	17.0	49.1	31.5	68.3
Non-Religious	11.6	38.8	36.5	13.1	53.7	5.7	23.9	47.8	22.6	63.3
Catholic	12.3	31.2	35.8	20.7	56.9	1.4	15.6	52.4	30.6	69.4
Anglican	8.5	29.1	39.8	22.6	59.8	2.0	16.1	49.5	32.4	69.0
Non-Conformist	7.0	28.4	42.0	22.6	60.7	3.8	18.0	42.9	35.3	67.9

Table 12.55 **What thermometer rating would the Labour/Conservative member give the CBI ? (%)**

Religion	Labour					Conservative				
	Cd	Cl	W	H	M	Cd	Cl	W	H	M
All	44.8	41.8	11.3	2.1	30.9	5.5	29.7	49.0	15.8	59.6
Non-Religious	52.7	39.0	7.6	0.7	26.1	6.7	34.4	49.7	9.2	55.7
Catholic	38.8	45.2	13.6	2.4	34.3	7.1	26.2	46.4	20.3	60.4
Anglican	36.4	43.6	15.7	4.3	36.2	5.0	28.7	49.9	16.4	60.5
Non-Conformist	38.9	45.2	13.4	2.5	34.6	7.0	36.0	39.5	17.5	56.7

Table 12.56 **What thermometer rating would the Labour/Conservative member give the Queen ? (%)**

Religion	Labour					Conservative				
	Cd	Cl	W	H	M	Cd	Cl	W	H	M
All	34.7	29.3	19.3	16.7	43.4	0.9	4.6	16.0	78.5	86.4
Non-Religious	49.7	31.3	13.7	5.3	30.9	3.7	12.0	24.4	59.9	77.1
Catholic	31.1	30.1	21.3	17.5	45.5	1.3	5.0	15.7	78.0	86.4
Anglican	17.0	26.4	24.1	32.5	58.5	0.3	3.6	14.7	81.4	87.9
Non-Conformist	25.4	28.0	25.4	21.2	50.5	2.9	5.0	18.7	73.4	83.3

Table 12.57   *What thermometer rating would the Labour/Conservative member*
give Judges ? (%)

Religion	Labour					Conservative				
	Cd	Cl	W	H	M	Cd	Cl	W	H	M
All	38.1	43.3	15.1	3.5	35.0	4.6	30.8	45.7	18.9	60.5
Non-Religious	49.4	40.4	8.9	1.3	28.3	7.0	41.4	40.5	11.1	54.8
Catholic	35.3	45.5	14.9	4.3	36.3	5.4	33.3	47.3	14.0	58.0
Anglican	24.9	46.1	23.3	5.7	42.9	3.7	29.5	46.0	20.8	61.8
Non-Conformist	30.4	45.3	18.6	5.7	39.6	9.5	26.2	48.4	15.9	57.1

13 Tenure

Table 13.1 *The Labour/Conservative party should try to capture the middle ground in politics (%)*

Tenure	Labour				Conservative			
	Agree	Neith-er	Dis-agree	N	Agree	Neith-er	Dis-agree	N
All	50.9	12.2	36.9	2839	69.7	13.3	17.0	2273
Own Property	49.0	12.5	38.7	2175	69.5	13.5	17.0	2074
Rent Property	62.1	10.1	27.8	515	75.0	9.6	15.4	136
Other	40.9	15.5	43.6	149	63.5	14.3	22.2	63

Table 13.2 *A Labour/Conservative government should introduce a prices and incomes policy as a means of controlling inflation (%)*

Tenure	Labour				Conservative			
	Agree	Neith-er	Dis-agree	N	Agree	Neith-er	Dis-agree	N
All	57.4	19.0	23.6	2841	42.0	11.5	46.5	2312
Own Property	49.0	12.3	38.7	2175	40.4	11.5	48.1	2105
Rent Property	62.1	10.1	27.8	515	66.0	7.8	26.2	141
Other	40.9	15.5	43.6	149	43.9	18.2	37.9	66

Table 13.3 *Income and wealth should be re-distributed towards ordinary working people (%)*

Tenure	Labour				Conservative			
	Agree	Neith-er	Dis-agree	N	Agree	Neith-er	Dis-agree	N
All	85.9	9.2	4.9	2874	25.3	20.2	54.5	2308
Own Property	86.8	8.6	4.6	2198	24.3	20.6	55.1	2107
Rent Property	84.4	9.7	5.9	525	40.3	11.9	47.8	134
Other	79.5	13.9	6.6	151	26.9	23.8	49.3	67

Table 13.4 *The Labour/Conservative Party should always stand by its principles even if this should lose it an election (%)*

Tenure	Labour				Conservative			
	Agree	Neith-er	Dis-agree	N	Agree	Neith-er	Dis-agree	N
All	67.9	11.9	20.2	2871	81.2	8.2	10.6	2365
Own Property	65.3	13.3	21.4	2194	80.7	8.5	10.8	2149
Rent Property	79.4	4.7	15.9	527	89.9	4.1	6.0	148
Other	65.3	16.7	18.0	150	77.9	10.3	11.8	68

Table 13.5 *Further nuclear energy development is essential for the future prosperity of Britain (%)*

Tenure	Labour				Conservative			
	Agree	Neith-er	Dis-agree	N	Agree	Neith-er	Dis-agree	N
All	14.0	11.8	74.2	2858	60.1	16.9	23.0	2326
Own Property	13.2	12.2	74.6	2197	60.6	16.8	22.6	2119
Rent Property	17.9	11.1	71.0	514	52.9	17.1	30.0	140
Other	11.6	9.5	78.9	147	58.2	19.4	22.4	67

Table 13.6 *A future Labour/Conservative government should not agree to a single European currency (%)*

Tenure	Labour				Conservative			
	Agree	Neith-er	Dis-agree	N	Agree	Neith-er	Dis-agree	N
All	25.4	18.9	55.7	2848	57.8	12.0	30.2	2346
Own Property	22.4	19.1	58.5	2183	56.9	12.0	31.1	2137
Rent Property	37.0	18.1	44.9	515	69.9	9.8	20.3	143
Other	29.3	18.0	52.7	150	60.6	16.7	22.7	66

Table 13.7   *High income tax makes people less willing to work hard (%)*

Tenure	Labour				Conservative			
	Agree	Neith-er	Dis-agree	N	Agree	Neith-er	Dis-agree	N
All	26.2	11.0	62.8	2876	82.0	6.0	12.0	2368
Own Property	22.5	10.8	66.7	2201	82.1	6.0	11.9	2156
Rent Property	41.9	12.0	46.1	525	84.7	2.8	12.5	144
Other	27.3	10.0	62.7	150	70.6	11.8	17.6	68

Table 13.8   *Britain's electoral system should be replaced by a system of proportional representation (%)*

Tenure	Labour				Conservative			
	Agree	Neith-er	Dis-agree	N	Agree	Neith-er	Dis-agree	N
All	57.8	13.2	29.0	2870	21.8	11.7	66.5	2334
Own Property	58.9	13.5	27.6	2196	21.8	11.4	66.8	2126
Rent Property	53.9	10.2	35.9	523	21.3	17.7	61.0	141
Other	56.3	19.9	23.8	151	20.9	11.9	67.2	67

Table 13.9   *Further moves towards integration within the European Community should be resisted (%)*

Tenure	Labour				Conservative			
	Agree	Neith-er	Dis-agree	N	Agree	Neith-er	Dis-agree	N
All	22.9	13.4	63.7	2067	54.5	15.0	30.5	1515
Own Property	16.2	10.9	72.9	680	54.1	14.9	31.0	1221
Rent Property	26.7	14.5	58.8	1327	59.6	14.2	26.2	267
Other	16.6	16.7	66.7	60	18.5	25.9	55.6	27

Table 13.10   There is no need for a Bill of Rights in this country (%)

Tenure	Labour				Conservative			
	Agree	Neith-er	Dis-agree	N	Agree	Neith-er	Dis-agree	N
All	11.4	10.0	78.6	2846	39.8	26.6	33.6	2261
Own Property	9.9	9.0	81.1	2178	40.0	26.9	33.1	2056
Rent Property	18.5	12.4	69.1	518	36.0	23.0	41.0	139
Other	8.7	15.3	76.0	150	40.9	24.2	34.9	66

Table 13.11   A future Labour/Conservative government should introduce a directly elected Scottish Assembly with taxing powers (%)

Tenure	Labour				Conservative			
	Agree	Neith-er	Dis-agree	N	Agree	Neith-er	Dis-agree	N
All	61.2	22.1	16.7	2869	22.7	26.4	50.9	2305
Own Property	60.9	22.9	16.2	2197	22.7	26.1	51.2	2097
Rent Property	61.7	17.8	20.5	522	25.5	24.8	49.7	141
Other	64.0	25.3	10.7	150	16.4	38.8	44.8	67

Table 13.12   Coalition governments are the best form of government for Britain (%)

Tenure	Labour				Conservative			
	Agree	Neith-er	Dis-agree	N	Agree	Neith-er	Dis-agree	N
All	8.7	16.7	74.6	2867	9.5	10.1	80.4	2374
Own Property	8.3	17.0	74.7	2194	9.0	10.0	81.0	2158
Rent Property	10.1	14.2	75.7	522	14.8	9.5	75.7	148
Other	9.2	21.9	68.9	151	13.2	14.7	72.1	68

Table 13.13 *A future Labour/Conservative government should/should not spend money to get rid of poverty (%)*

Tenure	Labour				Conservative			
	Should	Doesn't matter	Should not	N	Should	Doesn't matter	Should not	N
All	98.0	1.0	1.0	2868	80.1	8.4	11.5	2328
Own Property	98.2	0.8	1.0	2195	80.7	8.0	11.3	2121
Rent Property	97.2	1.7	1.1	523	75.3	12.7	12.0	142
Other	98.0	0.0	2.0	150	70.7	10.8	18.5	65

Table 13.14 *A future Labour/Conservative government should/should not encourage the growth of private medicine (%)*

Tenure	Labour				Conservative			
	Should	Doesn't matter	Should not	N	Should	Doesn't matter	Should not	N
All	3.7	4.7	91.6	2861	51.8	15.9	32.2	2338
Own Property	3.1	3.7	93.1	2187	51.7	15.9	32.4	2130
Rent Property	6.3	8.0	85.7	523	53.5	12.0	34.5	142
Other	4.0	6.6	89.4	151	53.0	24.2	22.7	66

Table 13.15 *A future Labour/Conservative government should/should not put more money into the National Health Service (%)*

Tenure	Labour				Conservative			
	Should	Doesn't matter	Should not	N	Should	Doesn't matter	Should not	N
All	98.0	0.7	1.3	2873	79.3	7.5	13.2	2347
Own Property	98.0	0.7	1.3	2195	79.4	7.4	13.2	2133
Rent Property	98.1	0.6	1.3	527	80.4	5.4	14.2	606
Other	97.4	0.7	1.9	895	74.2	15.2	10.6	468

Table 13.16   A future Labour/Conservative government should/should not reduce spending in general (%)

Tenure	Labour				Conservative			
	Should	Doesn't matter	Should not	N	Should	Doesn't matter	Should not	N
All	19.6	7.3	73.1	2826	60.7	8.6	30.7	2325
Own Property	18.2	6.5	75.3	2161	61.1	8.3	30.6	2121
Rent Property	27.2	9.7	63.1	514	60.4	10.1	29.5	139
Other	12.6	9.3	78.1	151	49.2	15.4	35.4	65

Table 13.17   A future Labour/Conservative government should/should not introduce stricter laws to regulate the trade unions (%)

Tenure	Labour				Conservative			
	Should	Doesn't matter	Should not	N	Should	Doesn't matter	Should not	N
All	10.2	14.7	75.1	2836	66.3	12.1	21.6	2353
Own Property	8.8	15.0	76.2	2169	65.7	12.3	22.0	2140
Rent Property	15.7	14.1	70.2	517	73.8	9.7	16.5	145
Other	12.7	13.3	74.0	150	66.2	11.8	22.0	68

Table 13.18   A future Labour/Conservative government should/should not give workers more say in the places where they work (%)

Tenure	Labour				Conservative			
	Should	Doesn't matter	Should not	N	Should	Doesn't matter	Should not	N
All	91.2	5.6	3.2	2863	63.6	13.4	23.0	2358
Own Property	91.3	5.2	3.5	2190	63.5	13.3	23.2	2143
Rent Property	91.8	6.3	1.9	522	65.3	13.6	21.1	147
Other	87.4	9.3	3.3	151	63.2	14.7	22.1	68

Table 13.19   *A future Labour/Conservative government should/should not spend*
less on defence (%)

Tenure	Labour				Conservative			
	Should	Doesn't matter	Should not	N	Should	Doesn't matter	Should not	N
All	82.7	4.6	12.7	2865	44.3	4.8	50.9	2345
Own Property	85.0	4.3	10.7	2193	45.1	4.5	50.4	2135
Rent Property	75.4	5.0	19.6	521	37.1	6.3	56.6	143
Other	75.5	7.9	16.6	151	32.8	10.4	56.8	67

Table 13.20   *Should a future Labour/Conservative government :*
(A) Reduce taxes & spend less on health, education & social benefits ?
(B) Keep taxes & spending on these services at the same levels as now ?
(C) Increase taxes & spend more on health, education & social benefits ?

Tenure	Labour				Conservative			
	A	B	C	N	A	B	C	N
All	2.7	6.5	90.8	2867	6.8	67.1	26.1	2371
Own Property	2.5	5.9	91.6	2197	6.7	67.3	26.0	2159
Rent Property	2.7	8.4	88.9	521	10.3	59.3	30.4	145
Other	5.4	7.4	87.2	149	1.5	80.6	17.9	67

Table 13.21   *On joining the Labour/Conservative party did the member approach*
the party (MA) or did the party approach the member (PA) ? (%)

Tenure	Labour				Conservative			
	MA	Don't Know	PA	N	MA	Don't Know	PA	N
All	77.5	19.9	2.6	2898	34.5	50.1	15.4	2381
Own Property	77.5	20.0	2.5	2210	33.8	51.3	14.9	2164
Rent Property	77.0	20.3	2.7	538	43.2	39.2	17.6	148
Other	78.7	18.7	2.6	150	39.1	36.2	24.7	69

310

Table 13.22   *How often has the member attended a party meeting in the last*
12 months ? (%)

Tenure	Labour				Conservative			
	Not at all	Occas-ionally	Frequ-ently	N	Not at all	Occas-ionally	Frequ-ently	N
All	41.7	30.3	28.0	2910	65.9	22.1	12.0	2398
Own Property	42.0	30.4	27.6	2224	66.1	22.0	11.9	2177
Rent Property	40.0	29.7	30.3	535	62.5	24.3	13.2	152
Other	44.4	32.5	23.1	151	66.7	20.3	13.0	69

Table 13.23   *Is the member more or less politically active than 5 years ago ? (%)*

Tenure	Labour				Conservative			
	More active	About same	Less active	N	More active	About same	Less active	N
All	12.9	38.5	48.6	2872	9.3	62.9	27.8	2016
Own Property	13.3	38.5	48.2	2198	9.2	63.6	27.2	1838
Rent Property	10.9	39.8	49.3	525	7.9	57.1	35.0	126
Other	14.8	33.6	51.6	149	15.4	53.8	30.8	52

Table 13.24   *Does the member hold any office within the Labour/Conservative*
Party ? (%)

Tenure	Labour			Conservative		
	Yes	No	N	Yes	No	N
All	15.9	84.1	2859	8.4	91.6	2364
Own Property	17.1	82.9	2188	8.5	91.5	2145
Rent Property	13.1	86.9	526	6.0	94.0	149
Other	8.3	91.7	145	10.0	90.0	70

Table 13.25   How much time does the member devote to party activities per month ? (%)

Tenure	Labour					Conservative				
	None	Up to 5 hrs	5 to 10 hrs	Over 10 hrs	N	None	Up to 5 hrs	5 to 10 hrs	Over 10 hrs	N
All	51.2	29.5	9.4	9.9	2869	76.2	15.3	4.4	4.1	2351
Own Property	50.9	29.9	9.7	9.5	2194	76.0	15.6	4.4	4.0	2136
Rent Property	52.7	27.8	9.3	10.2	526	76.0	14.4	4.8	4.8	146
Other	51.7	30.2	6.0	12.1	149	81.2	8.7	5.8	4.3	69

Table 13.26   What was the overall financial contribution made by the member in the last year ? (%)

Tenure	Labour				Conservative			
	0 to £10	£10 to £20	Over £20	N	0 to £10	£10 to £20	Over £20	N
All	24.3	19.7	56.0	2556	34.3	21.4	44.3	1783
Own Property	19.0	19.7	61.3	1984	33.4	21.7	44.9	1638
Rent Property	46.3	19.5	34.2	436	42.6	20.2	37.2	94
Other	31.6	19.9	48.5	136	47.1	13.7	39.2	51

Table 13.27   Is the member a local Labour/Conservative councillor ? (%)

Tenure	Labour			Conservative		
	Yes	No	N	Yes	No	N
All	7.8	92.2	2884	2.3	97.7	2379
Own Property	8.0	92.0	2201	2.5	97.5	2162
Rent Property	7.3	92.7	533	0.7	99.3	150
Other	6.7	93.3	150	0.0	100.0	67

Table 13.28   *The Labour/Conservative leader should be elected by a system of one party member/one vote (%)*

Tenure	Labour					Conservative			
	Agree	Neith-er	Dis-agree	N		Agree	Neith-er	Dis-agree	N
All	86.1	5.2	8.7	2878		49.8	14.4	35.8	2323
Own Property	85.5	5.5	9.0	2197		49.1	14.5	36.4	2114
Rent Property	88.9	4.0	7.1	531		62.2	11.9	25.9	143
Other	86.0	6.0	8.0	150		43.9	18.2	37.9	66

Table 13.29   *People like me can have a real influence in politics if they are prepared to get involved (%)*

Tenure	Labour					Conservative			
	Agree	Neith-er	Dis-agree	N		Agree	Neith-er	Dis-agree	N
All	65.9	16.0	18.1	2867		56.5	20.2	23.3	2335
Own Property	64.2	16.9	18.9	2192		57.1	19.8	23.1	2132
Rent Property	72.0	11.4	16.6	525		50.4	27.0	22.6	137
Other	69.3	19.3	11.4	150		51.5	18.2	30.3	66

Table 13.30   *Attending party meetings can be pretty tiring after a hard days work (%)*

Tenure	Labour					Conservative			
	Agree	Neith-er	Dis-agree	N		Agree	Neith-er	Dis-agree	N
All	77.2	11.4	11.4	2871		69.4	19.4	11.2	2314
Own Property	78.6	10.6	10.8	2198		69.4	19.7	10.9	2112
Rent Property	73.9	12.8	13.3	525		71.0	14.5	14.5	138
Other	67.6	18.2	14.2	148		65.6	20.3	14.1	64

Table 13.31   Someone like me could do a good job of being a local councillor (%)

Tenure	Labour				Conservative			
	Agree	Neith-er	Dis-agree	N	Agree	Neith-er	Dis-agree	N
All	48.7	21.8	29.5	2845	27.6	24.4	48.0	2305
Own Property	49.2	21.0	29.8	2180	28.0	24.5	47.5	2107
Rent Property	47.7	23.1	29.2	516	23.7	21.5	54.8	135
Other	45.6	29.5	24.9	149	22.2	28.6	49.2	63

Table 13.32   Being an active party member is a good way of meeting interesting people (%)

Tenure	Labour				Conservative			
	Agree	Neith-er	Dis-agree	N	Agree	Neith-er	Dis-agree	N
All	64.7	21.8	13.5	2869	59.2	30.1	10.7	2306
Own Property	62.7	23.0	14.3	2197	58.2	30.9	10.9	2104
Rent Property	74.5	16.2	9.3	524	71.9	20.9	7.2	139
Other	60.8	24.3	14.9	148	63.5	25.4	11.1	63

Table 13.33   The only way to be really educated about politics is to be a party activist (%)

Tenure	Labour				Conservative			
	Agree	Neith-er	Dis-agree	N	Agree	Neith-er	Dis-agree	N
All	42.1	11.2	46.7	2876	35.8	17.2	47.0	2309
Own Property	39.4	11.3	49.3	2200	35.4	17.1	47.5	2106
Rent Property	54.5	11.0	34.5	527	43.8	19.7	36.5	137
Other	38.9	9.4	51.7	149	31.8	13.6	54.6	66

Table 13.34   *The party leadership does not pay a lot of attention to ordinary party members (%)*

Tenure	Labour				Conservative			
	Agree	Neith-er	Dis-agree	N	Agree	Neith-er	Dis-agree	N
All	47.0	18.8	34.2	2875	42.2	24.1	33.7	2319
Own Property	44.6	20.5	34.9	2200	41.8	24.4	33.8	2116
Rent Property	55.7	12.2	32.1	526	49.6	19.0	31.4	137
Other	50.3	17.4	32.3	149	37.9	25.8	36.3	66

Table 13.35   *Party activity often takes time away from one's family (%)*

Tenure	Labour				Conservative			
	Agree	Neith-er	Dis-agree	N	Agree	Neith-er	Dis-agree	N
All	85.0	10.4	4.6	2869	67.1	25.5	7.4	2291
Own Property	85.9	9.5	4.6	2197	67.3	25.5	7.2	2091
Rent Property	84.4	11.0	4.6	525	66.9	22.8	10.3	136
Other	73.5	21.1	5.4	147	62.5	31.3	6.2	64

Table 13.36   *The Labour/Conservative party would be more successful if people like me were elected to parliament (%)*

Tenure	Labour				Conservative			
	Agree	Neith-er	Dis-agree	N	Agree	Neith-er	Dis-agree	N
All	33.8	34.0	32.2	2845	21.4	31.6	47.0	2282
Own Property	32.4	34.6	33.0	2176	21.1	31.9	47.0	2087
Rent Property	39.8	30.8	29.4	520	27.5	26.0	46.5	131
Other	32.9	36.9	30.2	149	18.8	32.8	48.4	64

Table 13.37   *During the last 5 years, how often has the member displayed an election poster in his/her window ? (%)*

Tenure	Labour					Conservative			
	Not at all	Occas- ionally	Freq- uently	N		Not at all	Occas- ionally	Freq- uently	N
All	9.6	21.7	68.7	2853		48.6	32.0	19.4	2270
Own Property	9.3	22.0	68.7	2185		48.4	32.3	19.3	2064
Rent Property	9.2	19.6	71.2	521		46.5	34.0	19.5	144
Other	15.6	23.8	60.6	147		59.7	19.4	20.9	62

Table 13.38   *During the last 5 years, how often has the member donated money to party funds ? (%)*

Tenure	Labour					Conservative			
	Not at all	Occas- ionally	Freq- uently	N		Not at all	Occas- ionally	Freq- uently	N
All	9.6	50.9	39.5	2847		14.9	55.3	29.8	2320
Own Property	7.7	51.1	41.2	2188		14.7	55.5	29.8	2114
Rent Property	16.6	49.9	33.5	511		16.1	54.5	29.4	143
Other	14.2	52.7	33.1	148		19.0	50.8	30.2	63

Table 13.39   *During the last 5 years, how often has the member delivered party leaflets ? (%)*

Tenure	Labour					Conservative			
	Not at all	Occas- ionally	Freq- uently	N		Not at all	Occas- ionally	Freq- uently	N
All	17.6	27.1	55.3	2799		61.0	17.1	21.9	2218
Own Property	16.1	27.8	56.1	2149		60.6	17.3	22.1	2019
Rent Property	24.1	24.1	51.8	502		67.9	14.6	17.5	137
Other	18.9	27.0	54.1	148		58.1	16.1	25.8	62

Table 13.40   *During the last 5 years, how often has the member attended a party*
                 meeting ? (%)

Tenure	Labour				Conservative			
	Not at all	Occas-ionally	Freq-uently	N	Not at all	Occas-ionally	Freq-uently	N
All	21.5	40.6	37.9	2803	50.6	32.8	16.6	2247
Own Property	20.9	41.7	37.4	2154	50.6	32.7	16.7	2042
Rent Property	23.1	35.2	41.7	503	54.5	30.3	15.2	145
Other	26.0	43.2	30.8	146	43.3	41.7	15.0	60

Table 13.41   *During the last 5 years, how often has the member canvassed voters*
                 on behalf of the party ? (%)

Tenure	Labour				Conservative			
	Not at all	Occas-ionally	Freq-uently	N	Not at all	Occas-ionally	Freq-uently	N
All	36.9	31.2	31.9	2779	74.9	14.8	10.3	2206
Own Property	37.1	31.9	31.0	2135	74.7	14.7	10.6	2011
Rent Property	35.7	27.5	36.8	498	77.4	13.9	8.7	137
Other	37.7	33.6	28.7	146	75.9	19.0	5.1	58

Table 13.42   *Where would you place yourself on a Left/Right scale within the*
                 Labour/Conservative party ? (%)

Tenure	Labour				Conservative			
	Left	Centre	Right	N	Left	Centre	Right	N
All	57.4	20.6	22.0	2878	13.4	26.0	60.6	2356
Own Property	58.9	20.6	20.5	2208	13.8	26.1	60.1	2144
Rent Property	51.0	21.8	27.2	522	9.0	22.8	68.2	145
Other	56.7	16.9	26.4	148	9.0	29.9	61.1	67

Table 13.43   *Where would you place yourself on a Left/Right scale within British Politics ? (%)*

Tenure	Labour				Conservative			
	Left	Centre	Right	N	Left	Centre	Right	N
All	79.9	10.4	9.7	2876	3.7	18.2	78.1	2351
Own Property	83.8	8.8	7.4	2205	3.6	18.1	78.3	2139
Rent Property	61.9	17.6	20.5	523	4.8	19.3	75.9	145
Other	83.7	9.5	6.8	148	4.5	19.4	76.1	67

Table 13.44   *What thermometer rating would the Labour/Conservative member give the Conservative Party ? (%)*

Tenure	Labour					Conservative				
	Cd	Cl	W	H	M	Cd	Cl	W	H	M
All	76.0	20.4	3.0	0.6	14.7	0.2	3.5	33.7	62.6	80.9
Own Property	77.5	19.4	2.7	0.4	13.9	0.2	3.5	33.7	62.6	80.7
Rent Property	69.5	24.9	3.9	1.7	18.5	0.0	3.4	34.2	62.4	82.7
Other	75.7	19.3	4.3	0.7	14.9	0.0	6.3	32.8	60.9	80.7

Table 13.45   *What thermometer rating would the Labour/Conservative member give the Labour Party ? (%)*

Tenure	Labour					Conservative				
	Cd	Cl	W	H	M	Cd	Cl	W	H	M
All	0.9	3.8	24.7	70.6	82.6	50.2	43.3	6.1	0.4	26.7
Own Property	0.9	3.4	26.0	69.7	82.2	50.1	43.3	6.2	0.4	26.7
Rent Property	0.9	4.5	19.8	74.8	85.0	53.3	40.9	5.1	0.7	25.9
Other	2.0	6.8	22.4	68.8	80.1	45.9	45.9	8.2	0.0	28.6

Table 13.46　　**What thermometer rating would the Labour/Conservative member give the Liberal Democratic Party ? (%)**

Tenure	Labour					Conservative				
	Cd	Cl	W	H	M	Cd	Cl	W	H	M
All	33.1	44.2	20.9	1.8	36.8	32.6	50.7	15.5	1.2	36.3
Own Property	32.9	44.9	20.6	1.6	36.6	32.2	50.6	15.8	1.4	36.4
Rent Property	34.0	42.6	20.4	3.0	37.4	37.2	48.9	13.1	0.8	35.3
Other	31.9	39.7	27.7	0.7	37.7	33.9	57.6	8.5	0.0	33.1

Table 13.47　　**What thermometer rating would the Labour/Conservative member give the Scottish Nationalist Party ? (%)**

Tenure	Labour					Conservative				
	Cd	Cl	W	H	M	Cd	Cl	W	H	M
All	43.9	37.2	16.0	2.9	32.1	69.0	26.7	4.1	0.2	19.1
Own Property	43.5	37.7	15.9	2.9	32.2	69.2	26.3	4.1	0.4	19.0
Rent Property	48.1	34.0	14.4	3.5	30.7	67.0	28.1	4.9	0.0	19.9
Other	35.5	40.3	22.6	1.6	35.8	64.1	35.9	0.0	0.0	18.6

Table 13.48　　**What thermometer rating would the Labour/Conservative member give Plaid Cymru ? (%)**

Tenure	Labour					Conservative				
	Cd	Cl	W	H	M	Cd	Cl	W	H	M
All	47.5	27.7	12.9	11.9	29.6	82.7	15.9	1.1	0.3	12.9
Own Property	46.2	39.1	12.7	2.0	30.1	82.6	15.8	1.2	0.4	13.0
Rent Property	53.8	33.9	11.1	1.2	26.8	84.9	15.1	0.0	0.0	11.9
Other	46.2	29.1	23.1	1.6	32.8	78.9	21.1	0.0	0.0	11.9

Table 13.49   *What thermometer rating would the Labour/Conservative member*
give the Green Party ? (%)

Tenure	Labour					Conservative				
	Cd	Cl	W	H	M	Cd	Cl	W	H	M
All	33.3	35.9	25.6	5.2	39.4	70.1	24.4	4.9	0.6	19.5
Own Property	31.2	37.0	26.4	5.4	40.3	70.2	24.1	5.1	0.6	19.5
Rent Property	43.3	34.4	18.3	4.0	34.1	66.7	28.7	4.6	0.0	19.6
Other	30.1	23.5	39.7	6.7	44.2	73.9	26.1	0.0	0.0	17.2

Table 13.50   *What thermometer rating would the Labour/Conservative member*
give the BBC ? (%)

Tenure	Labour					Conservative				
	Cd	Cl	W	H	M	Cd	Cl	W	H	M
All	9.4	26.2	39.7	24.7	60.3	8.4	30.6	40.6	20.4	59.3
Own Property	7.9	26.2	39.7	26.2	62.0	8.4	29.6	41.4	20.6	59.5
Rent Property	14.7	33.9	33.9	17.5	54.2	9.8	40.2	30.3	19.7	56.2
Other	12.8	31.5	34.2	21.5	56.6	6.3	42.2	35.9	15.6	57.8

Table 13.51   *What thermometer rating would the Labour/Conservative member*
give the European Community ? (%)

Tenure	Labour					Conservative				
	Cd	Cl	W	H	M	Cd	Cl	W	H	M
All	11.2	32.4	41.8	14.6	55.5	14.4	40.7	35.6	9.3	50.7
Own Property	10.3	32.3	43.1	14.3	55.8	13.9	40.2	36.4	9.5	51.1
Rent Property	14.5	32.7	35.5	17.3	54.3	20.5	45.5	23.9	10.1	46.6
Other	12.8	32.6	42.6	12.0	54.7	17.6	47.1	31.4	3.9	45.0

Table 13.52   *What thermometer rating would the Labour/Conservative member give the Trade Union Congress ? (%)*

Tenure	Labour					Conservative				
	Cd	Cl	W	H	M	Cd	Cl	W	H	M
All	5.6	29.0	47.6	17.8	60.1	53.6	39.8	5.7	0.9	26.3
Own Property	5.5	29.7	48.6	16.2	59.5	53.5	40.0	5.6	0.9	26.6
Rent Property	4.7	26.5	44.2	24.6	63.1	58.3	33.3	8.3	0.1	22.8
Other	10.6	27.5	45.1	16.8	58.5	48.7	48.7	2.6	0.0	24.5

Table 13.53   *What thermometer rating would the Labour/Conservative member give the Police ? (%)*

Tenure	Labour					Conservative				
	Cd	Cl	W	H	M	Cd	Cl	W	H	M
All	17.7	44.4	28.5	9.4	48.1	1.4	12.4	40.0	46.2	73.0
Own Property	17.3	46.8	28.6	7.3	47.1	1.5	12.5	40.5	45.5	72.6
Rent Property	17.7	35.0	29.5	17.8	51.9	1.4	10.7	35.7	52.2	76.2
Other	22.2	40.3	24.3	13.2	50.4	0.0	11.1	31.7	57.2	76.0

Table 13.54   *What thermometer rating would the Labour/Conservative member give the House of Commons ? (%)*

Tenure	Labour					Conservative				
	Cd	Cl	W	H	M	Cd	Cl	W	H	M
All	10.2	33.6	38.1	18.1	56.8	2.3	17.1	49.1	31.5	68.3
Own Property	9.3	33.5	40.1	17.1	57.0	2.3	17.3	49.4	31.0	68.2
Rent Property	12.1	33.3	31.2	23.4	57.3	2.4	12.1	46.8	38.7	70.8
Other	16.6	35.9	32.4	15.1	52.2	3.4	22.4	44.8	29.4	67.1

Table 13.55   *What thermometer rating would the Labour/Conservative member give the CBI ? (%)*

Tenure	Labour					Conservative				
	Cd	Cl	W	H	M	Cd	Cl	W	H	M
All	44.8	41.8	11.3	2.1	30.9	5.5	29.6	49.1	15.8	59.6
Own Property	45.7	42.6	10.1	1.6	30.0	5.3	29.8	49.4	15.5	59.6
Rent Property	41.9	36.5	17.2	4.4	34.2	9.1	23.6	47.3	20.0	59.6
Other	40.9	45.5	9.8	3.8	33.6	5.6	33.3	41.7	19.4	59.8

Table 13.56   *What thermometer rating would the Labour/Conservative member give the Queen ? (%)*

Tenure	Labour					Conservative				
	Cd	Cl	W	H	M	Cd	Cl	W	H	M
All	34.6	29.2	19.3	16.9	43.4	0.9	4.6	16.0	78.5	86.4
Own Property	36.1	31.2	18.7	14.0	41.3	0.9	4.8	16.4	77.9	86.1
Rent Property	27.5	21.2	20.8	30.5	53.0	0.7	3.5	9.2	86.6	90.0
Other	37.0	27.4	21.9	13.7	42.1	1.5	1.5	19.7	77.3	86.9

Table 13.57   *What thermometer rating would the Labour/Conservative member give Judges ? (%)*

Tenure	Labour					Conservative				
	Cd	Cl	W	H	M	Cd	Cl	W	H	M
All	38.0	43.5	14.9	3.6	35.1	4.5	30.9	45.6	19.0	60.5
Own Property	39.1	44.1	14.1	2.7	34.0	4.5	30.1	46.4	19.0	60.7
Rent Property	33.3	39.6	19.3	7.8	40.0	4.2	42.5	34.2	19.1	58.6
Other	36.9	46.8	12.1	4.2	33.4	5.5	34.5	43.6	16.4	59.0

14   Appendix

The following information details the construction and definition of all the variables used throughout this book. This includes frequency response rates in table format, original question wording, details of re-coded variables and further explanation of tables where necessary.

All the data used in this publication was taken from responses to the following political membership surveys :

(a) Political Activities and Attitudes of Labour Party Members in 1990
January 1990 - July 1990   *Response Rate*   *62.5%*

(b) Political Activities and Attitudes of Labour Party Members in 1992
May 1992 - August 1992   *Response Rate*   *60.9%*

(c) Political Activities and Attitudes of Conservative Party Members in 1992
January 1992 - April 1992   *Response rate*   *63.0%*

In an attempt to make the comparisons between Labour and Conservative party members as applicable as possible, most of the data was taken from the surveys that were carried out in 1992 because of the proximity of their respective fieldwork dates. However, as the Labour Party survey of 1992 was a follow-up of the original respondents from 1990, it was not necessary to ask some of the questions for a second time, e.g. Age, Gender etc. Where this is the case, the data in question was taken from the 1990 survey of Labour Party Members and this is indicated in the notes.

At times it was necessary to analyse more than one question in order to determine the appropriate response. In these instances all the questions used are listed in order of significance. The original question wording is shown alongside the following tables and unless otherwise stated, appears in exactly the same format in all three surveys.

Table 14.1 Strength of Partisanship (%)

Would you call yourself a ...

(A)   *Very strong Labour/Conservative supporter ?*
(B)   *Not very strong Labour/Conservative supporter ?*
(C)   *Fairly strong Labour/Conservative supporter ?*
(D)   *Not at all strong Labour/Conservative supporter ?*

Labour						Conservative				
A	B	C	D	N		A	B	C	D	N
54.1	38.9	5.1	1.9	2926		32.8	49.8	13.6	3.8	2454

Table 14.2 Social Class (%)

(1) What is the title of your present job? (If you are not working please answer in terms of your last job)

(2) Would you describe in detail the type of work you do, being as specific as you can. (If you are not working please answer in terms of your last job)

(3) Which of these descriptions applies to what you were doing last week, that is, in the seven days ending last Sunday?

(A)   *Salariat*
(B)   *Routine Non-Manual*
(C)   *Petty Bourgeoisie*
(D)   *Foreman/Technician*
(E)   *Working Class*

Labour							Conservative					
A	B	C	D	E	N		A	B	C	D	E	N
58.6	14.9	2.6	6.0	17.9	2725		55.4	17.8	13.4	5.8	7.6	2095

Table 14.3 Market Research Grading (%)

(1) What is the title of your present job? (If you are not working please answer in terms of your last job)

(2) Would you describe in detail the type of work you do, being as specific as you can. (If you are not working please answer in terms of your last job)

(3) Which of these descriptions applies to what you were doing last week, that is, in the seven days ending last Sunday?

Where a respondent indicated that they were presently unemployed, this information was used in preference to the details of their last job.

Labour								Conservative						
A	B	C1	C2	D	E	N		A	B	C1	C2	D	E	N
10.7	44.2	17.0	13.3	11.3	3.5	2708		12.0	45.8	27.4	7.0	5.9	1.9	2095

Table 14.4 Subjective Class (%)

Do you ever think of yourself as belonging to any particular social class ? If yes, which class is that ?

In the survey of Labour party members, only three categories were used (*Middle class, Working class, Other*), whilst in the Conservative party survey an additional category (*Upper class*) was specified. In order to facilitate a direct comparison of party members, the *Upper class* category in the Conservative survey was combined with the *Middle class* category.

Labour					Conservative			
Middle Class	Working Class	Other	N		Middle Class	Working Class	Other	N
32.5	64.6	2.9	2112		80.5	17.8	1.7	1562

Table 14.5 Completion of Education (%)

How old were you when you finished continuous full-time education ?

The responses to this question were coded into three categories to reflect the earliest possible school leaving age (*16 and under*), those completing sixth-form/further education (*17 to 18*) and those going on to complete higher education (*19 and over*). Labour party membership data was taken from 1990 survey.

Labour					Conservative			
16 and under	17 to 18	19 and over	N		16 and under	17 to 18	19 and over	N
76.4	18.5	5.1	2923		90.7	6.4	2.9	2419

Table 14.6 Annual Income (%)

Which of the following categories represents the present total annual income of your household from all sources before tax?

In the survey of Labour party members the categories of earnings were in the range of *under £5,000* to *£40,000 plus*. In the survey of Conservative party members the range was *under £5,000* to *£80,000 plus*. The responses were re-coded into the following final categories for both sets of members :

(A)   under £10,000
(B)   £10,000 to £20,000
(C)   £20,000 to £30,000
(D)   £30,000 to £40,000
(E)   £40,000 plus

Labour							Conservative					
A	B	C	D	E	N		A	B	C	D	E	N
33.6	33.3	19.1	9.3	4.7	2887		26.4	32.6	18.7	9.8	12.5	2286

Table 14.7 Employment Sector (%)

Which type of organisation do you work for? (if you are not working now, please answer in terms of your last job)

The responses to this question were coded into six categories originally. The *Public sector* category was derived from the combination of those respondents working in *nationalised industries/public corporations, local authorities/local education authorities, health authorities/hospitals and central government/civil service.*

Labour					Conservative			
Private Sector	Public Sector	Other	N		Private Sector	Public Sector	Other	N
34.6	49.0	16.4	2716		59.4	30.8	9.8	2068

Table 14.8 Economic Sector (%)

Which of these descriptions applies to the what you were doing last week, that is, in the seven days ending last Sunday ?

Respondents indicating that they were *waiting to take up work, registered unemployed or unemployed (not registered)* were all re-coded as *Unemployed.* Those indicating that they were *on a government training scheme, sick and disabled or undertaking voluntary work* were all re-coded as *Other.* The final categories were as follows :

(A)   Full-time work ?
(B)   Part-time work ?
(C)   Unemployed ?
(D)   Retired ?
(E)   Looking after the home ?
(F)   Other ?

Labour							Conservative						
A	B	C	D	E	F	N		A	B	C	D	E	F	N
52.9	9.0	4.0	18.7	5.6	9.8	2828		27.4	9.4	1.9	40.3	15.6	5.4	2424

Table 14.9 Trade Union membership (%)

Are you currently a member of a trade union ?

Labour			Conservative		
Yes	No	N	Yes	No	N
63.6	36.4	2848	16.1	83.9	2337

Table 14.10 Gender (%)

Are you male or female ?

Labour party membership data was taken from 1990 survey.

Labour			Conservative		
Female	Male	N	Female	Male	N
41.0	59.0	2914	52.1	47.9	2404

Table 14.11 Age (%)

What was your age last birthday ?

Labour party membership data was taken from 1990 survey.

Labour					Conservative				
Under 25	26 to 45	46 to 65	66 and over	N	Under 25	26 to 45	46 to 65	66 and over	N
3.2	42.3	36.2	18.3	2903	0.9	14.2	40.2	44.7	2425

Table 14.12 Religion (%)

Do you regard yourself as belonging to any particular religion, if yes, which religion is that?

The following responses were amalgamated into the respective categories which were used in the final analysis :

Church of England, Church of Wales, Church of Scotland, Presbyterian, Anglican, Episcopalian are represented as *Anglican*. All other responses are represented by the *Non-conformist* category.

Labour					Conservative				
No Religion	Catholic	Anglican	Non con-formist	N	No religion	Catholic	Anglican	Non con-formist	N
45.2	10.4	28.9	15.5	2898	10.3	6.8	76.7	6.2	2433

Table 14.13 Tenure (%)

Think of the accommodation where you live now. Do you own the property, rent it from the council, rent it from a private landlord, rent it from a housing association or are you living with family and friends?

Those responses which indicated that the property was rented were all combined in one general *Rent the property* category. The *Other* category includes all those respondents indicating that they live with family and friends.

Labour				Conservative			
Own the property	Rent the property	Other	N	Own the property	Rent the property	Other	N
76.4	18.5	5.1	2923	90.7	6.4	2.9	2419

In the following tables (14.14 to 14.25) the original responses formed five categories (*strongly agree, agree, neither, disagree, strongly disagree*). The categories *strongly agree* and *agree* were re-coded as *agree* and the categories disagree and strongly disagree were re-coded as *disagree*

Table 14.14 Middle Ground / Political Strategy (%)

The Labour/Conservative party should try to capture the middle ground in politics

Labour				Conservative			
Agree	Neither	Disagree	N	Agree	Neither	Disagree	N
51.1	12.1	36.8	2854	69.7	13.3	17.0	2305

Table 14.15 Prices & Incomes Policy (%)

A Labour/Conservative government should introduce a prices and incomes policy as a means of controlling inflation

Labour				Conservative			
Agree	Neither	Disagree	N	Agree	Neither	Disagree	N
57.5	18.9	23.6	2855	42.2	11.6	46.2	2344

Table 14.16 Income & Wealth Redistribution (%)

Income and wealth should be re-distributed towards ordinary working people

Labour				Conservative			
Agree	Neither	Disagree	N	Agree	Neither	Disagree	N
86.0	9.1	4.9	2889	25.4	20.3	54.3	2344

Table 14.17 Election / Principles (%)

The Labour/Conservative party should always stand by its principles even if this should lose it an election

Labour				Conservative			
Agree	Neither	Disagree	N	Agree	Neither	Disagree	N
68.0	11.8	20.2	2885	81.2	8.2	10.6	2240

Table 14.18 Nuclear Energy (%)

Further nuclear energy development is essential for the future prosperity of Britain

Labour				Conservative			
Agree	Neither	Disagree	N	Agree	Neither	Disagree	N
14.1	11.8	74.1	2873	60.2	16.9	22.9	2361

Table 14.19 Single European Currency (%)

A future Labour/Conservative government should not agree to a single European currency

Labour				Conservative			
Agree	Neither	Disagree	N	Agree	Neither	Disagree	N
25.4	19.0	55.6	2862	57.9	12.0	30.1	2382

Table 14.20 Income Tax (%)

High income tax makes people less willing to work hard

Labour				Conservative			
Agree	Neither	Disagree	N	Agree	Neither	Disagree	N
26.3	10.9	62.8	2891	81.9	6.0	12.1	2407

Table 14.21 Proportional Representation (%)

Britain's electoral system should be replaced by a system of proportional representation

Labour				Conservative			
Agree	Neither	Disagree	N	Agree	Neither	Disagree	N
57.9	13.2	28.9	2885	21.7	11.9	66.4	2371

Table 14.22 European Integration (%)

Further moves towards integration within the European Community should be resisted

Labour				Conservative			
Agree	Neither	Disagree	N	Agree	Neither	Disagree	N
21.7	13.2	65.1	2877	54.1	15.5	30.4	2381

Table 14.23 Bill of Rights (%)

There is no need for a Bill of Rights in this country

Labour				Conservative			
Agree	Neither	Disagree	N	Agree	Neither	Disagree	N
11.4	10.0	78.6	2860	39.9	26.5	33.6	2293

Table 14.24 Scottish Assembly (%)

A future Labour/Conservative government should introduce a directly elected Scottish Assembly with taxing powers

Labour				Conservative			
Agree	Neither	Disagree	N	Agree	Neither	Disagree	N
61.3	22.1	16.6	2884	22.7	26.4	50.9	2341

Table 14.25 Coalition Government (%)

Coalition governments are the best form of government for Britain

Labour				Conservative			
Agree	Neither	Disagree	N	Agree	Neither	Disagree	N
8.6	16.8	74.6	2882	9.6	10.1	80.3	2410

In the following tables (14.26 to 14.32) the original responses formed five categories (*definitely should, probably should, doesn't matter, probably should not, definitely should not*). The categories *definitely should* and *probably should* were re-coded as *should* and the categories *probably should not* and *definitely should not* were re-coded as *should not* in the final tables.

Table 14.26 Poverty (%)

A future Labour/Conservative government should/should not spend money to get rid of poverty

Labour				Conservative			
Should	Doesn't matter	Should not	N	Should	Doesn't matter	Should not	N
98.1	0.9	1.0	2882	80.3	8.3	11.4	2362

Table 14.27 Private Medicine (%)

A future Labour/Conservative government should/should not encourage the growth of private medicine

Labour				Conservative			
Should	Doesn't matter	Should not	N	Should	Doesn't matter	Should not	N
3.8	4.7	91.5	2875	52.1	15.8	32.1	2372

Table 14.28 National Health Service (%)

A future Labour/Conservative government should/should not put more money into the National Health Service

Labour				Conservative			
Should	Doesn't matter	Should not	N	Should	Doesn't matter	Should not	N
98.0	0.7	1.3	2887	79.3	7.5	13.2	2379

Table 14.29 Government Spending (%)

A future Labour/Conservative government should/should not reduce spending in general

Labour				Conservative			
Should	Doesn't matter	Should not	N	Should	Doesn't matter	Should not	N
19.6	7.3	73.1	2840	60.6	8.8	30.6	2358

Table 14.30 Trade Union / Legal Regulations (%)

A future Labour/Conservative government should/should not introduce stricter laws to regulate the trade unions

Labour				Conservative			
Should	Doesn't matter	Should not	N	Should	Doesn't matter	Should not	N
10.2	14.7	75.1	2850	66.5	12.1	21.4	2387

Table 14.31 Workers' Workplace Rights (%)

A future Labour/Conservative government should/should not give workers more say in the places where they work

Labour				Conservative			
Should	Doesn't matter	Should not	N	Should	Doesn't matter	Should not	N
91.2	5.6	3.2	2877	63.8	13.4	22.8	2393

Table 14.32 Defence Spending (%)

A future Labour/Conservative government should/should not spend less on defence

Labour				Conservative			
Should	Doesn't matter	Should not	N	Should	Doesn't matter	Should not	N
82.6	4.7	12.7	2879	44.2	4.9	50.9	2380

Table 14.33 Services vs. Spending (%)

Suppose the government had to choose between the following three options. Which do you think it should choose?

(A) Reduce taxes & spend less on health, education & social benefits
(B) Keep taxes & spending on these services at the same levels as now
(C) Increase taxes & spend more on health, education & social benefits

Labour				Conservative			
A	B	C	N	A	B	C	N
2.7	6.4	90.9	2881	6.8	67.1	26.1	2377

Table 14.34 Joining Labour/Conservative Party (%)

Thinking back to first time you joined the Labour/Conservative party, did you approach the party to apply for membership or did they approach you?

In the Labour party survey, the respondents indicating that they *had made the approach* were able to specify whether this approach was made to the regional or national party, in the final table these responses were combined.

Labour party membership data was taken from 1990 survey.

MA - Member approached party
PA - Party approached member

Labour				Conservative			
MA	Don't Know	PA	N	MA	Don't Know	PA	N
77.3	20.1	2.6	2913	34.4	50.1	15.5	2427

Table 14.35 Attendance at Meetings (%)

Thinking back over the last year, how often have you attended a Labour/Conservative party meeting?

The original responses indicating *rarely* and *occasionally* were combined to form the *occasionally* category.

Labour					Conservative			
Not at all	Occas-ionally	Frequ-ently	N		Not at all	Occas-ionally	Frequ-ently	N
41.6	30.5	27.9	2925		66.1	22.0	11.9	2445

Table 14.36 Political Activity (%)

Are you more or less active within the party than you were five years ago, or about the same?

Labour					Conservative			
More active	About same	Less active	N		More active	About same	Less active	N
12.9	38.4	48.7	2886		9.3	62.8	27.9	2052

Table 14.37 Labour / Conservative Party Official (%)

Do you currently represent the Labour party on any official bodies?

The wording appeared in a slightly different format in the Conservative survey.

Do you at present hold any office(s) within the Conservative party?

Labour				Conservative		
Yes	No	N		Yes	No	N
15.9	84.1	2873		8.4	91.6	2406

Table 14.38 Time Devoted to Party Activities (%)

How much time do you devote to party activities in the average month ?

Labour					Conservative				
None	Up to 5 hrs	5 to 10 hrs	Over 10 hrs	N		None	Up to 5 hrs	5 to 10 hrs	Over 10 hrs	N
51.2	29.5	9.4	9.9	2883		76.2	15.2	4.5	4.1	2395

Table 14.39 Financial Contribution to Party (%)

What is your estimate of the total overall financial contribution which you make to the party each year?

Labour					Conservative			
0 to £10	£10 to £20	Over £20	N		0 to £10	£10 to £20	Over £20	N
24.4	19.7	55.9	2564		34.1	21.3	44.6	1805

Table 14.40 Labour / Conservative Councillor (%)

Are you currently a local Labour/Conservative councillor ?

Labour				Conservative		
Yes	No	N		Yes	No	N
7.9	92.1	2898		2.3	97.7	2422

In the following tables (14.41 to 14.49) the original responses formed five categories (*strongly agree, agree, neither, disagree, strongly disagree*). The categories *strongly agree* and *agree* were re-coded as *agree* and the categories *disagree* and *strongly disagree* were re-coded as *disagree* in the final tables.

Table 14.41 One Member / One Vote (%)

The Labour/Conservative leader should be elected by a system of one party member/one vote

Labour					Conservative			
Agree	Neither	Disagree	N		Agree	Neither	Disagree	N
86.1	5.3	8.6	2893		50.0	14.4	35.6	2360

Table 14.42 Political Influence (%)

People like me can have a real influence in politics if they are prepared to get involved

Labour					Conservative			
Agree	Neither	Disagree	N		Agree	Neither	Disagree	N
65.9	16.1	18.0	2882		56.5	20.1	23.4	2370

Table 14.43 Party Meetings Tiring (%)

Attending party meetings can be pretty tiring after a hard days work

Labour					Conservative			
Agree	Neither	Disagree	N		Agree	Neither	Disagree	N
77.2	11.4	11.4	2886		69.2	19.4	11.4	2348

Table 14.44 Local Councillor (%)

Someone like me could do a good job of being a local councillor

Labour					Conservative			
Agree	Neither	Disagree	N		Agree	Neither	Disagree	N
48.6	21.9	29.5	2860		27.5	24.4	48.1	2334

Table 14.45 Meeting Interesting People (%)

Being an active party member is a good way of meeting interesting people

Labour					Conservative			
Agree	Neither	Disagree	N		Agree	Neither	Disagree	N
64.7	21.9	13.4	2883		59.5	29.9	10.6	2340

Table 14.46 Activism/Political Education (%)

The only way to be really educated about politics is to be a party activist

Labour					Conservative			
Agree	Neither	Disagree	N		Agree	Neither	Disagree	N
42.0	11.2	46.8	2891		35.8	17.2	47.0	2344

Table 14.47 Leadership/Ordinary Members (%)

The party leadership does not pay a lot of attention to ordinary party members

Labour					Conservative			
Agree	Neither	Disagree	N		Agree	Neither	Disagree	N
47.1	18.8	34.1	2890		42.3	23.9	33.8	2355

Table 14.48 Activism/Family Time (%)

Party activity often takes time away from one's family

Labour				Conservative			
Agree	Neither	Disagree	N	Agree	Neither	Disagree	N
85.1	10.4	4.5	2883	67.1	25.5	7.4	2324

Table 14.49 Success of Party (%)

The Labour/Conservative party would be more successful if people like me were elected to parliament

Labour				Conservative			
Agree	Neither	Disagree	N	Agree	Neither	Disagree	N
33.8	34.1	32.1	2860	21.4	31.5	47.1	2313

In the following tables (14.50 to 14.54) the original responses formed four categories (*not at all, rarely, occasionally, frequently*). The categories *rarely* and *occasionally* were re-coded as *occasionally*.

Table 14.50 Activism - Election Poster (%)

We would like to ask you about political activities you may have taken part in during the last five years. How often have you displayed an election poster in a window

Labour				Conservative			
Not at all	Occas-ionally	Freq-uently	N	Not at all	Occas-ionally	Freq-uently	N
9.6	21.8	68.6	2868	48.9	31.8	19.3	2309

Table 14.51 Activism - Donated Money (%)

We would like to ask you about political activities you may have taken part in during the last five years. How often have you donated money to party funds ?

Labour				Conservative			
Not at all	Occas-ionally	Freq-uently	N	Not at all	Occas-ionally	Freq-uently	N
9.7	51.0	39.3	2862	14.9	55.3	29.8	2359

Table 14.52 Activism - Delivered Leaflets (%)

We would like to ask you about political activities you may have taken part in during the last five years. How often have you delivered party leaflets ?

Labour				Conservative			
Not at all	Occas-ionally	Freq-uently	N	Not at all	Occas-ionally	Freq-uently	N
17.6	27.1	55.3	2813	61.1	16.9	22.0	2253

Table 14.53 Activism - Attended Party Meetings (%)

We would like to ask you about political activities you may have taken part in during the last five years. How often have you attended a party meeting ?

Labour				Conservative			
Not at all	Occas-ionally	Freq-uently	N	Not at all	Occas-ionally	Freq-uently	N
21.5	40.7	37.8	2817	50.8	32.6	16.6	2284

Table 14.54 Activism - Canvassed Voters (%)

We would like to ask you about political activities you may have taken part in during the last five years. How often have you canvassed voters on behalf of the party ?

Labour				Conservative			
Not at all	Occas-ionally	Freq-uently	N	Not at all	Occas-ionally	Freq-uently	N
36.9	31.2	31.9	2793	74.9	14.7	10.4	2245

Table 14.55 Left/Right / Within Party (%)

In Labour/Conservative party politics people often talk about the 'left' and the 'right'. Compared with other Labour/Conservative party members, where would you place your views on this scale below?

The respondents were asked to place themselves on a scale of *1 to 9*, where *1* represented the far left and *9* represented the far right, *5* was the centre mark on the scale. In the final table, the responses were coded as follows :

338

1-3	left
4-6	centre
7-9	right

Labour					Conservative			
Left	Centre	Right	N		Left	Centre	Right	N
57.4	20.6	22.0	2893		13.3	25.9	60.8	2396

Table 14.56 Left/Right / Within Politics (%)

And where would you place your views in relation to British politics as a whole (not just the Labour/Conservative party)?

Again, the respondents were asked to place themselves on a scale of *1 to 9*, where *1* represented the far left and *9* represented the far right, *5* was the centre mark on the scale. In the final table, the responses were coded as follows :

1-3	left
4-6	centre
7-9	right

Labour					Conservative			
Left	Centre	Right	N		Left	Centre	Right	N
79.9	10.4	9.7	2891		3.7	18.2	78.1	2390

In the tables 14.57 to 14.70 the original wording was as follows :

Please think for a moment of a thermometer scale that runs from 0 to 100 degrees, where 50 is the neutral point. If your feelings are warm and sympathetic towards something or someone, give them a score higher than 50; the warmer the feelings, the higher the score. If your feelings are cold and unsympathetic, give them a score less than 50; the colder your feelings, the lower the score.

For the purposes of this book the following thermometer ranges were ascribed headings :

Thermometer rating	0-25	*Cold (Cd)*
Thermometer rating	26-50	*Cool (Cl)*
Thermometer rating	51-75	*Warm (W)*
Thermometer rating	76-100	*Hot (H)*

M = the mean thermometer rating of the organisation/person and as such is the only figure that should not be read as a percentage.

Table 14.57 Thermometer: Conservative Party (%)

Labour					Conservative				
Cd	Cl	W	H	M	Cd	Cl	W	H	M
76.0	20.4	3.0	0.6	14.8	0.2	3.6	33.6	62.6	80.9

Table 14.58 Thermometer rating: Labour Party (%)

Labour					Conservative				
Cd	Cl	W	H	M	Cd	Cl	W	H	M
1.0	3.8	24.7	70.5	82.7	50.2	43.3	6.1	0.4	26.7

Table 14.59 Thermometer rating: Liberal Democratic Party (%)

Labour					Conservative				
Cd	Cl	W	H	M	Cd	Cl	W	H	M
33.0	44.3	20.9	1.8	36.9	32.7	50.8	15.3	1.2	36.2

Table 14.60 Thermometer rating: Scottish Nationalist Party (%)

Labour					Conservative				
Cd	Cl	W	H	M	Cd	Cl	W	H	M
43.8	37.2	16.0	3.0	32.2	69.0	26.7	4.0	0.3	19.1

Table 14.61 Thermometer rating : Plaid Cymru (%)

Labour					Conservative				
Cd	Cl	W	H	M	Cd	Cl	W	H	M
47.5	37.7	12.9	1.9	29.7	82.6	16.0	1.1	0.3	12.9

Table 14.62 Thermometer rating : The Green Party (%)

Labour					Conservative				
Cd	Cl	W	H	M	Cd	Cl	W	H	M
33.3	35.9	25.7	5.1	39.4	70.2	24.3	4.9	0.6	19.5

Table 14.63 Thermometer rating : BBC (%)

	Labour					Conservative			
Cd	Cl	W	H	M	Cd	Cl	W	H	M
9.4	26.3	39.7	24.6	60.3	8.4	30.5	40.4	20.7	59.3

Table 14.64 Thermometer rating : European Community (%)

	Labour					Conservative			
Cd	Cl	W	H	M	Cd	Cl	W	H	M
11.1	32.4	41.8	14.7	55.6	14.3	40.7	35.7	9.3	50.8

Table 14.65 Thermometer rating : Trade Union Congress (%)

	Labour					Conservative			
Cd	Cl	W	H	M	Cd	Cl	W	H	M
5.7	29.0	47.5	17.8	60.1	53.7	39.8	5.6	0.9	26.3

Table 14.66 Thermometer rating : Police (%)

	Labour					Conservative			
Cd	Cl	W	H	M	Cd	Cl	W	H	M
17.8	44.3	28.5	9.4	48.2	1.4	12.5	39.8	46.3	73.0

Table 14.67 Thermometer rating : House of Commons (%)

	Labour					Conservative			
Cd	Cl	W	H	M	Cd	Cl	W	H	M
10.2	33.6	38.1	18.1	56.8	2.4	17.1	49.1	31.4	68.3

Table 14.68 Thermometer rating : CBI (%)

	Labour					Conservative			
Cd	Cl	W	H	M	Cd	Cl	W	H	M
44.8	41.7	11.3	2.2	31.0	5.5	29.7	49.1	15.7	59.6

Table 14.69 Thermometer rating: Queen (%)

Labour						Conservative				
Cd	Cl	W	H	M		Cd	Cl	W	H	M
34.5	29.2	19.3	17.0	43.5		0.9	4.6	16.0	78.5	86.4

Table 14.70 Thermometer rating: Judges (%)

Labour						Conservative				
Cd	Cl	W	H	M		Cd	Cl	W	H	M
38.0	43.4	14.9	3.7	35.1		4.5	30.9	45.6	19.0	60.5

15 References

Burch, M. and Moran, M. (1987), British Politics - A Reader (Manchester University Press)

Crewe, I. (1983), Why Labour Lost the British Election, Public Opinion Quarterly, June/July 1983, pp 7-9 and pp 56-60

Forrester, T. (1976), The Labour Party and the Working Class (London: Heinemann)

Gamble, Andrew (1974), The Conservative Nation (London: Routledge and Kegan Paul)

Heath, A., Jowell, R. and Curtice, J. (1994), Labour's Last Chance (Aldershot: Dartmouth)

Heath, A., Jowell, R. and Curtice, J. (1991) How Britain Votes (Oxford: Permagon Press)

Hindess, B. (1971), The Decline of Working Class Politics (London: MacGibbon and Kee)

Norris, P, and Lovenduski, J (1995), Political Recruitment - Gender Race and Class in the British Parliament (Cambridge University Press)

Reid, Ivan, (1989), Social Class Differences in Britain (Fontana Press)

Seyd, P., and Whiteley, P. (1992), Labour's Grass Roots (Oxford: Clarendon Press)

Whiteley, P., Seyd, P. and Richardson, J. (1994), True Blues (Oxford: Clarendon Press)

16 Index